P9-CER-062

THEIR MISSION:

ASSASSINATE ELEVEN
TOP-RANKING CHINESE AND
NORTH VIETNAMESE
LEADERS, INCLUDING
THE NOTORIOUS GENERAL GIAP,
CHIEF OF STAFF.

I WOULD DIE FIGHTING

We were creating a diversion to cover a major drive by the Seventh Airborne. We blew two bridges and a railway link, and on the return we stumbled over a Viet Cong arms cache hidden in a tunnel . . . Six Viet Cong turned up, but most survived our ambush and got down the tunnel. They would not surface, so we knew they were retreating through the tunnel, which could stretch for miles underground. Half a mile away they blew the tunnel out . . . and tried to escape into the jungle. We went after them. We ran smack into a battalion of North Vietnamese regulars. One of our guys was killed immediately, and the second got his side ripped out by automatic fire . . . I fought a rearguard action to cover his retreat. I got pinned down against a cliff. I had only my shotgun . . . They closed on me and began to rush me. I was low on ammunition, under tremendous pressure. The final answer was complete contempt for the enemy; I would fight with my knife and my gun butt and take as many as I could with me. I would die fighting . . .

THE FIVE FINGERS

GAYLE RIVERS AND JAMES HUDSON

✌

THE FIVE FINGERS

*A Bantam Book / published by arrangement with
Doubleday & Company, Inc.*

PRINTING HISTORY
Doubleday edition published March 1978
Bantam edition / June 1979
2nd printing

*Bantam Books are published by Bantam Books, Inc. Its trade-
mark, consisting of the words "Bantam Books" and the por-
trayal of a bantam, is Registered in U.S. Patent and Trademark
Office and in other countries. Marca Registrada. Bantam
Books, Inc., 666 Fifth Avenue, New York, New York 10019.*

PRINTED IN THE UNITED STATES OF AMERICA

THE FIVE FINGERS

Part 1

THE MISSION

CHAPTER 1

What was the Englishman doing here? Everyone else looked appropriate for the setting. But a British SAS operative was as out of place at Bien Hoa as he would have been in the middle of Peking. When I had stepped in the door and spotted his pale blue beret, I thought at first that he was a New Zealand helicopter pilot. But that was a different shade of blue.

It was 0600 hours on the last Friday of April 1969. Barry Wiley and I stood in the door of a briefing room in the "south side" at Bien Hoa, the big United States tactical air base fifteen minutes by helicopter north of Saigon. Bien Hoa was a front-line tactical base, but American air bases were not quite so prefabricated as people might imagine. No Nissen hut knocked together with wood and string; this was a proper building. Air conditioned. Room 40B looked like a classroom or a hotel conference room. Several rows of chairs with pivotal desk arms faced a long conference table with a blackboard above it. Standing behind the table was a U.S. lieutenant colonel; he nodded curtly when we entered. Seated to the right of the colonel were a U.S. major and a second lieutenant, to his left four men in civilian dress. The lieutenant rose, handed us each two maps and a briefing pad. He directed us to two desks behind the five men already seated facing the colonel. The colonel ordered the lieutenant to shut the door, then turned to us. He did not mess about.

"Gentlemen," he said, "you have been selected for a special mission. The mission is of the highest security and will be so treated. Apart from training exercises, you will be confined to quarters until mission-start. We'll be seeing a lot of each other in the coming days, so we'd better get acquainted. Please rise as I introduce you. Major Toliver will be your commanding officer."

The colonel indicated the American Green Beret major seated in the front row. The major rose, half turned, and nodded at us.

"Lieutenant Tan." A wiry Korean Ranger stood briefly, then sat down.

"Master Sergeant Jackson." U. S. Green Beret. Lots of ribbons, lots of hash marks. He looked very sharp, very much a sergeant.

"Warrant Officer Rivers." I rose.

"Corporal Wiley." Somehow Barry looked a little wrong for this company.

"Private First Class Morrosco." A Green Beret medic. A big man with broad shoulders. Quite young. He appeared relaxed.

The colonel had skipped over the man we all wanted to know about.

"You will have an observer assigned to the mission from the British SAS. Regimental Sergeant Major Prather." Prather looked older than even the major. Mid-forties, I guessed. The SAS patch and the ribbons meant he was good. But he had been away from this sort of environment for some time. His skin was pale; the rest of us were burned coffee brown. And he looked fresh. His face did not have the appropriate strain for a man of recent combat experience. I did not like seeing him here. "Observer" could mean anything, but one of its meanings was "baggage," like a war correspondent. We all hated baggage. Prather would know that. He appeared as uncomfortable about being here as we were about having him.

"Let's see what it is all about, gentlemen," the colonel said, pulling down a map over the blackboard. He had not introduced himself nor any of the people beside him. I noticed he had removed the name tag from his uniform.

The colonel launched into a full-scale briefing. He proceeded to tell us everything but what we were there for. We were shown films similar to ones I had seen in Saigon earlier in the week. It was brought out that we had all recently heard more or less the same political background briefing. It seemed obvious at first that we were being briefed to go back to our separate units and brief them. As the films were of the same people we had seen before, I assumed new units were being formed in Laos and North Vietnam, and we were going in to displace these units. My assumption was reinforced when we got a topographical briefing on northern Laos and the adjacent North Vietnamese frontier. This was not an area that saw much insurgency activity, because it was too far north for dependable support. If the units were being formed up there, it would take several RFI teams to keep them spotted.

After more than an hour of nonstop briefing and still no hard information, I began having second thoughts. I had noticed a sequence of unusual things since Barry and I had reported for the briefing. I stopped listening and started watching. The colonel was very agitated, almost anxious. He kept glancing nervously at the civilians, who were oblivious of his lecture; they never took their eyes off us except to scribble quickly in a notebook. These were hard men, but even they could not suppress the tension in the room. At last I realized that this was a commitment briefing. For something very big. We seven were in this as a team. The men up front were monitoring our responses to one another; if we did not mesh, we could be sent back to our units none the wiser. There would be no hard information forthcoming until they had decided we worked as a team.

If it was important enough to shake these men, I wanted to know who I was going out with. I started doing my personals, my psychological assessments of the other six. They must be doing the same by now. The introductions had been abrupt, icy. Now the colonel began to draw on our experiences to open up the briefing with well-timed questions. Based on your previous trips to Laos, how would you move in this area, Rivers? As a radio operator, how would you handle this situation, Tan? We were soon talking back and forth across the room, closely watched by the briefing team. After another hour, the civilians left, and the briefing became purely military. We studied topographical models of Laos and were briefed on military activity there. We were briefed on the special jobs in the team. The young American, Morrosco, was our medic. Tan, the Korean lieutenant, would operate our radio. To my surprise, I was nominated second-in-command. I was outranked by Tan and Prather and, as an "adviser," held equal rank with Master Sergeant Jackson. Prather could not command, because he was officially an observer, but there was no obvious explanation for my commanding the others. It was not uncommon for a junior to hold rank in a special forces unit if the people in charge thought he was the right man for the job. Jackson did not look very pleased about it.

The briefing lasted four hours, after which we were dismissed for the day. Our next briefing was the following morning. We were being given time to get to know one another while the briefers analyzed their assessments of us. The major stayed behind when we were taken to new quarters within the south side compound. Our gear was already there. We spent the afternoon sorting our gear, just fooling around.

We talked tentatively over our evening meal, feeling

one another out. When people have spent a lot of time alone in combat, it takes a while for them to open up. We needed a couple of days to get used to one another. With the exception of the Englishman, Prather, who kept very quiet, it turned out we all had pulled off things that were well known among special forces people.

About nine o'clock, Toliver came into the barracks and dropped his guard a little. At the briefing he had remained silent, watching us as carefully as the men up front. Now he went on to first names and started to draw from us how we felt about working together. He had obviously been briefed to do this; I saw it was part of a psychological buildup of the unit to combat readiness, for the time when it would dawn on us well into preparation that none of us might make it back. I knew it was that kind of a mission as soon as I found out who the other guys were; this was too good a team to bring together for any ordinary job. Mind you, nobody went out on suicide missions. If it was that close a mission profile, they certainly were not going to let us know.

The purpose of isolating us, apart from security, was to give us time to get to know one another, to get over our initial distrust. When you have kept yourself alive for any length of time in our environment, you do not trust anyone. No one else is going to look after you the way you look after yourself. The first thing I did with any new unit was to file in the back of my mind the unit's weaknesses, from probables to possibles. This was an automatic function, because every unit had its weaknesses. The sloppy soldier was always a probable. If a guy was lackadaisical in the mess or barracks, he was the one you expected to make a mistake in combat, to throw his pack down rather than set it down, to overlook the trip wire that sends the mines up. You became acutely aware, almost in a paranoid way, that the tiniest mistake gets people killed. Even overcaution. A man who was too careful could work a time delay into a maneuver that would throw the rest of the party off balance. In combat, the only safe thing around you was your own awareness.

There was not one sloppy man among this lot. Wiley bordered on it. He was also a chain smoker, which told me he had an inward problem he had not worked out. I knew from experience that Wiley was good. But I could not allow myself the luxury of relying on past experience. If you get used to a man, you start relying on his reactions based on your last mission with him. He may have gone through something in the meanwhile, and the man's reactions may have changed. I had to consider him a possible.

I had first met Barry Wiley at Terendak, a British base in Malaysia which was headquarters for the combined British-Malaysian activities against Indonesian insurgents. We were both undergoing acclimitization and combat readiness for Vietnam. Barry and I worked together on a joint exercise with the Gurkhas. Barry was a raw squadee with the Australian infantry then, a very green soldier. I was training as a member of the Third Squadron Twenty-first SAS of the New Zealand Army. I never felt green for one day. I adapted completely, just as I had at Wairora, where I underwent SAS training. Just as I had to every new situation since I struck off on my own. I don't do things halfway.

I grew up on a hill farm on North Island. My father was Irish, my mother English. They immigrated from Birmingham shortly after they were married. We were five children on the farm. It was a hard life, and the only peace I knew as a child was when I hunted game in the mountains with a small-bore rifle. In summer I worked as a shepherd. I put my life savings into a rusty old two-stroke motorbike. One hot December day in 1960, I rode the bike home, straight into a violent argument with my father. That same day, I packed my belongings on the back and rode away. I was fifteen.

I worked as a manuel laborer by day. By night I

raced bikes on dirt tracks all over New Zealand. Some people liked the slightly deadly approach I took to racing. The Wellington Hell's Angels made me an honorary member. I did not ride with the Angels.

I had quite a few fights, mostly on the job. I was small and looked even younger than my years, and I could turn out more work than anybody else. Sometimes the older men resented me for that, and for being such a solitary figure. I fought to win, with whatever was at hand. I suppose I was lucky I never killed a man. By eighteen, I was flying without a license, dusting crops in planes too dangerous to leave the ground. Insecticide ate away the rudder controls of one old biplane. I crashed into a tree. I was trapped in the cockpit for over an hour, with hot engine oil blistering my body. I broke some ribs that time. After that, I got my license and flew as a bush pilot, in slightly better planes.

In 1967 the American fleet was in Wellington, and the Yanks were tearing up the town. A drunken sailor bounced a beer bottle off the bonnet of my new truck. I whipped a U-turn and ran the truck up on the pavement. I caught him with the front wing and broke both his legs. He turned out to be a New Zealand sailor. I escaped a prison sentence by the good graces of a sympathetic judge. He told me to volunteer for the army.

As soon as I began basic training with the First Infantry Battalion, I knew I could never make it as a regular squadee. That was a life for morons and zombies. I volunteered for the Special Air Services. I was twenty years old.

From basic training, twenty-five of us were selected for SAS training at Wairora as the First Twenty-third SAS Squadron. We were told straight off that our unit was selected for Southeast Asian combat training. That meant Vietnam. There were already New Zealand artillery and infantry regiments fighting there, as well as numerous SAS squadrons seconded as a unit or individually to the Americans or Australians. From Wairora, we transferred to Terendak to get ourselves ready for Vietnam.

I spent six months at Terendak, being based out of there for two missions into Vietnam. I had a natural leadership quality; I found myself taking over sometimes when strictly I should not have. I was among men who were the best, and I seemed to become leader without actually being given command. I do not know why this is; it is a thing that happens with me. Maybe it was because I liked the SAS and found my work absorbing; my earlier life was far behind me now, only a dim memory. Quick promotion followed. Maximum use of its manpower is the psychology behind any successful army. It must have the capacity to recognize and develop favorable attributes in an individual. It was certainly true in my case. Special forces people usually have a combination of higher intelligence and a technical specialization. My specialization was more general, an over-all spectrum analysis—an insight into various aspects of what an assignment was about and a detached view toward carrying it off in the best way possible. That incorporated two vital elements: leadership and an individual endurance factor that made me a character of slightly deadly capacity. More simply, I had the killer instinct. And an instinct for survival. And the ability to make other people think the same way. I had no special skill. I knew a bit about explosives. I was very good at unarmed combat. I was an expert marksman; I had a natural reflex action which just allowed me to be good at firing weapons. But I understood the technical application of weaponry to a particular theater of warfare; I had a knack for adapting weapons to obtain the most devastating effect.

After six months, the First Twenty-third was transferred to Saigon. We started going out on missions that lasted a month, sometimes two. We went out as small sections, or on joint operations with the Australians or Americans or Korean Rangers. We never worked with the Vietnamese. Their Panther Rangers were supposed to be elite. As far as I was concerned, they were not up to RFI standards. They were no better than the U. S. Marines. The Marines were just shit. So were the ARVN, but at least they knew it. I had seen Marines fight harder for a Coca-Cola truck than for ammunition.

We did all sorts of jobs. RFI mostly—search and destroy. We often took out small parties of fresh Green Berets to give them their first taste of combat. We would go looking for a unit that had terrorized a district or were operating out of some friendly village where they kept a cache of arms. We hunted them down and destroyed them.

A year after, I volunteered for a second tour of duty in Vietnam and was transferred to the Americans as an "adviser." I was bumped up to warrant officer second class so that I would hold rank over the U.S. sergeants I was leading in the field.

I rarely carried more than twenty men on any mission, and half that number if they were special forces. The enemy could be Viet Cong or North Vietnamese regulars or Montgards working for the other side. We might track quite massive units, then call in air support to hit them. But often we would by-pass the main body. The North Vietnamese officers would brief the NCOs separately from their men; it was a bit like having a field headquarters unit on the move. We would go in right under the nose of the main unit, hit the officers, and disappear.

We worked as bodyguards, escort patrols, observers. We went into high country where we could spot movement and relay it to headquarters. We had to avoid contact then, because we had all sorts of people looking for us. When you are in a combat zone, surrounded by enemy, you survive largely by your discreetness. We had to do crazy things like bury the enemy dead so that no one would spot our kill patterns. Missions might last several weeks, but they were not open-ended like some Green Beret missions. The end would be dictated by our getting the people we were after, or by a large regimental movement, or headquarters simply deciding we had been in long enough.

One of the great strains of being in Vietnam was the mental discipline a man put on himself in order to stay alive. There were times he had a war of nerves going on, when he had to maintain peak alertness, and every part of his body was crying to knock it off. A man became slightly detached from himself. Sooner or later, this must have emotional repercussions.

If we came off a mission in decent shape, we might get a couple of days' rest and go straight back into combat. But we could come back from an extended mission in terrible shape. Heat and humidity quickly spread infection from any wound. We were likely as not to have malaria or dysentery, or both. We sweated the salt out of our systems, and our metabolism was shot to hell. Then we got a couple of weeks' or a month's leave, and our health recovered remarkably fast. Saigon was off limits to us, so normally we went out to Japan.

Early in 1969, I went out with another New Zealander and a Green Beret to zero in on the Fifth, Sixth, and Eighth North Vietnamese Rangers. We followed them for about three weeks, keeping headquarters informed of their movements as they crossed the seventeenth parallel into South Vietnam. We were in bad shape, low on food and ammunition, and on our way to a pickup point when the other two got killed. I was five days on my own before I got back.

I came in from that one raging with fever, my nerves in tatters. I got a month's leave and hopped a ride on a MAC medic ship to Osaka. I knew a Korean nurse in Osaka, Sai Pei, a gorgeous dame. I intended to stay with her. It did not work out that way. I ran into a couple of guys I knew at the airport.

The Coliseum was what we called the hotel that was Mark Anthony's headquarters. Mark Anthony was the New Zealand adjutant in Japan. God knows what his real name was. He was a very friendly, very efficient guy. He was there to get the last couple of months out of us. To keep us or, often enough, to get us out of trouble. To keep track of us. SAS operatives were not expendable people outside combat. We were an expensive war item. We were supposed to keep Mark Anthony informed where we were at all times. I often went up to the mountains. I would just tell him what resort hotel I would be staying in. But when I was really done in, I would push off and say stuff it. This was one area where we were undisciplined, but it was harmless enough.

This time I went to a geisha house with these two guys. We started drinking hot rice wine, and I got drunker than I had ever been in my life. These three sisters took us to a house a hundred miles north of Osaka. I do not know how they got us on the train. Or why. We were in no shape to sleep with them. They were just doing a decent thing. I did not come around until three days later, when the U. S. MPs arrested us and dragged us back to Osaka.

There had been a big panic on. Mark Anthony had gotten orders to return me to Saigon, and he could not find me anywhere. So he told the U.S. authorities the three of us were AWOL. The girls learned they were looking for us and turned us over to the MPs, but not before they thought we were in shape to go back. Mark Anthony bailed me out of the stockade. He told me I was returning to Saigon in two days. An American officer interviewed me at the Coliseum to see if I had gotten into any trouble, but there was little I could tell him. He was cleaning up behind me.

I picked up my gear at the Coliseum and took it to Sai Pei's flat. I always carried with me my prime weapon, a pistol, and my machete. This was one of the privileges of being what we were. The Japanese never looked in our kit bags. We were sensible; we did not flash the stuff around in public. But these were all weapons I had adapted to suit me. I would not have left them behind in Saigon. Sai Pei and I had two days together. I cleaned my gear when she was at the hospital.

Tuesday morning, I went back to Saigon the way I had come, on a MAC flight. I reported to my commanding officer, Lieutenant Colonel Ian Stacey, at the Hotel Enfilade, which is what we called the U.S. headquarters. Stacey was an old Vietnam hand; he had been there since before New Zealand had an official presence. He told me to attend a briefing at 0700 hours the next day, then report to him. I went back to quarters and made my gear ready.

But the briefing the next morning was not for combat. It was a highly detailed political backgrounder delivered by an American colonel for New Zealand and Australian officers and NCOs. The hard-liners and soft-liners in Hanoi, he said, were locked in a power-struggle that was being brought to a head by two related movements. First was the growing strength of the doves in America; the American public was getting fed up with a no-victory war. Political pressure at home could force the Americans to leave Vietnam, as the French had, if they were to suffer a major battle-field defeat. Or following a negotiated peace, which Washington could use as an excuse to go. Secondly, there were rumors of détente feelers between Peking and Washington. A genuine détente would leave the North Vietnamese out on a limb. The pressure was on the North Vietnamese hard-liners to make a decisive move. The colonel's remarks, I noted, were as appropriate for the Americans as the North Vietnamese.

While the doves were talking détente, he went on, there had been a general upsurge in communist activity all over the world, but particularly in Africa and the Middle East where pro-Peking and pro-Moscow factions vied to outdo one another. Things were getting a bit naughty everywhere, and strong reactions were called for. There was a humming question that Britain might get involved in Vietnam.

The colonel's speech was interrupted by films and graphs that documented the patterns of movement on all sides. The briefing was a synthesis of the fantastic amount of data American intelligence had been gathering for six months. We saw some very interesting films that must have been shot by the Lockheed SR-71 over Peking and Hanoi; it carries cameras that can pick up a car registration number at 100,000 feet. The films were mostly of rallies and public celebrations. The shots would start at a sharp angle, then roll slowly over a group of people standing on a balcony or going up a flight of stairs. The frame would freeze and the colonel would explain who the people were and when and where they had met in recent months. He could not spell out the specific purpose of these meetings, though he implied they appertained to events of immense importance in the immediate future.

I reported back to Stacey, and he questioned me closely about the briefing, though he had been there as well. I took a great interest in our political briefings, because I was in Vietnam to fight communists, and these briefings increased my sense of purpose.

"We've got a special one on for you, Rivers," Stacey said, handing me my orders. "You're on a flight to Bien Hoa at 1100 hours tomorrow. We'll see you when you get back."

Bien Hoa was a familiar sight to me when I landed the next morning. There were a lot of tactical support missions out of there, fighters and gunships. We often used airborne infantry from Bien Hoa on RFI missions. I was not due to report in until 1600 hours, so I spent the afternoon wandering among the aircraft. I had lunch with some chopper pilots who had flown me and knew what I was.

I reported to the south side, a broken string of low buildings inside a heavily guarded barbed-wire enclosure. The south side was a self-contained headquarters unit for special missions, with its own administration, armory, film unit, mess, and living quarters. It was inside the southern perimeter of Bien Hoa, near the fuel and ammunition dumps. As the occasional mortar fell on Bien Hoa, unauthorized personnel stayed well away. Though the south side primarily ran Green Beret teams, it was staffed by regular officers. I reported to an American captain, who did a double-take when he saw my assignment number. He gave me confirmation of orders, assigned me quarters outside the perimeter, and ordered me to report for a briefing at 0600 hours the following morning.

I put my gear away, and as I left the barracks for the PX to get a hamburger, I ran into Barry Wiley coming in. He was assigned the room next to mine. He dumped his gear and came with me for a beer.

Barry and I talked about everything but what we were doing at Bien Hoa. Stacey told me my orders were top secret. When that happens, you do not even talk to people you know are secure.

"How long are you here for?" Barry asked me.

"I'm going out tomorrow," was all I said, which normally would have been the case; a briefing in the morning and upcountry by that afternoon.

"I'm going out tomorrow as well," Barry replied. Nothing more was said about our assignments.

Barry was a typical young Australian: tall, lean, slightly brash. There was no mystique about the man; he was an obvious person, easy to anticipate. Barry was intelligent but slightly immature. He had a keen, if somewhat heavy, sense of humor and was very likable.

What disturbed me about Barry was that he had retained his human reactions. He was not so hard that things did not scare him anymore. From one moment to the next, he could find himself operating right out of his depth.

Barry was an excellent soldier. He was an expert with explosives, and for a man who wore glasses, a remarkable shot with a rifle. Barry was superb when he could do things automatically. But when he had time to kill somebody . . . if he could see a man's eyes . . . he had this dangerous pause. He would do the job, but sometimes afterward he would go moody, as if in delayed shock. Then he felt he had to prove himself anew, which was ridiculous. His SAS badge was proof enough of his courage for any man. Heroes were unpopular in the special forces; they tended to endanger themselves and the men with them.

Sooner or later, Barry would have to talk about his fear. This was why he and I were not really close. I was totally insensitive to this. SAS men seldom talk about combat, because once it is over, it is no longer important except insofar as it can keep a man alive the next time. You locked that lesson into your memory, but you did not discuss it.

When we operated together, Barry's faults never caused me to lose sight of the fact that he was a very good soldier. I just kept my eyes on him for mistakes. He was that odd combination of a very human guy and an expert special forces operative. He was not terribly ambitious as far as the Army was concerned; he saw a termination to his involvement in Vietnam, which most of us did not. In camp, he was more interested in ball games and clay pigeon shooting than soldiering. He shared my passion for guns. We got on well together, though neither understood the other very well.

"What time is your briefing?" Barry asked me as we walked back from breakfast the following morning.

"0600 hours."

"Room 40B," he said.

"Shit," I said, "I'm lumbered with you again."

There followed a sequence of events that were not quite usual. When we reported to the OD and asked for room 40B, he called a second lieutenant who led us to an anteroom and asked us to wait. The lieutenant placed a guard on the door, then left. In five minutes he came back in and tried to jolly us up.

When you are put on alert for a mission, you go through an upsurge in readiness, a sequence of detaching yourself from everything but the mission itself. An up-graded office boy running around trying to kid you is one of the hardest things to take. I was more subdued than Barry, who began to get very agitated.

"Lieutenant," I said, "we're not going anywhere. You can leave us alone." He started to speak, then nodded abruptly and left the room. He sat outside in a chair where he could see us through the open door.

"Hey, Kiwi," Barry said, "did you notice how many civilians there are around the place today?"

"And rank."

"Did you see the choppers on the outside?"

"What about them?" Bien Hoa was like Heathrow, choppers coming in constantly, jets taking off.

"Command ships. Big Chinooks. CH-54s. Not the Iroquois."

Another second lieutenant came to the door. "Please follow me, gentlemen," he said.

The lieutenant led us to room 40B.

CHAPTER 2

The major came in, greeted us amiably, and had a chat around. At first, we carried the residue of tension we had all felt in the briefing room. Slowly we broke off into groups, in the natural order of things.

Jackson and Morrosco and Wiley talked about non-mission-oriented matters: women, cars, leave towns. Prather questioned me about Vietnam, with Tan sitting in as a silent partner. The major moved among us all, but he gave Prather and me most of his attention. We already had our delegation of thinking, which was how it was meant to be; a leadership party of four men, and then the followers. People pair off even in small units, not because some are inferior to others, but because of just how much they want to get involved.

Morrosco, Wiley, and Jackson were there to do a job. The reasons why, they left to others; they were not interested in interpreting orders. Which was great, because it made them uncomplicated people. I wanted to know everything about everything, and I always seemed to exercise a leadership role. The trio were quite willing to let the rest of us do the leading.

Prather, the Englishman, and I had a long chat that first night. He was an easy man to settle in with: quiet, a gentleman, a man of intelligence and breeding. I had seen his combat ribbons at the briefing— Malaya, Aden, Borneo, even Korea. I saw at once that he was in many ways a traditional soldier. Everything about him was understated, disciplined, orderly. He was a man of habit, down to his one bowl of pipe tobacco and one glass of port at night. He was a handsome man with well-defined features; the graying temples beneath his stiff brown hair did not age the man but drew attention to his distinguished bearing. He was of average height and weighed about 150 pounds. Everything about Lew Prather was tidy in an understated English way, even his conversation.

Despite the favorable impression he made on me, Prather remained the other possibility in the unit, because he was an unknown quantity. Two points bothered me about him. How much jungle combat had he seen? Most of the British SAS jobs in recent years had been in the sand. That was a different kind of warfare. And to what extent was he an observer? Was he going to be a genuine observer, baggage none of us wanted along, or "observer" in name alone, so that if he got killed, he would be less an embarrassment for his government?

Prather had relatives in New Zealand, and he tried to question me about our involvement in Vietnam. He did not get any mileage out of me there; New Zealand was as far away to me as England was to him. My involvement in Vietnam was purely personal.

The talk turned to weapons. He had brought from England a self-loading rifle and a Sterling light machine gun. Toliver and I both frowned on hearing this.

"What's wrong with them?" he asked.

"The SLR is a good weapon," Toliver said, "but not for here. Too much velocity. We're fighting at about a fifth the distance you're used to in the desert. Half of what you're used to in Borneo. The bullets just don't stay in a man. And the barrel's too long. You'll get it hung up. And they're so goddamn noisy."

"The Sterling is all right for close work," I said, "but they're too prone to jamming. Take a look at what Wiley uses. He's as good as there is with an M-3. It's a lot like a Sterling. It's a little heavier, but it's more accurate and has better spread. And half again the firing rate."

"What do you use?" he asked me.

"Shotgun."

"Shotgun!"

"A twelve-bore pump with a shortened barrel. Number six shot with a spherical ball on top."

"You must have no range at all," he said.

"I like to work close."

"This isn't Malaya, Lew," Toliver told him. "That's jungle, but compared to here, it's almost civilized warfare. This is just pure shit. You have no comprehension of the lengths people will go to, to kill each other. It's absolutely amazing. Things are being used out here that haven't even entered the minds of the people back home training guys to stay alive. So we do what we can the best we know how."

Prather was shocked. He was used to operating within the fixed confines of British warfare. The British SAS did not have the leeway for individual tastes that the rest of us had. That very discipline held the British Army together better than any other army in the world in mass combat. But it might mean a lack of adaptability in a special unit, where a combination of individuals with special ways of doing things could make a very powerful collective group.

"Well," said Prather, "I suppose I should try a grease gun."

Toliver briefed us informally at breakfast the next morning prior to our second scheduled briefing. He was working hard to integrate himself and make an imprint on us as unit leader, which normally was not done prior to combat. Even in the special forces, unit leaders did not fraternize much with their troops; the more aloof they remained, the less they encouraged contempt. We were all getting to like Toliver. He was definitely in command, even when he told us to call him Vic. And he was a perfectionist, as the rest of us were. There is nothing that brings a party of perfectionists closer than to have a perfectionist in command.

"This mission," he told us, "is going to be observed by the very highest authority. Outside Vietnam."

Prather cut his eyes at me in question. The highest authority was the White House. I did not overlook the fact that Toliver had said "observed by," not "initiated" or "conducted by." It sounded like somebody ready to take credit if it worked, but not the blame if it went wrong.

"Briefing and mission readiness will take us several weeks, perhaps three weeks," he continued. This took me by surprise. We did not need training for anything.

"What sort of situation are we getting into, Major? We've been under guard since we got here. And nobody tells us nothing. Now you're talking about several weeks. If we're being locked up, I think we deserve to know why," Jackson said.

"All I can say," he replied, "is that the nature of the mission will require that much preparation. Let me add that there are people coming in from the outside to brief us. And they have schedules like anybody else. They can't drop everything to brief us." That deflated me considerably. If we were being locked up until somebody had time for us, then we were not as important as I had imagined.

Toliver hammered at us, feeding us bits and pieces of information, fending off our questions with vague answers that would nevertheless preclude our raising them in the formal briefing.

Among the average foot soldier, speculation runs rampant. It is a form of verbal panic. People run off at the mouth and come up with completely misdirected ideas, which is extremely dangerous. But in a group like ours, people would come up with very accurate assumptions about what was going on. Briefers did not want any of that. They wanted to feed out the information at their own pace, in the most psychologically suitable sequence. This would be governed by security, unit buildup, and target date. They would have a briefing program worked out so that our curiosity would reach a peak just prior to the final briefing, then subside as we went on to physical preparation. Toliver was telling us enough to disarm us, so that we would not hit the briefers with the wrong questions.

He said the mission would call on our individual talents. That he, Tan, and I would be the first team, with Prather to back us up. So much for Prather being baggage. He said we would leave from and return to Thailand. We would be a couple of months behind enemy lines. He inferred it would be in Laos. Jackson pointed out that the briefing had touched on terrain and topography in northern North Vietnam.

"There may be enemy troop movement from there which could affect our mission, so look for more North Vietnam-Laotian border briefings," he said. He went on, "It will become obvious that some of you like to do things in an unorthodox way. In this unit, you can operate any way you want, so long as it doesn't interfere with the smooth operation of the team. I think we'll learn, in fact, that our little idiosyncrasies complement one another."

He said that some of us would have individual briefings, what we called mission recognition briefings. We would often go in somewhere as a unit, then separate to carry out individual assignments, after which we would rendezvous for the pickup. We got individual recognition briefings from the intelligence people about tactical obstructions protecting our target. That could be anything from a bridge to an enemy unit to a mountain. But from what Toliver said about the unit working together, it did not appear to me that we would be splitting up. Toliver finished by emphasizing again that the mission would be "observed by highest authority, outside the immediate theater." We broke up and went straight to the scheduled briefing.

It was Saturday now. The funny thing was that weekend passes existed in the American Army in Vietnam, even in a combat zone. The base was quiet for two days. Guys had gone to Saigon. People played baseball. The base had a weekend feel.

The weather was at its best, cool at night, not yet suffocatingly hot and wet by day. Things felt relaxed. We were not accepting the briefings under pressure. Sometimes you felt like you were going over the top, you had had a gutful, and small things like weather or the rumble of a distant battle seemed to stretch your nerves to the snapping point. When a man had been cut off from any friendly human contact, living on his nerves, forced to retain a cool exterior just to survive ... when that man came back in, he could be explosive. Some could let it out by talking. If you did not like to talk, it was harder.

The second briefing came in hard. Only two of the civilians returned; they handled the political side and the colonel the military. A couple of lieutenants served as aides. But this was no commitment briefing. We must have passed muster, because we were in it now. We got down to business.

The first civilian told us there was tremendous pressure on the U.S. high command for a decisive stroke in Vietnam. The war was becoming daily more unpopular in America, and press reports in the States of communist military successes were demoralizing the allied forces at a fantastic rate. If the Americans were going to win in Vietnam, they needed a bold stroke to gain the initiative. And soon.

The colonel stated straight off that the mission would be extremely dangerous and of the highest secrecy. The combat spectrum would allow us to take advantage of our individual ways of doing things, but we would function as a unit. This told me we were not getting individual briefings because we were splitting up. The colonel said we had been specially selected for this mission because of our individual talents, thus sidestepping the question of the national mix. We already had our medic and radio operator. Other specific responsibilities would be forthcoming at future briefings. We would depart and return to Thailand. Caches would be prepared for us in Laos, and we could have field linkup with one Green Beret unit in central Laos. The team would have absolutely no linkup outside the special forces network. My ears perked up when I heard this. Normally we would have been able to call on friendly Laotian infantry or airborne units to help us out if we got in trouble. High command did not want even friends to know what we were doing. The mission was being oriented more and more toward North Vietnam, though the colonel was not ready to admit it, and toward an elimination role. It began to look as if we were going to hit a unit of North Vietnamese officers.

He went on to say we would be provided certain weapons and armament for which we had shown personal preference. We would be taken off the base for a week to familiarize ourselves with these weapons.

We hit the maps for zone briefings that incorporated co-ordinates of our route in Laos. We were briefed on military obstructions in northern Laos and then shown, without explanation, two aerial reconnaissance films of northern North Vietnam. That was very deep into enemy territory, very near China. Some of us had been west of Hanoi, but never that far north.

We were briefed on future briefings. We would be confined to quarters until Monday, when we would have two briefings from people coming from the States, followed by a three-week training period interspersed with individual briefings. Finally, a departure briefing.

All this was taken without a single question from the team. First, we did not know what was happening, and second, we had learned from Toliver's breakfast meeting that we would get more answers from him than from the colonel. The colonel knew we were getting all we could from the briefing; we were not dumb listeners to be put in tin cans and shipped into combat. But he was getting no feedback from us. I thought at first it was our silence that was making the colonel uneasy. He began to sweat as the mission edged toward North Vietnam. Then I noticed that the rest of the briefing team were anxious as well. This I had never seen before. My first thought was that the mission was still being debated somewhere. Or someone was having second thoughts. They were getting close to telling what it was all about; if they were going to kill it, they would have to do it soon. One thing I knew for sure. If the mission was on, we were going in against the rain. We all began to get uneasy as we mirrored the tension at the front of the room. Jackson drummed his fingers lightly on his desk. Prather cleaned his pipe for the third time without lighting it.

When Toliver took us back to quarters, his gear was there. He was part of the team now. After we had eaten, he called us together in the day room. In his hands he had a dossier on each of us.

"If you have any questions, let's hear them. I'll answer them if I can."

"What did the colonel mean when he said 'certain weapons' of our preference would be used?" I asked.

"You men have been chosen for this mission because, apart from being excellent special forces operatives, you have each an area of special competence which will be useful. Kiwi, you are a top marksman."

He had not told me anything yet. There were a lot of those around. "Tan, you can operate a radio in five languages," he went on. "Prather is an excellent topographer, climatologist, and pioneer. Morrosco, besides being a medic, is very good with explosives. As is Wiley. And Jackson has an eye for deflection like nobody's business."

Jackson grinned. He knew what Toliver meant.

"To answer your question, Kiwi, you're getting a Sahka."

"A what?" asked Morrosco. "And what's a kiwi?"

"A Sahka," Prather answered him, "is a 7-mm. hunting rifle. Czechoslovakian. A kiwi is a New Zealand bird, and the nickname for anyone who ever left." Prather looked slightly worried. He must have been wondering if his people knew what he had gotten himself into.

"A scope for the Sahka," Toliver said. That meant it was a hit job. "And you get your rocket launcher, Jackson."

"Do you know how many rockets we'll be carrying?" Jackson asked.

"As many as you need. And not one more. Wiley and Morrosco will help you disperse the load."

This was promising to be the kind of job I relished. The Sahka meant I was to hit someone who badly needed hitting. My last assignment like this had been to hit some real villains, a ragtag band of Montgard mercenaries in the pay of the United States. Their leader had worked for me before, and I hated and distrusted the bastard on sight. They had turned over and led an American patrol into an ambush that had wiped them out. With no survivors, they did not know we had learned about the sell-out. So we hired them as one flank of a phony ambush of a VC unit. I borrowed a sniping rifle. When they were in position, we hit them. I put a dumdum through the head man and blew him apart like a melon.

Toliver led us out into the barracks yard for an hour of calisthenics. For a major, he could do a lot of sit-ups. I was not much more than half his age, and I was exhausted. We broke and went into the barracks to attend to personal details.

We were all getting to like Toliver. He was a strong leader without wearing his rank on his sleeve. When it did not matter, his discipline was almost casual. And he was obviously being as frank with us about the mission as he was allowed.

Toliver was a hell of a man in every way. Tall and lean—he was well over six feet—he was fit in the extreme. He had a swarthy complexion which was more than a deep tan. He had a typical army head with closely cropped hair streaked in gray and brown. This was a common sight in Vietnam, where even youths of eighteen who had been in too much high-density combat found their hair turning white. There was a scar under Toliver's left eye, and he was missing part of the little finger on his left hand. He was powerfully built, a man of constant physical awareness; every move he made seemed calculated. His uniforms were noticeably more immaculate than even other special forces people. I guessed his age as late thirties. He had a Korean ribbon, so the Army had been his life from a very early age.

He impressed me as a man of his own style, a man used to doing things his way. Without stretching the bounds of military respect, his self-confidence made him as casual with superior rank as with his juniors. The people who briefed us showed great respect for Toliver; he had done a lot of missions, and it showed. A man who had been through as much as Toliver never let go completely. He could appear to be totally relaxed, but the edge was always there.

My feelings for him had changed abruptly from that first briefing. Then he had been assessing us because, to my knowledge, it was the first time he had seen any of us. When a person did that to me, I rejected him immediately; I felt contempt for him. There was no question of his expertise. One look around the briefing room told me I was with the best. But some are always better at being the best. After what I had been through for a year, I felt threatened by no other human being. I felt contempt because his assessment of me was irrelevant. I could not be belittled by superior rank, because a situation would arise sooner or later where we would recognize and respect one another's capabilities, or one of us would prove to be the better man. If there was mutual recognition of that fact, then you respected one another as equals. If not, you had the leader and the led. But from that very first breakfast meeting, Toliver had made it clear he knew what I was.

I grew to recognize that his brilliance as a commander was directly allied to mission concept, to using the people under him to maximum advantage. He was expert with explosives and weapons and in unarmed combat, but his greatest talent lay in delegating the experts he had at his fingertips. That meant knowing a little about everything. A man could not be trained for this; it came from experience and having a certain knack. Years in Vietnam meant Toliver had both.

By Saturday evening, the base was filling up again with soldiers on shortened weekend passes who started preparing for a Monday morning inspection. We stayed in the quarters, quietly tending to our personal detail, figuring out just what we wanted to take with us. We knew enough by now to make a lot of educated guesses. The Sahka meant it was to be a hit job. The time allowed meant a long walk somewhere. I would need a lot of ammunition for the shotgun. The others were working out their own gear in the same way.

All day Sunday, the base buzzed with activity as it prepared for the Monday inspection. The south side was cleared completely of all unauthorized personnel.

Early Monday, we were led under guard to our briefing room. Awaiting us were the two civilians, the colonel, and a major we had never seen before. The rest of the briefing party were absent. As we started to take our seats, the colonel called us to attention.

"Gentlemen," he said, "the general has a few words to say to you."

General Westmoreland had been sitting at the rear of the room, and we had not seen him when we filed in. He was supposed to be in Washington, and here he was greeting us. He came forward and made the usual vague speech about the importance of the mission. This was largely ignored because he said nothing concrete but implied that he knew what it was all about. I did not know and I did not care what he thought about it. While the general was speaking, I found myself listening to the big choppers. Iroquois and Cayusas were coming and going all the time at Bien Hoa, and I was accustomed to the familiar beat of their rotors. What I heard now was the distant but unmistakable rumbling of the Chinooks, several of them. Westmoreland stopped in midsentence, glanced at the colonel and his own aide, then continued. The colonel trembled visibly as he rustled the papers in front of him. I heard the faintest tremor of anxiety in the general's voice. When the choppers touched down near our building, the general cut his speech short and returned to his seat. I heard a party of men storm into the building, the sound of their heels rushing ahead of them as they strode through the corridors. In the distance, I heard several jeeps driving off in another direction.

A moment later, the door flew open. Two civilians burst in. They both carried brief cases and wore raincoats against the chill of the early morning helicopter ride. They were followed by several military aides. I had never seen either of these men before, but from the way they came upon us, I knew they were very powerful people. They bubbled with confidence and authority. The first man sat down facing us. The other stepped forward without bothering to wait for an introduction.

"General"—he nodded in a perfunctory bow to protocol—"gentlemen, we won't waste time. You have a basic outline of the mission. Let's get down to what it is all about."

In three minutes, he sketched everything we knew to date. He stopped and looked up at the general.

"Gentlemen," Westmoreland said, "I wish I could spend more time with you. Unfortunately, I must attend to a base inspection. Your mission is of the utmost urgency. I wish you every success, and a safe return."

The general left the room with an aide. I suddenly realized that the inspection had been a decoy to get these two men on the base without attracting attention. Bien Hoa was very much a front-line base, under constant observation by the enemy. Somebody was going to a great deal of trouble over us. But I was not given time to reflect on this.

"Faces!" the speaker snapped. The second man removed a brown envelope from his brief case. The envelope contained photographs which he pinned, five in a line, then seven beneath, to a bulletin board set up at the front of the room. These were head and shoulder shots, portraits of communist officials. The faces suddenly became familiar; we had seen them repeatedly in films over the past week. General Nguyen Van Giap, the North Vietnamese Chief of Staff, was the only one I knew by name. His had been the first picture to go up. The American raked a pointer across the top line of five photographs.

"Prime targets," he said sharply. "Secondary targets," he said, quickly thumping each photo in the lower line. He gave us no time for reflection. He stepped closer and rapped General Giap's photograph with his index finger.

"Rivers!" he called out.

He made a V with his fingers and touched the next two photos, both Chinese officials.

"Toliver," he said.

He made the same V beneath the last two primary targets.

"Tan," he said, turning slightly to look at the man.

The first of Tan's targets was Chinese, the second Korean. Tan stiffened visibly in his chair and leaned forward. The speaker dropped his hand to the second row.

"Rivers," he said, again spreading his fingers to indicate two targets for me. The next three went to Jackson, then one each to Tan and Toliver.

I could not tear my eyes away from the first photograph. I had been up against Giap a lot in the past year, facing units he was directing in the field. He was the man who made the NVA work, the cleverest fighting man in Southeast Asia. Here stood a stranger in a raincoat giving me license to hit him. I found myself shaking with excitement. The blood seemed to rush to my head, to my fingertips. The back of my neck burned fiery hot. Jesus, I thought, this is it. Then the thrill subsided as quickly as it had come.

And suddenly I was amazed at what we had gotten into. All the analysis, all the assumptions we had been making for a week began to fall into place. Prather was the one who broke the concentration. He packed his pipe, then looked up without lighting it.

"Sir," he said, "does my government know about this?"

The man gave a mirthless smile which told me he was not going to answer Prather's question.

"Your unit designation is the Five Fingers, the mission designation the Five Fingers Exercise. You have been selected for the mission because of your individual talents . . . allied to your five nationalities. It must be obvious from your political briefings that there has been an upsurge in political activity among the Southeast Asian communist rulers appertaining to this theater. A plan of action is at this very moment being debated among the communist hierarchy which, if implemented, would have global repercussions. Forty-five days from this date, a conference will be called by the adherents of this plan to finalize its form and content. It has been decided to combine the interests of the principal anticommunist powers to effect joint counter measures. You have been assigned to this mission as representatives of your various nations to take positive pre-emptive action against this conference to prevent this plan being carried forward. Your job, gentlemen, is to erase the conference site and to terminate with extreme prejudice the faces you see before you."

"Sir," interrupted Prather, "by whose authority are we ordered to do so?"

"By highest authority," the American said. "The Supreme Commander."

"I am sorry to persist, sir, but your Supreme Commander and mine are not the same. The photo top left is of the highest-ranking military officer in North Vietnam. Most of the others are Chinese military and government officials of high office. Has my government given its blessing to their termination?"

"You're not here under your government's blessing, Prather. You are here under its order."

"Yes, sir."

"Sir, there is no Vietnamese representation on the unit," said Morrosco.

"It has been agreed that the United States will represent South Vietnamese interests."

This was a polite way of saying that South Vietnamese security was so leaky the mission would be compromised by their inclusion.

"Gentlemen, you are being presented the opportunity for an active role in one of the key moves in the entire physical arena. What you do, or fail to do, may determine whether we seal the envelope on Vietnam or go on to a global holocaust. I welcome your questions, when they concern mission detail. I am not interested in conjecture or speculation. If I may proceed . . . The prime targets have been meeting in twos and threes for the past six months, formulating plans for the opening of simultaneous military campaigns in Vietnam and Korea. These campaigns are to proceed under an umbrella of Chinese nuclear rockets. I can assure you, gentlemen, that the Chinese have the hardware to hit any spot in Southeast Asia from the Chinese mainland. In short, they have chosen a strategy to draw the entire world into Vietnam. If agreement is reached at the forthcoming conference, we've begun the rundown to World War III. The cards will come up on the table. Western withdrawal from Southeast Asia or nuclear holocaust. You know who these men are whose photos you see before you. You know the power they hold. And you know they are capable of making such a decision."

I found it hard to accept that so clever a soldier as Giap would risk everything on one roll of the dice. But Teng Ping and Lin Piao—for I was sure I recognized them as two of the three Chinese prime targets—were a different kettle of fish. They were politicians, communist theoreticians, above all, civilians. And no longer young men. They might welcome the chance to see it all happen within their lifetime.

The man hammered at us for another hour in his powerful, almost hypnotic way . . . an expanded arena . . . a drive to involve the entire world in Vietnam . . . nuclear war . . . or surrender by the West to Chinese blackmail . . . every man at the conference a power unto himself . . . they would never meet again in one group . . . they must be eliminated, the threat terminated now. It was so convincing, the man so persuasive, we were all on the boil. My adrenals were racing, my heart pounding with excitement. Giap was the best soldier I would ever go up against. In the hierarchy of communist mythology, he ranked up there with Mao and Ho and Chou En Lai. He had been making the fighting in Vietnam for thirty years. And I was the one, out of all the men in Indochina, they had picked to hit him.

The other targets were as important as Giap, one rung down the ladder from running their countries, or marshals of their armies. We were going to change the face of power for a billion people, this team of ours, these Five Fingers.

I sensed that the others were feeling the same. Each one of us was a very powerful man on his own. They had brought us together to work us as a unit and make us work as a unit. When that happened, we would be more effective than a regiment, we could lay down more fire power than two hundred men firing in the bloody air. Nobody could stop us.

I was surprised, when we broke for lunch and went back to quarters, how quiet we all were. A certain deflation had set in, I think, because there was still so much they had not told us. We talked little during the meal. There was some discussion that the whole thing might be a ploy, a devious way to get Giap, that I was the reason the mission had been mounted. I argued that there were too many easier ways to get him, too many times and places it could be done without this elaborate deception, without hitting the Chinese. I had been concerned by Prather's reaction at the briefing, but he made it clear over lunch that he was not troubled by the mission. What concerned him was getting involved in a political move that his government was not privy to.

When we returned to the briefing room, the desks had been pushed against the walls to make room for a table on which rested a padlocked wooden box about six feet square. A larger table held what was obviously a topographical model of the route which was covered with a cloth. The moment I stepped into the room, the rush returned. The others looked as edgy and excited as I felt. The second American took charge now, hitting us just as hard and fast as his associate, with the same punch all the way through. We began to get DD—destination date: elapsed time, specific routings; zone briefings. A wall map was pulled down to show our route in Laos; the red line that was our route disappeared into the map roller at the North Vietnamese frontier. The American briefed us for another half hour on our route in, detailing our two caches in Laos; he hit us again and again with the discreetness of the mission. We were to avoid combat whenever possible. There would be an upsurge in Green Beret activity in Laos to camouflage our movement. Finally he gave us the date.

"Seven June. At 0800 hours, all the principals will gather for the opening ceremony. You will hit at that exact moment. You have your date, gentlemen—0800 hours on seven June." He paused, almost like a man having second thoughts. "I think it is time for you to look at the impact area."

He pulled down the map behind him. The route through Laos cut the North Vietnamese border and continued north by northeast toward the Red River border between North Vietnam and China. It pierced the Red River and thrust due north for several kilometers before ending in a red-shaded box.

We were going to China.

CHAPTER 3

No one moved. The American grinned at us. Again Prather was the first to speak.

"Sir," he said, "am I correct in understanding that the impact area is in China?" For some reason, Prather's question sounded funny. We all laughed and relaxed.

"That is correct, Prather. The Five Fingers will be the first joint allied insurgency team to operate inside China. You will proceed to Ta shu tang township in Yunnan Province. There, gentlemen, you will forestall a nuclear confrontation. Let's take a look at your route and the red zone."

The sheet went off the large table to reveal a three-dimensional model of our route all the way up. It had been made from aerial photos with extreme attention to detail. And it was rugged all the way, with a steady climb up to about five thousand feet, where Ta shu tang nestled on a fairly open plateau with its back against a mountain range. It was wild country. What was not mountain was jungle; often it was both. There was a bad patch of swamp in Laos and another in North Vietnam near the Chinese border. A lot of the route was sparsely populated, but mountains and rivers would make it hard to keep to schedule. There was no question of support after northern Laos; we would be on our own. But we were going somewhere nobody had ever been before, to do a job that only we could do. We knew the consequences of going into China. It was the end of the line. But I dismissed that thought immediately. We all would have fought communists from the tropics to the ice caps. I was in Vietnam to do that job. And what a way to finish.

"Gentlemen, I am here to brief you on mission purpose and give you your routing to the impact area, which is the twenty-mile radius around Ta shu tang. I am not here to tell you how to carry out the mission. It will be your responsibility to work out the most suitable plan for hitting the conference site. If that had to be explained to you, you wouldn't be good enough to be on this team. You will receive detailed group and individual briefings on the conference site, projected security, and profiles on your targets. You have almost three weeks to work out your plan of attack and rehearse it down to the second. But, gentlemen, these men must be terminated. I don't have to tell you that you are expected to be as flexible as you are precise. Your prime objective is the impact area. Once there, you will be free to alter the hit in any way that corresponds to changing circumstances. If the parties are delayed by a blown bridge or wind of you in the area or whatever; if you have to change the lineup because some of you have been hit; whatever the reason, once in the impact zone, we expect the mission to be carried out. We will be monitoring your progress by the usual procedures—aerial reconnaissance, ground observation, the movement of enemy troops against you —but no units will be able to help you on the ground. Yours will be one of the key moves of the entire

Southeast Asian campaign. That is why we picked you. And that is why we expect you to succeed.

"For security reasons, you will be operating with the minimum backup. That means two caches in Laos. After that, you will be on your own. The communists don't know we are aware of the existence of this conference. Any sign of movement in that direction would bring instant cancellation. That is why you must maintain the lowest profile possible. Avoid all combat when possible. Any questions?"

"Will you have a backup unit in the field if we don't make it?" Jackson asked.

"You, gentlemen, are it. You'd only have to catch a snag somewhere, get slowed down and have a backup unit overtake you, and we would have confusion in the battle zone."

"If this conference is that important, why risk having us get hit and not carrying out the job," Morrosco asked, "when B-52s can do it in an hour."

"We're trying to stop a war, not start one," the American answered. "If we sent B-52s into China, we'd have buttons being pushed everywhere in five minutes. You do your job properly and the Chinese will never know, or be able to prove, who was there."

"What about abort?" Wiley asked.

"Lieutenant Tan will carry a crystal-locked receiver. That receiver is for one signal only. Abort. You will listen for it daily between 1515 hours and 1545 hours to allow for error in your watches. The signal will be broadcast one time only, at 1530 hours. The abort signal is . . . v . . . e. Repeated three times. Followed by three v's. Finally three e's. If your movement is plotted by the enemy, or if for any other reason it is no go, you will be broadcast your abort."

We all began to shout at once.

"You can't abort us in China!"

"The radio monitors will pick us up!"

"Calm down," the man said. "Under no circumstances will the mission be aborted in China. In fact, it won't be aborted after you have crossed into North Vietnam. You will have a mission-in time of twenty-four days. Seventeen of those will be in Laos. Once you have left Laos, the mission is on."

"Then I can throw the receiver away after we cross into North Vietnam," said Tan.

"You will listen for abort every day from the day you depart until six June. Under no circumstances will you fail to listen for abort."

"Why, if it's not coming?"

"To allow for all contingencies."

"Apart from our discovery why would the mission be canceled?" asked Wiley.

"Just cancellation. Your job is to complete the mission. Cancellation is the responsibility of higher authority. There is no place on this mission for conjecture, Wiley. That goes for you as well, Prather, and for all of you. Everything you need to know and don't learn in this briefing, you will learn in the training program. Don't concern yourself with what you don't need to know. Any more questions?"

There were none.

"Two more points. If you do your job right, with some luck you'll all get away. At the conference site, there will be nothing, I repeat nothing, left behind that will point a finger at you, or your countries, as being responsible for this mission. No personal items are to be taken with you. No photographs. No letters. No rings. No good luck charms. And especially no dog tags. The rest of the world can speculate all it wants, but nothing is to prove you were there. This is a two-edged sword. If the Chinese can't prove you were there, they may want to keep the whole thing quiet. It would be very embarrassing to have to announce that their friends weren't safe inside the Chinese borders. Some people may speculate with our help, that it was the result of a power struggle within China.

"Point two. What I have just said is meaningless if one of you happens to be captured. You are seven men. You are too few to be carrying wounded. The

Five Fingers Exercise is a mission of total unit closure. You are expected to establish your own protocol in that regard.

"Finally, upon a successful conclusion to the mission, you can anticipate extraordinary benefits accruing from your various military commands. Good day, gentlemen. Good luck."

Before we had time to catch our breaths, the two Americans were gone. We stayed in the briefing room. The major opened the wooden box and brought out a very precise scale model of Ta shu tang, with every house, garden shed, and tree reproduced to scale. The conference hall was the one large building in the town. We hit the models and maps with Toliver and the colonel. By the questions they asked, I could see that the others were as enthusiastic as I was. The more than slightly suicidal nature of the mission was ignored completely. We were all experiencing the excitement of knowing that we were the best. But what a challenge this one was, even for the best.

We were jumping off from an airfield north of Chiang Khan, Thailand, a few kilometers from the Mekong River border with Laos. We would have one hidden cache at a riverhead in southern Laos and a second one in northern Laos at the safe village of M Ngoi. From M Ngoi we would have to take enough to get us to China and back. We would resupply again at M Ngoi on the return and strike from there for the Mekong. With luck we might contact a Green Beret unit in southern Laos which could get us hauled out by chopper. From Chiang Khan to Ta shu tang was just at 420 miles, all uphill.

"Why didn't they pick an easier place for us to get to?" said Morrosco.

"Yeah," said Jackson. "Why are they meeting in such a little bitty place as that?"

"If you look at the map," said Toliver, "you'll see that Ta shu tang is about five kilometers north of the railroad line that runs from Hanoi to Kun Ming in China. They don't want the world knowing about the meeting, so Peking and so forth are out. They can't hold it in Vietnam for security reasons. Now Ta shu tang is the boondocks, even for China. Who's going to know they were there? The Koreans and Chinese can come there in complete safety, and the Vietnamese party can all go up together on one train. And when the meeting is over, in half an hour they're back in Vietnam. We tried to arrange it for New York, Morrosco, but the delegates didn't feel safe on the streets."

"Damn right, Major. They better stay out of my old neighborhood."

"Why do we have to start so far off the mark?" Wiley asked. "Choppers could take us up to central Laos and save ten days' walk."

"The enemy doesn't know we know about the meeting. If we lift a unit way up in Laos, and they start walking toward China, the meeting will be off in five seconds."

"We could do it with drag chutes at night," I said. We were all trained to jump from five hundred feet with small chutes. They brought you down fast, but it was the best way not to be seen.

"We'd have to send too big a team to leave seven of us without broken legs. We'd have injured scattered all over the jungle. Then they would have to be picked up."

"How do we make the hit?" Jackson asked.

"We'll work that out ourselves." Toliver looked around. "Tan, you haven't asked a single question since you got here."

"When can we leave?"

"When we're ready."

"I'm ready now."

"Give the rest of us a few days."

By the time we got back to barracks, Prather was ready to explode.

"That last bloke was a right bastard," he said.

"What's bugging you, Prather?" Jackson asked.

"It was the bloody offhand way he talked about

'unit closure.' How can he stand there so coolly and tell us to wipe ourselves out?"

"Why not?" I said. This was Prather's lack of acclimatization showing through. The rest of us had heard it more than once before. I could see Prather was confused by me. I knew he had found me to be a normal guy, with normal passions, human emotions. Yet I was accepting unit closure as casually as it had been presented.

"Are you having doubts about your ability to carry out your role on the mission, Prather?" Toliver asked him.

"You know I'm not, Vic," he replied. "I'm having doubts about whether I'm meant to be on the mission. You know, I was quite extensively briefed by my government before I came out here. There was no suggestion of a mission of this magnitude. I'm told to hit half the communist military command in Asia. I question that my government is party to this. I was seconded here as an observer. This is a suicide mission."

"So what?" I said.

"Don't you want to live, Gayle?" he asked.

"Lew, I don't worry about dying at the best of times. I work to stay alive, but I don't worry. And these aren't exactly the best of times."

Prather looked around, but he received sympathy from no quarter. "I for one am not going to wipe myself out," he said.

"Don't worry, Lew," I said, "if need be, I'll do you in myself." There was a long silence.

"What did that guy mean about 'extraordinary benefits,' Major?" Morrosco asked.

"It means you'll get promoted."

"Can he promote me all the way to civilian?" Morrosco said.

"Think you'd make a good one, Morrosco?" Toliver asked.

"I've made a few in the past, Major. I'd like to try some more."

I had been watching Pete Morrosco very closely. He

was impossible to dislike: good-humored, colorful, funny, a man with a relaxed outlook on life. And that was why I had watched him, to see if he was too relaxed. But at the briefings, he had listened intently, and I soon realized that Morrosco took pride in being a Green Beret and worked hard at being a good one.

He was short and, rare among special forces, very stocky. The rest of us were lean; our bodies were built for endurance. At first sight, I had thought he was overweight. But what might have been fat was muscle. Morrosco was a body-builder. There were no weights around now, so whenever he found something heavy enough, he would hoist it up and press it over his head.

Morrosco looked like a soldier should look: the uniform clean and well pressed, the hair the right length. He had a swarthy complexion even deeper than Toliver's. His parents had immigrated to New York from Puerto Rico, and he often broke into Spanish when he was excited. He referred jokingly to himself as a wetback and a spic, though he never gave leave to the rest of us to do so.

"Hey, kid," Jackson had said that first night. "What kind of name is Morrosco?"

"A last name, Jackson," he had replied. "Just leave it at that."

Pete came from a big family, from one of the poor sections of New York. He talked like I imagine tough New York kids talk. Violence was nothing new to Pete. Vietnam was just an extension of what he had known all his life. He was not married, and his pay went straight home to help support the younger children. I got the impression that he was a bit of a hero in his neighborhood. He planned on going to medical school when he got out of the Army.

"Why do you want to be a doctor?" I asked him.

"I been playing doctor since I was three years old, Kiwi. I was the most famous gynecologist on the block by the time I was ten. A man does what he knows best. Right?"

A training program began at once. We spent all the next day studying the model of the impact area without coming up with a plan. It was not lost time. We were working together for the first time as a unit, establishing our work methods, sorting out our relationships to one another. Jackson set at once trying to stamp his authority on Wiley and Morrosco in a very rigid military way. He wanted it understood that he was the sergeant. They were both too good-natured to fight it this early on, but I did not believe Jackson would be able to maintain this posture in our unit. He must have been an excellent sergeant for the regular army, but a team like ours had to function as one mind. That could not happen in a strictly regulated military atmosphere. It was essential that we have a breakdown in discipline. Despite what we might call the major, there was no question of his authority. The trio would need the same relationship, if it was to function smoothly, both internally and with the rest of us. I was not concerned yet, because I could see that Jackson was a very capable soldier, and he worked well with Toliver.

I had taken an instant dislike to Jackson. He became a sergeant the moment he walked in a room. He looked hard, and he looked mean. He was loud, but he had a reputation for getting things done. He was also a man with a tremendous amount of experience, which I respected.

Jackson would have been about Toliver's age, in his mid- or late thirties. He was of average height and build. He was a well-turned-out soldier, his mousy brown hair short and neat, his uniforms impeccable. He had a thin face with jaw muscles that flexed when he was concentrating. He rarely smiled, and his face was lined by the strain of three years' combat in Vietnam. He had a quick mind and had absorbed the briefings with a minimum of questions. He was just as quick to absorb the data from Toliver and the colonel.

That first day we rejected plan after tentative plan. We were working from a few fundamental facts, but we could not come up with the right combination. The conference would take place in an open-sided building facing a rising plateau which would be our obvious avenue of approach. All the prime targets, and hopefully most of the secondary targets, would be gathered in front of the hall to greet Giap when he arrived last. The attack would be initiated by my shooting Giap as he got out of his car. The prime targets were the responsibility of marksmen—Tan, Toliver, and myself. At the same time, the trio would blow the building with rockets, hopefully hit their targets, and create mass confusion among the defenders. They then would provide covering fire for our withdrawal. But no one came up with the right combinations to get us close enough to do the job thoroughly and give us half a chance to get away. We broke up without deciding anything.

CHAPTER 4

We spent the following morning at individual briefings on our targets, then went back in the conference room after lunch.

"I'd like to suggest a plan," Prather said.

"So you're back on the team," said Toliver laughing.

"I never was off the team. I just wish someone would tell me I am meant to be on the team."

The individual briefing that morning had really bowled me over. American intelligence accumulates an unbelievable amount of data. They had been observing Giap closely for five years, and they knew the man better than he knew himself. I was the last and potentially the only weak link in this chain of assassination, because I was the human link. When they got through briefing me, I would be as close to being a machine for assassination, a human computer, as they could manufacture. I would spend almost a month walking into a scene which might last thirty minutes, a month in which the climax would stretch over three seconds.

I had to be more attuned than the Sahka to the target.

I was the first man the colonel briefed individually, and when he came in the film room with a file twelve inches thick, and the projectionist began to set up his equipment, I knew what it meant. I got the thrill again of knowing that I was the very best man they could find for this job. I felt a rush of blood to my shoulders and to the back of my neck; I started to tune in, in a very high-pitched way, to what I was going to do. My target proved a very interesting subject for study.

Giap was a vain man. He reveled in his role of public hero. In the films, he seemed genuinely to be enjoying himself, whether at a formal occasion like a parade or merely accepting the adulation of the crowd in more casual street scenes. I saw the same three films again and again. The first was a propaganda film in which he was reviewing a military parade in Hanoi. The other two were newsreel footage. One was of Giap directing military operations from a field headquarters. He was doing a field officer's job—counseling with his junior officers, congratulating his men, maintaining contact with the troops and battle-front conditions. The third film was of Giap on the streets in some city, probably Hanoi. He was standing on the steps of a military building, and the civilians were pressing forward to meet him. The film did not appear to be concocted and, boy, were these people carrying on. They were kissing his hand and bowing, and some just hung back, like it was too much for them, meeting him. He never stopped smiling. He was encouraging them.

The films ran about half an hour each, but I would stop them and ask for certain shots to be reproduced and blown up for target recognition and character analysis. The films were silent; while they ran, the colonel fed me information about the man.

I studied Giap down to the color of his eyes, even to learning that he did not wear contact lenses. If a man climbed out of the car and into my scope, and his eyes were not the right color, I might hesitate for half a second. Long enough to miss. I learned how he got out of a car, how he walked, how his aides walked with him. I studied the man's history, his personality, anything that would make that target grow and steady itself between the hairs of my scope.

Regardless of the final plan, the colonel and I worked from a few basic premises. Giap, as the highest-ranking military official, would arrive last. Everyone else would be gathered in a reception party to greet him. He would arrive by car on the only road from the railway. We would be positioned somewhere on a hill to the south. This road came from my due right, or east, then turned northwest to about 2230 hours on the hand of a clock a hundred yards before the building. The car would stop with its left side facing us, but turned away at a forty-five-degree angle, exposing both sides of the rear of the car to us. Giap would be by the right rear door of the car, with an aide to his left. Another aide would accompany the driver in the front. The only safe time to hit Giap with everyone present was when he got out of the car.

Unlike most men, Giap had a habit of putting on his hat before he got out of a car. Consequently, he bent lower than the average man, and his head was the first part of his body to exit a car. My first sight of Giap would be the round crown of his hat. I would have half a second to put a bullet through the crown, but it was very risky because that span of time would show almost no definite contour through the scope. Certain movements of certain colors give a very poor contour. I might shatter the side of his head and not kill him. One second later, I would see his profile, which would present far better definition. I could shoot him through the cheek and send the round through his head.

Giap had something wrong with his right arm that caused it to hang stiffly at his side. It was thought to be arthritis or an injury of some kind, nothing permanent. When I heard this, I climbed out of a closed car a few times with my arm stiffened. I found I had to turn a bit farther out from the car to climb out, and once on my feet, I came to a complete stop before stepping off. If Giap responded likewise, it was another half second gained.

When Giap's car came to a stop at the reception party, the driver would jump out and open Giap's door. He would exit the car from the right rear quarter to enter a building facing him. His aides would both be seated on the other side of the car. Intelligence told us that in this case, Giap always waited by the car door for his aides to fall in behind him. With luck, I was going to have a stationary target for four or five seconds, when Giap would then be joined by an aide who was one of my secondary targets. My last target would be some distance away in the receiving line. Sometimes it almost seemed easy, sitting there in the film room.

From where we assumed the car would stop and the reception committee assemble, I would have to move the rifle through a maximum arc of thirty degrees to get all three targets; it could be much less. Allowing two seconds for three rounds into Giap, then two rounds for each of the others, I should be able to hit all three targets inside ten seconds. There was no doubt in my mind that the first shot would kill Giap, but he got three bullets regardless. He would be hit in the head by an explosive shell, a 7-mm. crossed bullet. That would kill him. The next two rounds would take his body out and eliminate any chance that bone deflection or premature explosion or decompression of the bullet would let him live. Premature explosion occurred when the bullet broke up on impact, decompression, when it broke up just under the surface of the skin. In either case, the fragments could dissipate in the outer casing of the body rather than spreading through it. A 7-mm. bullet is not exactly small, and it could have more deflection on bone than a smaller round. Used right, it had a devastating effect. But the body can take a tremendous amount of punishment.

It was my decision to put the first bullet into his head. Judging by the topographical model, the closest point with cover would be a rocky outcrop some 160 to 180 meters distant. I would be prone, with my pack as a gun rest, using an accurate rifle and a thirty-power horsehair scope. With luck, I would have a stationary target and could fire when ready. I could not imagine failing.

The second and third shots would be far more difficult. The first shot would fling Giap clear of the car, but I did not know where he would land. The body has a high lever motion on impact. Giap was a short man, so I could take him out in the head. A short man will somersault; if a tall man takes a head shot, his body will move in a far wider arc, which makes it hard to enter the body shots. Where my secondary targets might be two seconds after I had fired off the first round was a matter of conjecture; it would depend on how quickly they could respond to the firing. I would have to decide at what moment I had Giap in my center of vision and know the others were exposed and close enough to move my shots on. That would be a decision of the moment.

That afternoon we worked through Prather's plan on the model and, with some alteration, accepted it until we could run through it on the ground. There was messing about now; we were all edgy, feeling the press of time.

Our only reasonable approach to Ta shu tang was due north up a mountain pass from the Red River, some seventeen miles away. We would crest a hill, and Ta shu tang would lie on the far side of a shallow bowl, backed by a sharply rising contour of hills which rose rapidly into high mountains to the north. We would be hidden by a tree line to within three hundred meters of the hamlet; there the trees ended, and the land dropped away rapidly around outcrops, the closest of which were as near as 150 meters of the community hall. We would have to shelter behind them for fire cover.

Ta shu tang was a typical plateau hamlet. At its center was a community hall surrounded by an ever-increasing circle of houses that contained in all a population of a couple of thousand. The houses were brown or gray stucco, very plain, some with pitched slate roofs, others with flat roofs for catching water. The community hall, which was to be the conference site, was a wooden structure about eighty feet by forty, open on all four sides but with slatted blinds which when lowered made a weather wall. The building was un-decorated and had a flat roof, but I got the impression that it might once have been a Buddhist temple with a pitched roof. The hall was situated slightly above and separate from the village houses.

Though the hamlet radiated out from the hall, most of the buildings were south of the area we wanted to gain, toward the railway line which we would have to cross. The houses that obstructed us numbered fifteen. A third were between us and the hall. Another ten, which we hoped to use for retreating cover, lay behind the hall. The houses in front were low and scattered enough to give us a clear view of the hall and the road leading to it. Every arable piece of ground around the hamlet was being farmed. There was one large rice paddy; the rest was vegetable gardening. There were some wandering livestock and domestic fowl. This was marginal farmland; the people spent most of their time in the fields. Away from the hamlet, it was pretty wild country. On our approach route from the south were the remains of a fortified perimeter, an old town wall. In some places, it had fallen down, in others it was being used as a water stop; the peasants had built the ground up on either side and farmed it. We could walk through and around the old wall without difficulty.

Jackson had suggested early on that we set up between the last houses and the community hall. The trio would fire mortars into the hamlet as well as their rockets into the hall, thereby creating mass confusion and allowing the four of us to go in and get our targets at point-blank range. It was not a bad plan, but it meant carrying mortars as well as rockets for three weeks. Tan pointed out that the security for the meeting would be oriented off the tarmac road south of the hamlet; there were likely to be heavy vehicles and armor. If they spread out to protect the hamlet, we would be forced to go north into the mountains rather than risk cutting their lines. None of us was keen on retreating farther into China. If we just hit the hall, security would come straight there, and we had a chance of circling around them.

Wiley suggested as an alternative to Jackson's plan that the trio stay well south of Ta shu tang and hit the township with rockets just as Giap arrived. That would momentarily divert even the immediate security and give us the chance to get our targets from very close. The four of us would break out north for a few hundred yards, and the trio would fight their way southward to rendezvous with us as quickly as we could circle the hamlet. It was a sound idea, because it meant our carrying the minimum amount of gear into the fire zone; the balance could be left with the trio. But Prather and I objected to it, and Toliver rejected it because it separated the unit. If we got pinned down, we would need the others to help us, and vice versa. If one party got trapped, the other would never know they were dead. They could be pinned down and sieged out of ammunition. This mission had total closure. If any man stayed behind, we had to know he was dead.

Prather pointed out that if we were going north of the hamlet, the rocket team could fire from there. If we set up our fire zone two hundred meters northeast of where we had planned, using parts of the same outcrop for cover, the four of us would have our targets presented virtually in the same way. By putting the trio at our right flank, they would already be north of the hamlet.

Tan would take the first position, I would move fifty meters to Tan's right, and Toliver another fifty meters beyond me. Prather would take a position about thirty meters behind me, where he could provide covering fire for all three of us. The trio would be grouped a hundred meters beyond Toliver, where they had a clear view of the hall over the tops of the houses.

I would initiate the attack by shooting Giap at the most propitious moment. Tan and Toliver would already have their weapons trained on prime targets. By the time my second bullet was entering Giap, their first would be hitting their targets. Jackson would immediately launch antipersonnel rockets into the hall. The majority of the secondary targets would be inside or on the steps, we hoped standing in a line. It could present problems if they were in a loose group. Jackson's rockets would be devastating in the flimsy building. We would close on the trio by overlapping; Tan, me, then Toliver, each of us covering the others. Then all seven of us would hit the building. With everything. Small arms. I would carry my shotgun. Everybody would bring down canvas dobie bags of explosives. With the charges primed to go off on a four-second delay, we would chuck them into the building from all directions. Go in behind the explosives if we recognized any targets still standing.

The secondary targets were rather more than a luxury. Some of them were security officials or local army commanders, the people who would organize the pursuit. The rockets should kill everyone inside and around the buildings, but it was worth our while to make sure. We were relying on maximum surprise and maximum impact. Spreading panic would be the principal objective to secure our getaway.

We anticipated that the guards in the immediate vicinity would number about sixty. They would be the Chinese equivalent of special forces. They would not panic for long, and we certainly could kill sixty of them.

"Let's don't get greedy," Jackson said. "The pigs get fat, and the hogs get slaughtered."

We had to assume that the main security forces would be down on the highway. After all, this was supposed to be a secure meeting. If the President of the United States was walking around the White House lawn with the Russian leader, they would have a few bodyguards about. But they would never expect a commando team to hit them with rockets and high explosives.

Once we had delivered our explosives, it was time to leave. We would have nothing but small arms to fight with now. The Sahka and rocket launcher rifle would stay behind; they were of no use to us. We had to pull this off in under ten minutes, before the security detachments on the road below could reach us. We would strike north into the mountains beyond, circle back south to our route in, and run for Thailand.

Withdrawal was very suspect for the first twenty minutes; we would be at close quarters and under observation all the time. Twenty minutes north of Ta shu tang, we would move into cover.

We worked on Prather's plan late into the night. With a few changes we made on the spot, it seemed sound in theory. If it worked in rehearsal, we would stick to it.

We were tense but relieved by the time we broke up. After a quick meal, we gathered in the day room for a chat.

"Toliver's a good English name," Prather commented.

"Taliaferro's a good Italian one," replied Toliver. "My father came to America when he was five. He changed his name the day he reached twenty-one. I may change it back one day."

"Where'd you get that southern accent?" Morrosco asked Jackson.

"What's it to you, soldier?"

" 'Soldier' won't do in this outfit," Toliver said.

"It's not southern. I'm from Texas. Anything wrong with that?"

"I don't know. You left it. Do you know why Texas was settled?"

"No, I don't know why Texas was settled."

"Neither do I."

"That supposed to be funny?"

"What happened was the wagon trains were headed for California, and when they got to Texas, the guides died."

"Why don't you go get Tan, Gayle," Toliver said to me. Tan had not joined us in the day room.

Tan's door was open, so I knocked and went straight in.

"Join us for a beer?" I said. Then I saw that Tan was sitting on the floor, gazing at a yellow candle flame. I had walked in on his nightly meditation. He was resting on a rush mat, his back very straight, his hands and legs in the lotus position. His only movement was a deep breathing and an ordered, slow blinking of the eyes. I left him. Half an hour later, he joined us.

"Hey, Kiwi," he said, "what's going on? Is Jackson letting these young boys know who the sergeant is?"

I had liked Tan from the first time I saw him, a sentiment which had been mirrored by him. I had spent less than a day with him before I recognized that Tan was about the best soldier I had ever seen. He was totally tuned into a combat environment and to doing the things he was good at. He was very talented and commanded a tremendous amount of respect right across the unit. And he immediately distrusted anything that he was not involved in or could not instantly identify. These were ideal qualifications for the special forces.

Though Tan was a lieutenant in the South Korean Army, he must have grown up in America, because he spoke American English with no trace of a Korean accent. His age was difficult to judge because, like so many Orientals, he had a mature face and a very youthful physique. He was a handsome man with a clean, shiny complexion; a lot of the Koreans were pock-marked, as if there was something in the climate that did not agree with them. Tan was not classically Oriental in appearance. His eyes were a bit rounder than the average Korean. He was about my height, five feet six or so, which was on the tall side for a Korean. He was unusually stocky, very strong but incredibly quick, with a total awareness of the immediate physical environment. Tan was the sort of person who seemed to catch something before it started to fall.

I supposed that Tan had gone to America after the Korean War. He must have trained with the American forces at some time, because he did things the American way. But Tan was a man with no history. I would never try to penetrate the armor of a man like Tan. His past was to be his own forever. He was a man with a hatred. The others speculated about what might have happened in Korea. I never bothered.

Tan was totally dedicated to being what he was. He was in Vietnam to kill communists. Sometimes it was as if he had no allegiance to anything but that, not even to Korea. He would fight communists until he died. Now he had been given this job, to kill the biggest Korean communist he would ever see. He was not keen on details; he wanted to go. The more involved things got, the less interested he was in the far-reaching effects of the mission. To Tan, Vietnam was a localized theater. He did not care what the Americans were up to, or the Russians, or the Chinese. He had an abstract interest in Asian politics; he was quite knowledgeable on communist political strategy, particularly at the peasant level. But he refused to allow that to be allied to the mission. He wanted to go north and kill his communist. And, if possible, come back and kill some more.

Tan was an intellectual, well educated in several cultures. He spent his spare time meditating or reading, mostly religious books. Despite whatever years in the States, he remained an Oriental, but with Western interpretations. He had the privilege of a Western education, which made him in my estimation a better man. Not out of conceit for the Western mind. Tan had grasped the best of Western technology, but if he had lost his Korean culture, he would have been a lesser man. Tan was not that.

Though Tan worked mostly for the Green Berets, he was permanently attached to a Korean Rangers squadron which operated under its own identity. The Koreans were about the best troops in Vietnam. Tan was virtually a free agent. He was given enormous latitude for a Korean, to the extent that while the ordinary Korean soldier had almost a shaved head, Tan had black hair that hung straight to his shoulder blades. In moments of relaxation, or when we were being briefed, it remained loose. In training, he tied it in a pony tail with a scarf and tucked it in his shirt.

An idiosyncrasy like the long hair emphasized Tan's self-confidence. Many of the Oriental soldiers, even good ones, were self-deprecating. Tan knew he was good, knew he commanded our respect. He did not have to prove a damned thing. Oddly enough, he was capable of a certain affection for the people around him. I could see it growing in the unit, for Toliver, for me.

CHAPTER 5

We stayed in the same quarters, under permanent guard, for the balance of the training period. We spent the first two days working out our plan under a shed in the barracks yard; after that, we flew out almost daily to a firing range a few miles away where we rehearsed in earnest.

Our day started with breakfast at 0530 hours. We were serviced in our own mess by the colonel's staff aides, senior NCOs who brought our food in from outside. We had anything we wanted. Toliver, Jackson, and Prather enjoyed a heavy breakfast of eggs, sausages, toast, juice, and coffee. Wiley ate the same, only more. Tan had nothing but fruit juice and coffee. Morrosco's massive frame burned more energy than the rest of us, and he could never fill his sweet tooth. For breakfast, he ate a pumpkinlike gourd smeared with jam and sugar. He stuffed his pockets with sweets to munch on during the day. I usually had wheat germ and milk, then tropical fruit: papaya, guava, tree tomatoes, a boiled sweet potato similar to the New Zealand kumara.

After breakfast, we carried out pack readiness while consolidating in our own minds and among ourselves what we wanted to accomplish for the day. Then a physical buildup. We ran, climbed ropes, vaulted a horse, did body contact work: pushing, wrestling, throwing. Stretching our bodies to the limit first thing in the morning made us rearing to go.

At 0900 hours, special forces choppers picked us up behind our barracks and ferried us to an open patch of land about five minutes northeast of the base. The spot was elevated and had tree cover at the perimeters, which made it difficult to observe; Bien Hoa was under continuous surveillance. The chopper crews stayed with us as a security guard. We laid out with sandbags and timbers the approximate dimensions of the conference hall and set to work.

We broke for lunch in the field; the chopper crews ate with us. They were very impressed with our weapons, especially when I started piling off with my shotgun. In the afternoon, we practiced anything we were not happy with from the morning.

The day ended when we called a halt. One by one we would decide we had reached our goal for the day. Over coffee, Toliver would debrief us in the field on how the day had gone. We planned the following day's program. Then we would loosen up a bit, perhaps play ball with the chopper crews until dusk. On the way back, I might have a go at flying a chopper. We showered and ate and a couple of hours later had an evening briefing with Toliver. Then Toliver would disappear for a briefing with the colonel, who was monitoring our progress very closely.

From the first moment, my objective was to personalize my target, to make it—not the mission— the most important thing in my existence. I studied the three films for hours alone, selecting certain shots to be blown up for facial and character analysis. On a couple of occasions, the colonel came in the film room and tried to chat. But preparing a target is a solitary exercise. I did not want him interrupting my pace of recognition and interpretation. Even among the unit, we did not discuss our targets or individual briefings. None of us wanted another's analysis of his target; it remained a very personal thing. A hit like ours was rare, even in special forces. It might happen once in a career. We were being allowed the time to think it through. I spent hours pacing the impact area, inwardly working out my attitude, dissecting the target mentally and physically. I would work on a vein of thought, then test it to see if it worked in practice. Or I would spend a morning timing myself over a certain distance, as often alone as with the others.

I stuck the blown-up photos on sandbags, paced off 180 meters, and started firing. Zeroing in for the first shot was a mechanical operation that took ten minutes the first day. The only thing not allowed for was the elevation, which I would have to determine on the spot. I began tuning my weapon for my fire rate, allowing myself the flexibility to adjust to altered conditions at the site. I could never train to absolute perfection, because things are never exactly as they are supposed to be. But I could try. There were areas that had to be strictly timed. After I had made my shots, I had to disconnect from my weapon. Do I secure it? Drop it? Throw it clear of the area? I would make the shot from a prone position, using my pack as a gun rest. My other weapons would be behind me; I could not risk something swinging under my arm as I fired. I had to detach myself from my prime weapon, gather my gear, and take off for the trio. Our lives were counted in seconds here. Four of us practiced alone, the trio as a team, until each knew he had reached the limits to which he could perfect his role.

Then we came together on the linkup. There was nothing difficult here. It was a matter of working out how well we could coordinate, which after three weeks together on the march would become an automatic function anyway.

We rehearsed withdrawal tactics, but there was little we could train for, because it became purely operational, for which we were already at peak training. A fire fight was almost a matter of habit for us. Once we had memorized instructions, the rest came naturally. Mission-in and mission-out were going to be fairly commonplace, though harder than usual. Details were reduced to mechanical factors like daily progress, the two caches, the abort signal. There were no rendezvous to make, so our progress would be charted by coordinates.

We rehearsed the hit day after day until we were all satisfied. Then we began on its permutations to compensate for anyone who got hit on the way. If I got killed, Toliver took my targets, and Prather took Toliver's. Prather would join the trio if one of them was hit. In the absence of Tan, Prather would hit his prime targets, and I was responsible for his secondaries. And so it went. If we got to the site, anyone could take any other's job. If all three of us with prime targets were killed, the mission was aborted. All this was not training appertaining to this particular mission; this was basic mission readiness, excepting that we were training to carry out a very important job in a very short time, and we were given the luxury to prepare it to perfection.

As soon as we had the hit rehearsal going smoothly —about the middle of the second week—when we should have started to relax, I felt the unit tightening up. We had time to think about more than the physical mission, and I heard snatches of conversation about "stopping the Third World War" and "changing history." When the issues thrust themselves forward like this, they were too big for people like Morrosco and Wiley to handle. Their edginess was reflected across the unit. We all grew tense. Toliver and the colonel started to detune us psychologically from the importance of our targets. The purpose of the mission became to remove certain individuals meeting together on a fixed date. The motivations for the mission reached so far beyond the immediate theater of Vietnam that to allow us to relate our job to the possible consequences would have focused our interest on political repercussions rather than the mission itself. This could create endless delay factors, both in preparation, where we might overdo our training, and at the site, where the possible repercussions might make one of us hesitate a second before pulling the trigger. They did not want us preoccupied with the extremity of what we were doing.

The emphasis was put on the threat we had been made aware of, and its diminishment by taking out these parties. Immediately it became a military mission, no longer sabotage or political assassination. We were being asked to do what special forces do best, but on a grander scale.

Our incursion into China was always very clear. We were doing something that had not been done before, and we had been chosen because we were the only people good enough to do it. This underlined the drastic measures that were being taken: it elevated the whole affair above a lot of discussion. The mission, we were told repeatedly, had been initiated at the very highest authority. No one ever named the White House, but what else could we assume?

How could the Western allies gamble so much on one bold stroke that would be measured in seconds? They could do so because we dealt in time spans that were incomprehensible to the average man. Some people— pilots of high-performance aircraft, auto racers, downhill skiers—have a different visual perception from the rest. They can stretch time with their eyes. In combat I often experienced this, as did other long-time combat veterans. Events around me could suddenly be thrown into slow motion while my mind was sorting problems and finding solutions at a fantastic rate. As if I had time to calculate what should have been reflex actions in a normal time span. The brain would start interpreting at the speed of light; my eye and my mind would take charge, directing my body with total detachment. Nothing happened too quickly; it was as if time stood still, waiting for me to respond.

That was what survival in combat was about. You would be jumped by surprise; if you were that sort of detuned person, you allowed your body to function automatically. You just naturally moved the right way. That left your mind free for problem-solving. If a man was laying an arc with an AK-47, somehow you knew if you were part of the next sweep. You moved. Or hit that gun. And you got away with it. Because you had more time than he did.

We needed that edge to survive this mission, because we were going to be out in the cold for a long time. We had already drawn the conclusion that we were expendable. In military terms, not the stark realization of what that meant. We had no linkups beyond central Laos. We were not given access to the espionage network in China, which must have been extensive just north of Vietnam, judging from the intelligence data we were being fed. The colonel told us the mission justified exposing a network that had been built up over the past twenty years. The first plan had been to us Chinese. We were chosen as a better alternative. We could do the job as well, and we did not compromise the network.

As training progressed and we became more integrated on a personal level, we found we shared mutual respect for one another's talents. Morrosco and Wiley were unit support; they had been brought in as aides for Jackson. But believe me, they were as important as the rest of us. Without them, there was no mission complete, no unit survival.

Often one of us would show another something he did not know. Weapons instructions came natural to me. Wiley was superb with an M-3. Prather watched Barry a day or two and chose that as his prime weapon. I taught him to zero in with short bursts rather than sweeping the weapon . . . how to get a good spread by vertical instead of horizontal arcing, thus not creating self-inflicted deflection of the bullet.

Jackson and Morrosco got Toliver to show them how to cut a boar's-tooth pattern at the top of the barrel of their Armalites. The boar's teeth caused the round to expand unevenly as it left the barrel. This set it in a tumbling motion which shortened its range but did not affect velocity greatly. On impact the round was tumbling and spinning and, by jees, it would rip a tree apart. We all tried it, and I got quite accurate using an adopted Armalite. Jackson taught us all how to use the rocket launcher and passed along some of his sighting techniques.

Weapons fascinated me, because they are subject to endless adaptation. I showed Prather and Wiley how to use explosive bullets, crossed dumdums, to best advantage. Dumdums might be illegal under the Geneva Convention, but there was no question about our not using them. If you hit a man with a solid round, and missed bone, he kept coming. He might die later, but in the meanwhile he could kill you. The hollow-nose bullet was more effective, but it could flatten against bone and be deflected. The dumdum exploded on impact and just disintegrated in the man. Almost the ideal round. But any time you tampered with a bullet, you unbalanced it. Unbalanced rounds caused guns to jam. So you kept altered rounds to a minimum. You did not need every round to be explosive. This was overdoing a technique which was highly effective used in a balanced way. There was no point in having a prime weapon with prime ammunition if you used it en masse. In a fire fight, if you were using all explosive bullets, you would have shit flying everywhere. And when it all settled down, you would be surprised to see how little damage you had done. With one in three rounds explosive, you would pick your area of destruction and do twice the damage. It was partly psychological, partly to do with weapon application. The same was true with tracers. Used exclusively, it was like running a rope from your barrel to the target. You would not concentrate your fire within the natural confines of your arc, and you would be pin-pointed immediately. So you spread adapted ammunition across the conventional load, spacing it to be effective.

Individual unit training was interspersed with unit briefings from Toliver. At first we concentrated on our targets and the impact zone. Later we turned to route detail; expected opposition, topography, terrain, climatic conditions. Slowly a general unit pattern started to form.

The colonel watched us closely. He was particularly interested in my Sahka. Once the hit-zone training was going smoothly, I spent hours in the armory setting the weapon up. If the trigger were too stiff, I might jerk off the first round rather than squeeze; too sensitive, and I could find my reflexes sending off the second round before the completion of my arc. But at 180 meters, with a five-meter horsehair scope, I needed an ultralight trigger action, regardless of consequences. By the time I was satisfied, I only had to exhale and the bloody thing would go off.

I was out on the range late one afternoon. The others had just broken off, and I was firing at photos. The colonel arrived by chopper and came straight to me.

"How are you, Rivers?"

"Fine, sir."

"How do you like your weapon?"

"I've just about got it the way I want it, sir."

"Mind if I try?"

He loaded the weapon with three rounds, rammed one in the chamber, and took aim from a standing position. The first round rang off, followed immediately by the second while the rifle was still jumping in the colonel's hands. Half a second later, the third round went into the ground fifty meters in front of the target.

"For Christ's sake!" the colonel said. "That's a hot trigger you've got there, Rivers."

"Yes, sir."

"Can you handle it?"

I fired three rounds into the target in three seconds.

"Do you mind if I show this to some people, Rivers?"

"No, sir," I said, minding very much.

"Good. I'll have it back to you tonight."

It was after supper the next evening before a corporal brought the Sahka to our quarters. When he had disappeared, I tested the weapon. The trigger was about as sensitive as a gate latch. I tore the trigger mechanism out of the weapon.

"Toliver!" I shouted. My hands were trembling. He came in my room.

"What the hell is going on? I spent two days getting this weapon the way I wanted it, and now the colonel has got it right fucked!"

"He doesn't want you to miss."

"I'd do better using it like a cricket bat."

"Well, let's go fix it, Kiwi."

He led me to the armory and stayed there until dawn while I repaired the damage.

Mission training continued in an almost unnaturally pleasant atmosphere, without undue pressure, though we all felt a sense of urgency. We each found our motivation, our personal involvement, totally absorbing. As the days passed, we became a very close-knit unit.

No one got badly hurt in training, though there was the occasional turned ankle or twisted knee. Jackson tried a direct eye-level shot with the rocket launcher against his shoulder, and the recoil tore his ear open.

Tempers grew shorter as mission-depart approached. Wiley and I had words on the range when I was trying to sight in the Sahka, and he was spraying M-3 rounds around the place. It was not stupidity; it was lack of thought on both our parts.

There were two more serious incidents during hand-to-hand combat training. Toliver and I were talking at one end of the clearing while the rest were training fifty yards from us. Suddenly, we heard Morrosco shouting, first in English, then Spanish. I turned around to see him thump Prather on the head with a big stick. Prather's knees buckled, then he fell over backward. Jackson and Wiley stood by watching. Prather was trying to get to his feet, and Morrosco was about to hit him again, when I tackled Pete from behind. Prather started for Morrosco and had to be brought down by Toliver.

Wiley told me later that Prather had been coolly throwing Morrosco every time they moved together. Morrosco grew excited, and it got serious. Fists and boots started flying, and Prather was taking Morrosco apart. Morrosco grabbed up his Armalite, and Prather took that away from him. Then Morrosco drew his knife, thought better of it, and crowned Prather with a stick he snatched off the ground. Jackson and Wiley had done nothing to discourage it, they were fighters themselves and could not see the far-reaching consequences.

The very next day we were doing close-quarter combat with fixed bayonets, two on one. Toliver came at me. I parried his thrust—if he had gotten through, he would have butted me on the ear to let me know I had done it wrong—and foot-tripped him. I spun around, and Jackson was almost on me. Instinctively I thrust at him. I went for his uniform, but the bayonet ripped into his forearm.

"You son-of-a-bitch!" he shouted and came at me with his bayonet. I got under his weapon and knocked it out of his hands, but my move put me off balance. Before I could recover, he came straight in and gave me a head butt in the face, turned himself around and caught me under the chin with the back of his boot. I went down, and he came back at me. But dirt was flying everywhere, and he got a fistful in his eyes. That gave me time to regain my feet, and we were about to tear into each other when Toliver jumped between us.

"Cool it," he said.

"Jesus, I'm glad to see you, Toliver," Jackson said. "I might have broken this kid's back."

"Better get your arm patched," I said. "Your Armalite is on the ground behind you."

Jackson and I did not like each other much, but

there was no hard feeling. We were all primed for combat, and we respected one another's capabilities. We were a bit like lions; they may muck one another around, but they never fight to the death within the pride. This was our way of shaking hands in a violent way.

In the evenings, we relaxed completely. We seldom talked about the mission or our training, though Jackson and Morrosco were born soldiers, and their conversation seldom strayed beyond the confines of a military existence. Prather told me about the Devon countryside, and he would often chat with Tan about Korean opera, for which he had developed a passion when stationed there years before. Tan and I were the quiet ones. I preferred reading to talking. Tan spent many hours with his books and meditation. Toliver reported every evening to the colonel, but when he returned, he joined in the chat with the rest of us.

"You seen my family?" Jackson said one night.

He had laid a photo beside him while he wrote home. He passed it around. It was a dinner-table snapshot. Two teen-agers—the American family seems to be a couple of kids—grinned at the camera, while Jackson's wife watched them, side-on to the camera. Jackson was not in the picture. They were obviously having a good time. They looked like good people.

"What sort of uniform is your son wearing?" I asked.

The son was a handsome boy, built very much like his father. He was dressed in what appeared to be a band uniform.

"He's in military school in Tennessee. He's the cadet captain. I think he's going to get in the Air Force Academy next year. I wanted him to go to the University of Texas and study law. But hell. You could do worse than the academy."

"What's his name?" asked Toliver politely in response to Jackson's obvious pride.

"Eugene. Eugene Lamar. We call him Bud. That's my wife, Judy, and my daughter, Susy. She's fifteen.

Just started high school." The daughter was a pretty girl, a fresh young teen-ager. It was difficult to see his wife because of the angle, but she seemed reasonably attractive. The impression I got was of a happy family.

"What about you, Lew? You got any family?" Jackson knew that Prather wore a wedding ring.

"I have four children. Only two are still at home. I have a boy at Duke of York."

"What's Duke of York?" asked Morrosco.

"A military school in England for sons of military families," I answered. "Your old school, Lew?"

"Yes."

"How many generations?"

"We've been regimental sergeant majors to the same unit for five generations."

"You got any pictures of your kids?" asked Jackson.

"No. I have a photo of my wife, though."

He brought out a photo of himself and a woman standing under a tree. Both were dressed in hunting tweeds. She looked to me like a woman of good breeding as well as being attractive. Two retrievers sat at her feet. In the background an expanse of green fields stretched at a distant tree line.

"Is that your farm?" I asked.

"We're agents. Someone in my family has managed that estate for as long as we have served in the British Army. My wife is living there now, down in Devon," he replied.

Prather held a deep affection for his wife. At times like these, he appeared such a stable character it was almost unnerving. This life in the photo, this provincial life, seemed his natural environment. Not Bien Hoa. He had a home and a family to return to when the mission was completed, which was more than the rest of us could count on. This was reflected in a calm collectedness which none of us could fail to like.

Toliver used to question Prather about the English family environment and compare it with the American, almost as if he were jealous. He talked in generalities about his own private life; he seldom mentioned his family. He had a son in college, so he must have married young. That was all I ever knew. I got the impression that he was widowed or divorced. But this was a posture taken by a lot of the married men who had been living Toliver's life for a while. They insulated themselves against the past.

In the evenings, we avoided talk about the mission ahead. Morrosco and Wiley chatted about New York and Sydney, not rockets. We drank beer. Played cards.

"You got gangs in Sydney?" Morrosco asked.

"My family's a gang. Six boys. Raised on the docks and all tough, believe me. Come stay with me in Sydney one day and meet a good family. They'll take care of you."

"Is your dad a longshoreman?"

"Is that a docker? . . . No, a cobbler. The best cobbler in Sydney. He learned his trade in England. He makes boots for the dockers. You could drop a lorry engine on them. They're good for putting the boot in. The steel caps will break a leg."

"What were you doing before Nam?"

"I worked oil rigs. Shot kangaroos for the bounty when I was skint. I was trying to get into the university at Melbourne when I was conscripted. I wanted to be an architect."

Prather tried on a couple of occasions to draw learned discussions about the political significance of the mission and was bewildered by our lack of response. We grew more tight-lipped as the mission approached. We were like a submarine crew securing every hatch before a dive; we became one with our own thoughts.

For us, there was no psyching up to be done; we were responding inwardly to an attitude of readiness. That had come early on, with the last two briefings. We did not pass on the power and expectation of the briefings to our training, because that was a matter of habit. We carried it out almost in an automated fashion. Prather could never understand this. Why were we not showing signs of anticipation and apprehension as he was? We were, but we kept it within us. He found a friend here in Wiley, who was feeling a bit the same way. It irritated me to hear them talk about it.

"What's the matter, Barry?" I asked one night. "Vietnam beginning to scare you?"

"Yeah, it is, Kiwi. It would scare you too, if you had any feelings."

I grew more silent as departure approached. Sometimes a conversation would be going on around me, and I would slip into a state of deep concentration about what we were going to do. Now and again I got the rush that this would be my last mission.

CHAPTER 6

As our departure date grew near, we had two personal
briefings with the colonel regarding our individual
targets. The first was a review of intelligence data and
a précis of our plan for the hit. Present at the second
was a captain in the medic corps, an army psychiatrist,
though he never said so. They were monitoring the
guys in the War Room in the Pentagon so it was no
surprise to see him. He launched a battery of questions
without introduction.

"How do you feel about this mission, Rivers?"

"It's a job."

"It's a lot more than a job. How do you feel about
the odds against?"

"They don't bother me. I've been up against the
odds before."

"Have you been experiencing any depression or
suffering doubts since training began?"

"No." Psychiatrists got very little mileage from me.

"What do you consider the hardest part of the
mission?"

"The mission-in."

"Not the hit?"

"That's the easiest."

"What about the mission-return?"

"Why should I worry about that? It would be pure hypothesis. We'll take it as it comes."

"How do you feel about the team?"

"The best I've ever worked with."

"What about your fight with Jackson?"

"What about it?"

"Are there hard feelings?"

"None."

"How do you feel about him?"

"I consider Jackson a junior. He got a little over-primed, a bit self-indulgent. There are no problems between us."

"How do you look at your prime target?"

"What do you mean?"

"As a man or as an animal?"

"A man."

"What kind of man?"

"A vain one. Basically insecure."

"How do you arrive at that conclusion?"

"From the film. He obviously adores the crowd worship. Vanity. And he seems to need it to boost his ego. Insecurity." The captain leaned forward. I was coming up with perfectly natural conclusions he had gone to school for years to learn. "A small-man complex coupled with great power. That adds up to instability. And decision-making from a personal, rather than strategic, viewpoint."

"How do you feel about eliminating him?"

"It will be a good thing for everyone concerned."

"Including yourself?"

"My motivation is the target. The moment he is eliminated, it will become my survival."

The last week was spent preparing gear: checking and binding weapons, distributing the load across the team, packing our individual packs.

Apart from the Sahka, which would not be a combat weapon, I carried an Armalite, a .38 automatic, and my twelve-bore Creener Remington pump-action shotgun with the barrel cut back to the end of the hand grip. For hand-to-hand combat and jungle survival, I wore both a machete and a double-edged sheath knife with a six-inch blade. Slung across each shoulder were two dobie bags. One contained a hundred prepared rounds for the shotgun, two hundred plastic casings, a thousand primed caps, loose number six shot, and a small tool for recapping rounds. The second bag held a thousand steel balls, plus my powder, which was not bulky as each shell took only a small amount. I expected to pick up shell casings in the field and repack cartridges when we broke to rest.

We wore U.S. fatigues of heavy canvas that would breathe in the daytime, provide warmth at night, and serve as armor against insect bites and skinned elbows and knees. Six of us wore U.S. jungle boots. Prather kept his SAS desert boots, which were of similar design but leather where ours were canvas; they offered good ankle support, and the leather breathed sufficiently for jungle use. We each kept our own beret, with the service flash removed.

Across my waist and shoulders, I wore magazine belts loaded with M-3 clips for Wiley and Prather and ammunition for my Armalite. The .38 was on my hip, with two clips attached to the holster. The Sahka went on my back. It was broken down in three pieces in a hard leather case which was mounted on a parachute support. The butt of the Sahka was hollowed to hold seven crossed rounds. The rifle case was protected in my waterproof body wrap, which would double as sleeping bag or rain shelter. On my back, below the Sahka, I wore a medical wrap that circled my chest and snapped in front. In the medical wrap was a kit containing morphine, elastic bandages, wadding for plugging wounds, two short pieces of dowling for making a temporary splint, Benzedrine, quinine, vitamins. One trouser pocket was stuffed with

.38 clips, another with three three-day K-ration packs. In a shirt pocket I had extra dry rations—barley sugar cubes, more quinine and vitamins, salt tablets, penicillin tablets. I carried dried figs and apricots in wax paper; these I would chew for moisture. I had two corks to burn and rub the charcoal into wounds to prevent infection. I had the usual body-care supplies—tar soap, toothbrush, toothpaste, chewing gum. On my belt, in addition to my mess kit and two canteens, I hooked ten grenades. On one wrist I wore a watch, on the other a wrist band with aspirin, swabs, yet more quinine, antinausea pills. Stitched into one arm of my fatigue shirt was a sewing kit of thread, needles, and plastic scissors. I had a gun-cleaning kit small enough to roll up in my hand; a rag, a string, a metal weight, a telescopic wire brush, tiny cans of oil, grease. A wee flint for sharpening the knives. Extra net underwear and socks were wrapped around my calves beneath my trousers. The others were dressed much as I was and carrying the same personal items.

Prather carried M-16 ammunition, M-3 clips, and lots of grenades. He took an M-3 as his prime weapon and an M-21 for use at the hit site in case he had to step into the firing line. He carried a lot of pipe tobacco.

Tan used an adapted M-3 both for the hit and as his prime weapon. He had lengthened the barrel and taken the flash retractor off. He would add a scope for the hit. In addition to standard ammunition, he took two magazines with explosive bullets. He had grenades and Armalite ammunition for Toliver and me. In a backpack, he carried the primers for Jackson's rockets. The small crystal-locked radio receiver he wore attached to the side of the pack. Tan's load was scarcely more than thirty pounds, the lightest any of us traveled. He slung a binocular case loosely over one shoulder; Toliver and I had done the same.

Jackson's load was twice that. He carried an Armalite and an adapted M-1 as his rocket launcher. He wore a flak jacket which he used to support a wooden rocket platform that fit across his back. The rockets were Jackson's handiwork. He had loaded them himself with shale wrapped in a light chain; every fourth link in the chain had been weakened with a saw. I had watched Jackson test his rockets on the range. They were devastating. When they went off, the chains whirred like razor blades. Jackson would not trust picking them up at either cache, so we carried them the entire way. They were broken down into three parts for safety and comfort, and he, Morrosco, and Wiley carried them on their backs.

Toliver carried an Armalite for combat, and M-21 with infrared night sight for sniping and for the hit. In addition to his own ammunition and powder for me, he had M-3 ammunition for the others. He wore a .38 Smith & Wesson revolver on his hip. He had the usual personal gear, plus a soft leather map case with map sections folded like pages in a book, each section in a plastic cover.

Morrosco carried two big Green Beret medical bags with syringes, morphine, tourniquets, sutures, sterilized knives, quinine, Benzedrine, antiseptic cream, extra insect repellent, all of it packed in sterilized plastic containers. He took an Armalite.

Wiley carried in addition to his M-3 and ammunition, explosive charges for the rockets, Armalite ammunition, and more medical supplies. He, Jackson, and Toliver carried the satchels of explosives.

Virtually all our weapons had been adapted for the mission—barrels lengthened or shortened, stocks lightened, flash retractors removed. The M-1 rocket launcher broke down into two parts and was carried like my Sahka.

Despite orders, I took my dog tags, and the others probably did as well. They held my blood type. I was not going to bleed to death for security.

We trained in full pack over the last several days, learning to disperse the load across our bodies and across the unit. Departure date was May 13. As that day approached, and we rehearsed our moves for the hundredth time, the old excitement was rekindled. We wanted to get on with it. But not a man among us was suffering from the tension; that diminished as departure grew near.

The night of the eleventh, I could not sleep. Toliver gave us a final briefing, a summary of everything we had done. There were no questions, and each of us went silently to his room. My head was whirling. Had I overlooked anything? Had I perfected my moves to the maximum degree possible?

The last day was like exam time; it was too late to worry. We had done everything we could to prepare ourselves. The colonel gave us a departure briefing which was nothing more than a summary, reassurance, and a chat around. That night I slept better than I had done in three weeks.

Part 2

THE HUNTERS

remained impassive; they had heard the speech many times before. The crowd slowly broke up. The women dragged the smaller children to play around ... while they carried on with the cooking and wash-

CHAPTER 7

At 0430 on the thirteenth, we were jeeped to a waiting C-130 military transport. Our gear was stored in mission packs like canvas yachting bags, then packed in wooden cases. We walked to the aircraft carrying only our weapons. No one came to see us off, not even the colonel. Five minutes later, we had lifted off. The big plane swung out over the China Sea. We were airborne for four hours on a roundabout route to northern Thailand.

We landed at a small dusty air base between Chiang Khan and the Mekong that the allies used as a jumping-off point for special forces incursions into the north. We attracted little attention; there were lots of Americans about. We piled our gear under a shed, trying to be as inconspicuous as possible. While Toliver went to get confirmation from the base radio that our caches had been deposited, we ate, did some last-minute waterproofing, made our loads more comfortable. He returned, then went off to the river three miles to our north to arrange a discreet crossing. We were talking little now. The plane ride had passed in almost complete silence.

We left the air base just after midnight and reached our crossing point at 0100 hours. We climbed into a Bailey amphibious craft operated by an American crew. Half an hour later, we beached in Laos, in a dry riverbed. The crossing was so simple as to be almost casual.

We struck up what must have been the bed of a feeder stream to the Mekong. The stream cut through a shallow valley that was sparsely populated. We moved quickly, protected by thick undergrowth along both banks. A few miles inland we left the stream bed to turn due north. We were pioneering, taking bearings almost at the run, moving at a tremendous pace. We skirted a few farms and the occasional hamlet without being observed.

We marched in total silence until 1100 hours the next morning. We were not concerned greatly yet about a low profile; most of the combat activity was southeast of us toward Cambodia, which was one reason why we had cast off from Thailand rather than walking up the neck of Laos. We made steady progress north, moving on a low-lying ground west of a range of hills that was spotted with farming hamlets. We broke and slept for four hours through the heat of the day.

For three days we walked on riverbeds up a wide valley, around the village of Ban Hinkang Na, and past several riverheads that spilled into the main stream. We came to a fast-running tributary on the east bank that corresponded on our maps to a stream passing the village of Ban Muang Fuong several miles east of us. We walked two miles up the tributary stream, found the hill we were looking for, took a bearing, and walked its reciprocal. In ten minutes we had found our first cache, well hidden in the riverside foliage.

There was material enough for us to re-equip completely, with the exception of Jackson's rockets and my shotgun ammunition. All we could use were three rucksacks of food—salt beef in gauze, dried meat, canned and dehydrated vegetables, malt biscuits—and fresh canteens to replace ours, which were quickly oxidizing. We pushed what we did not want far into the undergrowth and moved back down to the main stream at double time. We did not know who might be watching the cache.

We walked from bearing to bearing ten hours at a stretch, with a fifteen-minute break every four or five hours and a half-hour pause every afternoon for radio transmission. It was easy going now; we were route-marching almost at the double. We kept a party head two hundred yards out in front who never stopped moving. If anyone dropped out to drink or relieve himself, he had to catch up; the line never stood still. We ate on the march.

The pace was not tiring us. It was pleasant in a way, almost like a glorified hunting party, except that we were under forced march. There was no time to negotiate small inclines; we ran up them. No leisurely wading in a cool stream; we cut them and kept moving.

We were marching at ten-yard intervals, very vigilant, weapons always at the ready. This was the easiest way to carry our arms on a quick march; a slung weapon was clumsy and uncomfortable.

We talked very little. We were primed, like sprinters just broken from the block. Time became a substance we were pushing against. We had three weeks. We wanted to break the back of the race early on and allow for delay later.

We moved half a day from the cache and stopped for our first meal. As we walked, we gathered broad beans and a sweet wild cabbage similar to pua. We threw these in a pot with the meat and cooked up a delicious stew.

On the fourth day, we moved into higher ground. There were peasants about. We were in close country now, too thick to penetrate except by river bottom or jungle trail; we were exposed to head-on confrontation at every twist in our route. The riverbeds were the safest place to move at this time of year. The rivers were reduced to trickling streams that wound back and forth across wide, flat shingle beds. Heavy undergrowth near the banks made fine cover. The washes would be roaring rivers in the rainy season, but they were virtually hard-surfaced highways now. We had to be cautious; the peasants washed and fished in the rivers and used them for roads. We approached the Nam Lik—"Nam" meaning "river" in Laotian and Vietnamese. We covered eighty miles in three and a half days, but we accepted that the easiest was behind us.

So far, our movement had been remarkably close to the hypothetical timetable we had set. We had come across the hamlets where and when we expected to find them; we had moved cautiously around them, then streaked across the empty landscape. The sparse population had been confined to small, self-contained farming communities, with few people straying far from home. We came off the high ground nine miles short of the Lik and joined a trail that led to our crossing point.

When we got a glimpse of the Lik in the distance, we left the trail for the trees, then moved forward in silence. Toliver, walking point, suddenly turned and waved us down. He disappeared in the ground cover and crawled back to us.

"There's people in the river," he said.

"Military?" asked Jackson.

"I don't know. They haven't posted any guard. There's about a dozen men and a woman. Bathing and swimming around. They look like peasants." That meant only that they were not in Pathet Lao or government uniform. Half the opposition we faced were peasant armies of one kind or another.

We inched forward to the riverbank. The bed of the Lik was a hundred yards from shore to shore, the running stream often no more than ten yards wide as it coursed among the flat stones. Just in front of where we hid, the water had scooped a small bowl from the shingles, making a chest-deep pool for the naked men who were splashing in it. They were young, mostly teen-agers. A young woman squatted fully dressed on the opposite bank by a pile of clothing. There was no way to know if they were a peasant work party, a Pathet Lao patrol, or free-booting tribal mercenaries.

Whoever they were, they were cutting our only route. The terrain to the east was very close. We would have difficulty in reaching the river floor, which ran in a ravine for several miles. A detour to the west would cost us half a day.

"We'll give them twenty minutes," Toliver said.

"Jackson, you and Wiley take the left flank. If we go, hit the woman first. Tan, you and Rivers take the right. We'll cover the middle. I don't want any of them leaving the water."

As we started to break up, I saw Tan grab Toliver's arm.

"Look!" he said. A second woman had joined the first. She was carrying half a dozen automatic weapons cradled in her arms.

"Hit them," Toliver said.

I had just taken a firing position when Jackson and Wiley downed the two women with what sounded like one shot. The men in the river started shouting and scrambling toward their weapons, which lay scattered around the two women. The men were tightly bunched; as they struggled against the weight of the water, Tan blew them over with automatic fire. Wiley stood up and biffed two grenades among them. The naked bodies lifted in the swell from the muffled explosions, then rolled over and drifted slowly downstream. Jackson shot the last two as they dragged themselves out on the rocks. The rest of us never fired our weapons.

We slid down the bank and sprinted toward the stream that now ran red with blood for a hundred yards, checking quickly that no man was left alive. I ran to the two women. Both lay dead with gaping holes in their chests. Toliver waved, and we moved out to the east along the riverbed. We made no attempt to hide the action; it could have been the result of any regional dispute. We wanted distance, and we moved at a jog for about an hour before breaking. I knew there would be little said about this action even though it was our blooding as a unit, because it was a classic ambush executed with the precision I had expected from the unit. One round each took out the people with weapons. Two grenades and spare automatic fire had put down ten men in less than three minutes. No one had survived to expose our presence. And we did not have a scratch. There was nothing to say about it. Special forces men talked about the ones that went wrong. I felt no more than that peculiar emptiness that followed in the wake of my first killing, eighteen months earlier.

It was my first combat mission, a reconnaissance patrol into Indonesia from Terendak. We were in the jungle at night. Eight of us ran head-on into twenty Indonesian terrorists moving in an arrowhead formation. We saw them and went to ground before we were spotted. The main party went through us. But one of the out-riders came straight at me, face-on. He was going to walk on top of me.

The simple logic was that if I did not kill him, he was going to kill me. I did not have the luxury of analyzing why he and I were fighting each other. That had been done before the mission began.

I let him walk right up on me. I stood up, grabbed him by the hair, and broke him backward over my knee. The myth about cutting a man's throat is not quite accurate. If I had done it the way people imagine, he would have been heard by everyone on Sunday. I stabbed my knife in the side of his neck and ripped it out the front, severing the windpipe and jugular with one quick stroke. He could not even make a choking sound. The whole thing took about five seconds. I leaned too far over the man, and when I did him, a fountain of blood exploded in my face. Somehow I managed to cut two fingers on my left hand. I was a proper mess. The Indonesians never missed the man. We got clean away.

We hugged the north wall of a steeply sided ravine as Toliver led us down the dry bed of the Nam Lik. The sheer cliffs shielded us from a trail paralleling the river but committed us to the Lik for the next twenty miles. The Lik wove a capricious course, traveling northeast for several miles, then bending swiftly to the north, then east again, and once more to the north. Then the river divided, one arm continuing north, a branch more directly on our route swinging sharply eastward. We took the northern arm toward Ban Namon; the eastern branch swept past Vangvieng, a regional headquarters for the Pathet Lao and tribal mercenaries working south and west of the Plain of Jarres.

Our plan was to stay with the Lik until near its junction with Highway 13, then walk the lower slopes of the ranges paralleling the highway to the west, keeping the river between us and Highway 13 all the way to its junction with highways 4 and 7. When the new highway formed by these three turned due west toward Luang Prabang, we would cut river and highway and strike north. This meant leaving the Lik at the last hamlet below Ban Namon. We were scheduled to skirt the hamlet by night, but we were already there by late afternoon of the fifth day. We watched the hamlet, no more than a few scattered huts at river's edge, from the opposite bank while waiting for night to fall. In the hours before dark, two Pathet Lao patrols passed through. Both left toward the west, where we were headed. Beyond the hamlet our maps indicated at least two hours of open ground to cover. We would have to move with extreme caution.

"Eighteen men," Tan counted as the second party left. The first had been half that size. Tan watched through a pair of enormous binoculars.

"What in hell are those?" Morrosco asked him.

"They are World War II glasses. They belonged to a German admiral."

"Where did you get them?"

"I bought them in Tokyo."

"See any battleships?" Morrosco asked.

"I see eighteen men moving out on our route," Tan answered.

Morrosco's smile faded away.

I watched the departing patrol through my own small, high-powered German glasses. The party was led by an agitated young man who pushed and shouted at the men as they filed out of the hamlet. The higher-ranking Pathet Lao officers were sophisticated and knew how to command respect. The young officers were often peasants and had a hard time exercising their rank coolly. It gave them an almost comic appearance to the initiated. I knew better. These small units—usually thirty men or fewer—were highly disciplined and dedicated to their cause and, despite appearances, there was a well-defined chain of command. Even in combat they were so strictly controlled that their fire patterns could be almost stingy. They maintained good regional communications and intelligence. They were very tough, but they fought a conventional type of guerrilla warfare, unlike their mercenary counterparts, that I found bordered sometimes on the predictable.

When night fell, we slipped down to the river. The safest crossing point was five hundred yards upstream, where the banks on both sides were less than a man's height. Between lay a hundred-yard dash across flat pebbles, with a narrow knee-deep stream near its middle.

We stayed under cover until past midnight, when the hamlet finally grew still. Toliver sent Jackson and Morrosco across. They were down the banks, over the flat stones, and up on the other side in less than a minute. We all lay silent for fifteen minutes before Wiley and Prather moved. Then Tan went alone. Three quarters of an hour had passed before Toliver and I moved out last.

I was pleased with Toliver's obsession for cover.

The only way we could survive was by remaining invisible. A small team could walk through an enemy patrol, breathe right down its neck; if they were not known, they could pull it off. But when people were looking for a seven-man team, the world was not big enough to hide it.

I scrambled up the riverbank, then fell still on the ground. We were bunched tightly on the bank, and I suddenly realized we were three too many bodies. They were peasant men, their clothes soaked in blood. Without a word, Jackson and I pulled the bodies into the undergrowth and stripped them of their rings and wallets, which we would throw away on the march. The villagers would blame bandits.

Above the hamlet, the river forest gave way to a rock-strewn landscape of sparse grass. We moved northwest until we hit the foothills of the western range, then turned north to follow its lower slopes. Toliver wanted to cross Highway 13 just above Muang Kasi to put distance between us and Luang Prabang. Muang Kasi lay fifteen miles to the north over steep and rugged terrain, but we were traveling fast. After a hard two-hour climb, the foothills leveled out into a forested plateau. The trees grew together overhead as the vegetation thinned at ground level. At times we broke out of the trees and moved across vast expanses of tussock. We had little cover, but the country was empty of human life, and we made good time. We reached Muang Kasi half a day ahead of our scheduled night crossing. We set up camp overlooking the village and listened for the abort signal. We rested all afternoon and into the night. I took out a dried fig, started to chew on it, and turned to Toliver. He and I had fallen into a pattern of taking our breaks together.

"Who killed those three guys?" I asked.

"I did." Jackson answered. "Me and Morrosco. When I came up out of the water, this guy was just sitting on the bank, and he got up and came over to see what was happening. He walked right onto the end of my knife. But he made some kind of a noise. He must have been with them other two. They came running out of the bush, and Morrosco and me took them out."

From where we rested, we could see Highway 13 as it followed the opposite bank of the Lik through Muang Kasi. There were two bridges in the village that joined tracks on the west bank to the highway. Both bridges were carrying traffic; oxen- and horse-drawn carts, an occasional jeep, peasants on foot. Beyond the second bridge, our maps showed a shallow stretch of river that would make a safe crossing. Night came, and the village grew quiet. We dropped down into the riverbed above the village, hugging the western banks. Before we could move, several peasant men strolled out on the highway on the far bank. We ducked quickly into the chest-deep stream. Only the elevated bank of the highway shielded us from view.

We stayed in the water until we came under the first bridge, then scrambled into a tight bunch on the bank. Wiley moved out first. Just as we started to follow, he went down, pulling Toliver with him. In the pale light, I saw a small wooden boat drifting directly toward us. We all slid silently back into the water. There were three men in the boat, talking quietly and trolling behind them while the boat drifted stern-first. It came within feet of Wiley, then veered away and slipped back into the deep water. We stood without moving for a quarter of an hour in the gentle current, then Toliver tapped Wiley, and we moved off.

We crossed under the second bridge without incident, but just beyond we came upon a pontoon bridge that was not on our maps; it was a fish trap or boat dock of recent construction. It was built of barrel-sized corks lashed together with rope, with a wooden structure and slatted flooring above. The floor of the bridge stood seven feet above us. We studied the bridge a few moments, then Toliver turned to Prather.

"Lew," he said, "see if you can get under that thing."

Prather slipped out of his gear and handed it to

Tan and Morrosco. He took a breath and dropped out of sight. After thirty seconds, he surfaced long enough to gulp a lungful of air and disappeared again. He did this twice more. He came up gasping after the fourth attempt.

"There are a lot of support beams under there. I couldn't find my way through. We can manage it if we take enough time, but someone may drown under there. I don't believe it is worth the risk."

"We have to go up and over," Toliver said. "Take a look, Lew."

A riverside path approached the bridge from both ends, so we would be totally exposed until we dropped back onto the river on the other side. We had to get over in a hurry. Prather strapped on his knife. Morrosco and Wiley boosted him as he scrambled up the steep ten feet of the mudbank. Suddenly his wet boots slipped in the soft dirt, and he slid halfway down the bank before grabbing a root that held firm. He scrambled back up and had his hands over the edges of the bank when we heard someone approaching. I saw Prather poke his head up, then heard a man speak in a voice that was more curious than suspicious. Prather tried to pull himself up onto the path, but his feet kept slipping beneath him. As he struggled to keep from falling, the man spoke again.

"What the hell am I supposed to say to him?" Prather said without turning his head.

"For Christ sake, get him!" Toliver said in a whisper.

"I can't get up," Prather said. The man suddenly appeared at the edge of the bank, standing beside Prather's head. Dressed in a makeshift uniform, he held a rifle casually at quarter, pointing out over Prather's head. He must have seen the seven of us quite clearly, but he seemed totally relaxed. He was typical of peasant militia everywhere, refusing to believe in the reality of war even as it stared him in the face.

At that moment, Prather's boot found a rock. He

strode up the bank as if he were mounting a staircase three steps at a time. The man must have recognized from Prather's silhouette against the sky that he was not Oriental.

He sprang back, half stumbling, and tried to bring his weapon to bear, but his movements were jerky and overcompensating in his fear. There was a loud crack when Prather hit him a straight-arm punch that seemed to split the man's face open. Blood gushed from his nose and mouth. As he fell, Prather caught his shirt with one hand, slipped the man's head under his armpit, locked wrist in forearm, and gave a tremendous thrust back and downward. The man's neck snapped like dry timber. His body sank under its own weight. Prather fell down out of our sight line, and we all lay still. We waited in the water with weapons at the ready. Prather stuck his head over the edge of the embankment.

"He was alone," he said.

We handed up the gear, then Prather hauled us one at a time up the slippery slope. We dropped as quickly into the water on the far side. Prather pushed the dead soldier down to us, and Tan and Morrosco lashed the body with torn shirting to the bridge supports beneath the water. It would be days before it surfaced.

We followed the riverbed for a mile, then forded the shallows and crossed Highway 13. We struck northwest on the slopes paralleling the road. We all felt a sense of relief that we now had the highway between us and any activity out of Luang Prabang. We moved onto open ground for three miles, then climbed a series of low hills where the vegetation grew dense again and gave us enough cover to relax. Prather lit his pipe, and Wiley fell out to roll a cigarette. We began to talk softly. I caught up with Toliver and fell in beside him.

"Too much luck," I said.

"You're right," Toliver said. "That guy should have blown Lew right off the riverbank."

"We can't make it on luck," I said.

"I don't intend to," Toliver said. He sounded slightly annoyed.

"If that bloke had been any kind of a soldier, all hell would have let loose," I said.

"He wasn't," Toliver said, then moved on up the line.

It frustrated and angered me that so many unpredictable elements controlled our destiny. At the bridge, why had we lived and the peasant soldier died? The fortunes of war? It made the pit of my stomach burn when I saw the worst soldier in the field go on surviving mistake after mistake and the best walk into a stray bullet. There was no rationale to death.

The thick grass quickly gave way to jungle as we climbed. At first the jungle was soft and green, the thick foliage growing above us as it reached out for sunlight. As we moved higher, it grew dryer and closer to the ground. Soon we were pushing through heavy undergrowth that tugged at our uniforms and scratched our hands and faces. We broke out onto a rugged hillside carpeted in hard knee-deep tussock. We walked for three hours over exposed ground without seeing any signs of human life.

We were closing on the village of Ban Pho Khuan, which we wanted to skirt, then join Highway 13 beyond it. By midnight, we began to encounter hill tracks again and stumbled across isolated rice fields with a few huts clustered nearby. We grew quiet again. I heard Wiley coughing softly. Toliver heard it as well, and he dropped back to walk alongside Wiley.

"I didn't dry out. I'm coming down with a cold," he said without being prompted.

"We'd better bivouac and get some rest," Toliver said.

We had maintained a tremendous pace for six days. Only our high spirits were driving off the signs of physical exhaustion that must set in soon. Toliver moved to point to scout for a proper bivouac.

"We'll break here," he said when we caught up with him in a small clearing in the now almost impenetrable jungle.

We were tending our weapons before the first man had sat down. We had little trouble with oxidization in the jungle, but the heat and humidity made the weapons slippery in our sweaty hands. We coated them very lightly with oil, then wiped them almost dry. Moving parts got a drop of oil, then were coated in a dry charcoal-based paste similar to boot black that left a peculiar matte finish.

Tan and I lashed half a dozen boughs together and draped groundsheets over them to make a *hootchlai* large enough for all of us to sleep under. Within minutes of halting, fatigue seemed to sweep through the unit. We chewed slowly at cold rations. Morrosco dressed a small scalp wound Prather had somehow picked up when he killed the man by the bridge.

"Hey, baby, we're making time," Morrosco said, giving Wiley a thump on the shoulder. "Mucho miles in six days."

"We're bloody invisible," said Wiley.

"Let's stay that way," said Toliver. He was studying the maps. "We've got five miles to cover on the highway between Ban Pho Khuan and the junction with Highway 7. We've got to do it in the dark." Toliver looked at his watch. "It's 0100 hours. We'll take three hours' rest. Jackson, you split watch with Morrosco. Wake me at 0400." It was better that five men rest and two go short than all seven be deprived of sleep.

The night was black when Morrosco shook me awake. We loaded the gear and broke camp within minutes. We dropped quickly out of the hills onto the valley floor just behind Ban Pho Khuan. We circled the village, tracking through the rice fields on the south side where we caught several chickens without much ruckus. We strung the chickens from our packs for a hot meal later. We were clear of the village before the first peasant stirred. Half a mile north of Ban Pho Khuan, the village trail dropped down onto Highway

13. We still had an hour before sunup. The highway was empty.

We spaced out at ten-yard intervals at the edge of the road and struck out at a tremendous pace. I could feel the tension falling away with every step, now that we were not fighting through the undergrowth. The blood was flowing freely through my calves and thighs, easing the cramps that had plagued me all night. I had known few pleasures in combat; walking this road by morning was sheer joy. As the faint light that precedes dawn spread over the landscape, what had been a forced march became almost a stroll. For the first time in a week, I had the freedom to think. I could forgo the mental application to push myself up and down hills, to survive an endless series of localized pressure zones. Hills and rivers frayed the nerves. Fire fights stretched them to the breaking point and left them limp and inelastic. As we walked the highway at dawn, I felt as if twenty-five pounds had been lifted from my shoulders. My stride lengthened. My hip joint seemed to throw off six days' accumulation of dirt and grit.

Tan was out in front, pulling us along fast. I could see in the way the others moved ahead of me that they were rejuvenated as well. But this did not affect our readiness. A man did not lose his edge six days into enemy territory. But there was a spring in our step, as if we had all recognized we were being offered a brief respite. We would grab it and be stronger for what lay ahead.

We were within a few miles of the junction with Highway 7; both roads carried a lot of military traffic. For a long while, we heard nothing but the sounds of the forest and the noises of canvas and leather and metal we carried with us. The first traffic arrived just as the colors appeared in the landscape. We heard a jeep approaching from a great distance and stepped into the trees as it sped past. It was followed immediately by a second. The land was coming to life. We left the highway and walked the lower slopes of the hills to the east, then climbed higher to reconnoiter the country. The jungle was busy with movement: birds, insects, animals, all hidden from view by the heavy foliage. As we walked, I watched the morning sun slipping down the hills to the west. I thought of other mornings—colder, the air sharp rather than heavy —when I had walked as a boy with a party of men in the mountains. I had known a freedom then that vanished when we came back down from the hills. These men . . . this mountain . . . that feeling was reborn now.

A brilliantly colored bird lifted noisily out of the trees ahead. It turned and circled, beating furiously past at treetop level fifty feet below us on the steeply sloping hillside. I felt against my cheek the stock of the tiny 410-bore single-shot. I took aim just ahead of the speeding bird. I waited, then pulled slowly at the trigger. The bird spun, tumbling toward the ground, a shower of feathers in its wake. . . . Prather slowed down to let me catch up with him.

"It's a beautiful sight, hills in the morning," he said. I nodded. For a moment I had been a boy in New Zealand again.

"Were you thinking of home?" Prather asked.

"Morning is a good time to be on the trail," I said.

Prather pointed to the west, where the sun had just touched the stream that meandered at the foot of the hills.

"If the light were softer, those hills could be in Devon," he said.

"You got much jungle in Devon?" Morrosco said. He had dropped back to walk with us. "It's funny," he said, "those hills remind me of the Lower East Side. My old man's got a little coconut farm on a hill just like that one. Near Washington Square."

"What does a city boy know about the country?"

"If a city boy had known, he'd be back in the city. You country boys got no excuses."

"Piss off, Morrosco," I said without malice. I had seen us all drawing closer over the past week. Down below, where every step took us closer to an invisible enemy, where every movement was a struggle against a hostile environment, I often felt completely alone, as if I were pushing my body, my thirst, my fatigue almost dumbly toward a fantastic and impossible goal. But up here, where we could see for miles, where every step was not a battle with vines or greasy hillsides, where we could breathe and talk, I felt us fusing into one close body of men. We were almost enjoying life. Morrosco's natural lightheartedness, which had been subdued for several days, was resurfacing. Prather was quiet; he was probably thinking about his family. Even Tan was unwinding a little; his eyes had lost some of their furtiveness. We were all walking upright for the first time in days. Our backs had straightened, our hunched shoulders fallen into a more relaxed posture.

Toliver took point and increased the pace. We raced across the green landscape as if we were soaring. The weight of the gear melted from my back. We climbed hills and tumbled down the valleys below, but we were not tired, nor thirsty, nor hungry.

Where Highway 13 turned sharply west toward Luang Prabang, we skirted Ban Pho Tout and drove due north along a steep river valley. We wanted to keep well east of the patrols that protected the capital, only thirty miles away. We climbed first a dirt road, then jungle trails that led up to scattered hamlets where the land was arable. We were moving more cautiously now. When the road took a lazy meander around a low hill, we cut over the top. Sliding back down to the road on the far side, we stumbled ito a small field hidden behind a screen of jungle vegetation.

"Poppies," said Tan.

Instinctively, we primed our weapons. Intelligence had not warned us of opium this far west. The opium poppy flowers private armies.

I hated drugs like I hated communists. One of my few brushes with authority had been over them. A group of us were working as a support detail for supplies coming from the Cambodian highlands. We wanted to know what we were doing; the more we knew, the better we could work on the odds against us. We broke into the consignment and found it to be opium. We destroyed it.

Our high command was all over us when we came in. We had caused an embarrassment with the Cambodian Government. No mention was made of the cargo. They slapped our hands and demanded close confinement to orders in the future. I paid no attention to that. I would have destroyed the next batch. I was not risking my life for opium.

We slipped through the trees at the edge of the field and dropped back onto the road below, then left it to follow a mountain path. The trail was firm and bore recent jeep tracks. Ahead, it rose rapidly and disappeared where it turned sharply to the right. Trees bordering the trail provided good cover, so we pushed ahead at a jog.

Without warning, three open military vehicles raced bumper-to-bumper around the bend and headed straight for us.

CHAPTER 8

The men inside were laughing and hanging on as the vehicle bounced in the ruts. A few wore the uniforms of tribal mercenaries; the rest were Pathet Lao. They were all drunk and all armed with automatic weapons. The jungle had muffled the racing engines until the vehicles burst upon us.

We broke for the trees. Prather and I automatically moved left from the center of the line, the others darted to the right. But the men in the lead car had seen us; they shouted to the others and pointed. The vehicles slowed momentarily, then the lead driver changed his mind and accelerated down the track directly toward us. The other cars followed, with the whole lot of them rounding off automatic fire from the bumping, speeding cars. When the first car was level with Tan, he hit it with a long burst from his M-3. The windshield exploded. The two men in front arched in their seats and tumbled backward. The car careened to the right, hit a rock, rolled back to the left, teetered, came upright again, and skidded fifty feet before stopping just in front of Prather and me. The second car crashed into the first and skidded to a stop. The third swerved off the road on the opposite side, bounced off a small tree, and came to rest against a dirt embankment.

"Four to a car!" Toliver shouted.

The first car had separated Prather and me from the rest of the team, but it shielded us from the other two vehicles. Two men were still alive in the front vehicle. One jumped out the open top and ducked for cover behind the car. The second searched frantically for a weapon.

"I'm going up," I shouted to Prather.

As I sprinted out of the trees, I could hear Prather laying down covering fire. The man behind the car never saw me. I waited until I was fifteen feet away, then fired at him from the hip at full run. The man's head was blown clean off his shoulders in a cloud of bone and flesh. I spun on the second man. He had a weapon in his hands and was trying to scramble out on the far side of the car. Before I could fire, he flew backward out of the car, hit in the chest by Prather's M-3. I fired, and the man's stomach opened and closed before he hit the ground. Prather ran up and fell down beside me. The Laotians had piled out of the other cars and were firing across the road, unaware of us at their backs. When Toliver saw us fire at the second car, he broke out of the trees and ran toward the third.

"Toliver is going!" Wiley shouted.

While Prather laid down covering fire, I pulled back into the trees and sprinted past the second car to the third. Toliver was opposite me on the other side, firing exposed from the edge of the road. He had killed two of the four in the third car; the other two were crouched down on my side, firing wildly in Toliver's direction. When I gained the trees directly behind them, Toliver broke into a run toward them. Both men stood up to fire. I went straight at them from the rear. A shout from the second car gave me away. Suddenly they were trying desperately to look both ways at once. I changed direction three times in the seventy-five feet that separated us without firing once; when I was near enough to know that my rounds would hit the targets, I blew them both apart. I was so close to the second man I could see the gold in his teeth. Bone and gristle stung my face, body matter clung to my fatigues. I ran past the two bodies, searching for more targets. Thirty seconds of deafening automatic fire was followed by the roar of three grenades exploding in quick succession. I dropped to one knee and waited. One grenade had blown the sides out of the second car. Sound and movement ceased as quickly as they had begun. Toliver sounded off. We replied hoarsely, still catching our breaths. No one was hurt.

"Weapons and personal effects!" Toliver hollered out.

It was senseless hiding the bodies; the vehicles would have to be accounted for. By stripping them, we became another band of tribal mercenaries. I was covered in the blood of the men I had killed, but there was no time to clean properly. When I untied my dog rag to dry my face, the tip of a thumb fell out of the twisted cloth. I wiped at the blood and the pieces of flesh that were fast sticking to my skin.

The others were already gathering weapons. I grabbed a body and pulled it free from one of the cars. I searched inside the man's waist for the slim leather wallet in which he carried his identification, money, and perhaps a photograph of his family. I tossed it aside without opening it. I stripped a cheap watch from the man's wrist and cut two fingers off one hand to get at a thin gold band.

A shot rang out. I dropped down beside the car and grabbed my shotgun. I saw Wiley with a pistol in his hand standing over a body. He must have come upon a wounded man still trying to fight. Wiley habitually cleaned up after a flash action with a pistol in his hand. I did the same on occasion. It was a spontaneous reaction; the pistol just seemed to fall into my hand. But we did not have the ammunition now to waste indiscriminately. Wiley would have used a knife if there had been time.

I stripped two more bodies quickly and carried the booty in my shirt to an opening Toliver had cleared in the thickest undergrowth. I tossed the things down and turned back to gather weapons. Wiley walked right into me without looking. Wallets and personal effects were cradled in the crook of his left arm. He was staring at a large piece of paper that fluttered in his right hand as he walked.

"Hey, Kiwi, look what one guy was carrying," he said. He handed me the paper. It was a centerfold nude from *Playboy,* creased and worn with age.

"He took it from some Yank," Wiley said.

He took the photograph out of my hand, refolded it carefully, and buttoned it in a flap pocket on his fatigues. Within ten minutes we had hidden everything fifty feet from the path in foliage so dense it might never be found. We had destroyed what were probably the only vehicles in the neighborhood. But the peasants from the village up the trail would have heard the action. We faded into the trees and headed for higher ground.

I looked back for one moment at the devastation we left behind. Not a man among us was carrying a wound. I had never been with a unit like this before, nothing like this. It was as if we were reading each other's minds. I had not been told that Toliver was exposing himself. But I was on my way almost before he moved. I had not asked Prather for covering fire, but he was throwing out a hail of it when I went up on one knee. I had never seen anything like the fire pattern we were laying down. We were communicating with our weapons as if they were extensions of our arms.

We struck due north on a line to the Suong River. We were only twenty-five miles east of Luang Prabang, close enough to be within the circle of activity fanning out from there. But we had a range of peaks up to nine thousand feet between us and the capital, and the population was thinning. We kept a hard pace to clear the battle zone. As we moved along the western slopes of a lower range, the jungle gave way to waist-high tussock and a thick shrublike grass spotted by an occasional hardwood forest. It began to seem that we never put a foot on a level surface; we were either climbing or running downhill for hours at a time. We covered twenty-five miles a day in mountains, walking around the clock with one break of two or three hours to eat, rest, and listen for the abort signal. The pace would have killed an ordinary soldier, but we were trained for it; we could move for weeks like this.

Wiley's cold became a fever. His eyes grew red and swollen, and his breathing came hard. But he never slowed us. Spirits and energy were soaring. Toliver doubled the pace. We pushed on without complaining. We rested in elevated positions, where we could relax with maximum security. Occasionally we boiled roots and wild vegetables, but most often we ate field rations to conserve energy during the breaks.

Just after dawn we hit a long ridge back and climbed without stopping until the sun was overhead. There was no water on the slope, and we were careful to conserve what we had in our canteens. The last hour to the summit had my thighs and calves screaming for rest. We stopped for fifteen minutes on the flat surface of the hill; there we had a clear view of the surrounding landscape. The back side of the hill sloped away from us in a gradual decline. We saw half a dozen farms scattered in the valley ahead.

A few hundred yards below us was a small clearing with a bamboo hut surrounded by cultivated fields. There were chickens in the fields and two goats tied up under a thatched shed, but no sign of a peasant family about anywhere.

"Let's get a decent feed," Toliver said.

We were all in need of fresh food to get our bowels moving and to replenish the minerals we had sweated out. We were well above the route of any normal patrol. If the family returned, they were expendable.

We fanned out around the clearing and waited in the trees for thirty minutes. When no one returned, Toliver and Tan moved in, then called the rest of us. Jackson and Wiley stood guard while we scavenged. Nothing was done hastily. Toliver had decided we needed a rest and a hot meal; we went about it in a relaxed, businesslike manner. Breaking in the open was a calculated risk; if a patrol wandered up, we were badly situated to get away. But maintaining the physical integrity of the unit was as much a part of the mission as marching thirty miles a day. This was just one of thousands of calculations Toliver had to make to keep us alive and pull off the mission. We had great confidence in his judgment, and were prepared to accept the consequences.

Toliver turned up a burlap bag of rice in the shack. He set part of it to boil in a clay pot and put the rest in his pack. I milked the goats in a large wooden bucket. Morrosco killed and cleaned two chickens and added them to the bubbling rice along with some vegetables he had dug from the fields. Tan broke eggs into the rice stew and packed half a dozen more in straw in his pack. We all washed and refilled our canteens from a shallow well. We ate, then rested for another hour before pushing on.

We came down off the slopes onto the valley trails. Some of the trail junctions were guarded by local militia or small Pathet Lao units. When the point spotted activity, we would back up for a mile or more and skirt a wide circle around it, then fan out quickly at trailside in a defensive position and dash across one at a time.

The going grew rougher as we approached the Nam Suong Valley, but we were relatively safe as we moved farther from Luang Prabang. The scattered farms gradually disappeared; the patrols grew fewer. We had been ducking enemy parties as often as twice a day, and the tension and hard mountain walking were draining us rapidly. Wiley's fever increased. His breathing was labored and his eyes puffy and blood-red. Finally he dropped out of the line ahead of me and took out his contact lenses.

"I can't wear them," he said, putting on his plastic-rimmed army-issue glasses.

I said nothing. The reflective power of two spectacle lenses were enormous. Wiley knew that. He would have them off as soon as he could wear the others. We marched all that night along the upper slopes of the valley. Early the next morning, as we worked our way toward lower contours, a following rain hit us without warning. We ignored it until we were thoroughly soaked, then one at a time buckled our body wraps around us.

It rained without stopping for three days while we struggled to reach our Nam Suong crossing. There was no solid footing anywhere. The earth was covered in a sheet of running ground water. Every small wash was a rushing stream that could sweep a man down a hillside. After the first day, I could feel my boots cracking up. We moved without talking, without stopping now. Yesterday's dust was six inches of greasy mud. Every fallen tree limb, every leaf was moss-slick and treacherous. The rain drove the mosquitoes down to the ground where they swarmed around us, diving for exposed flesh.

We stopped to hand the gear over a treacherous ford in a streaming gully. As Tan passed my shotgun across, I saw a small black lump fall from his beret onto his neck. I started up the hill, then realized what I had seen. I spun around, grabbed the lump off Tan's neck and threw it to the ground.

"Leech," I told Tan. I had managed to knock it away before it sank its two tiny hooks painlessly into Tan's neck, depositing disease and infection and drawing human blood to feed itself.

"Leeches!" Tan shouted up the line.

The others instinctively hunched their shoulders, then quickly buttoned fatigue collars and rolled down shirt sleeves. Prather drew out his pipe, and Davies rolled a cigarette, but neither would light in the rain.

The leeches dropped on us with no more impact than the huge incessant raindrops beating at our backs. Wiley traded his beret for a bush hat that covered his neck. Prather managed with great difficulty to get a flame going on a short piece of hardwood. He kept it dry and smoldering as we moved. Every time we stopped, he burned off the leeches with the hotstick. Jungle disease was a far more dangerous enemy than we had faced so far.

Our pace had slowed; we were now losing time to the schedule. We kept close together. There was no air. With my collar up and sleeves down, I felt the heat of the jungle pressing on me. It was like trying to run in a steam bath. When I breathed in, I was not getting air; I was getting something else that did not fill my lungs. The packs, ammunition belts, the weapons, the canvas and leather and metal pulled at my body and squeezed and choked it in a giant fist. I tore open my collar. I rolled up my sleeves. I would have to take care with the leeches.

The rain fell. Every step became more agonizing than the last. The mountainsides were broken by a series of raging streams, the banks slick with rotting foliage that crumbled beneath us. Toliver, at point, cautiously worked his way down a steep slope. It collapsed under him, and he slid a hundred feet before a tree checked his fall. He was not hurt, but one of his boots was ripped halfway up the ankle. We passed his mud-choked gear around and cleaned as much as we could on the spot before pushing on.

Our loads were constantly sliding about on our backs as we stumbled through the mud and slime. The rain hit the trees like gravel on a rooftop. We had to shout to be heard.

On the second day the rain stopped as suddenly as it had started. In an instant, we were blanketed by silence. Slowly the jungle noises—birds chattering, cicadas buzzing, the scurrying of unseen small creatures along a jungle floor—rose in a cacophony of sound. Minutes later, that too stopped as suddenly as it had begun, and the jungle was as silent as a cave. Silence is a danger signal in the jungle. We stopped and quietly primed our weapons. But it was that other silence that precedes a change in the weather. Without a warning drop, the rain fell in sheets.

Climbing, falling, fording a dozen streams in half a day, we struggled on, losing time to the mission schedule. Toliver tried to increase the pace, but he pushed up against the exhaustion barrier and had to slack off.

We had planned to reach the Suong River Valley in late afternoon and ford the river under cover of dusk, but it was hours past sundown before we began to descend to the valley floor. My body was crying for rest, and my nerves were drawn to the breaking point. I found myself startled by the snap of a twig underfoot or a branch that suddenly leapt out to brush against my face. We struggled on for hours, never exchanging a word.

The rain stopped while we were traversing the valley floor in total darkness, but when we reached the Suong, it was swollen to a raging torrent. Our ford was to have been an easy dash across a shallow stream; we found chest-deep rapids twisting and spilling across the rocks.

"We'll have to go across in a chain," Toliver said.

"We'll be completely exposed," Wiley said.

"For God's sake, Barry," Morrosco said, "who but us would be stupid enough to be here in this weather?"

We lashed driftwood into small rafts, onto which we strapped the gear. We crossed in a human chain, one hand clinging to the rafts, the other clutching the belt of the man in front. It took us half an hour to inch our way through the chill waters. Just off the opposite bank, a huge tree limb came tearing around a boulder. It hit me a glancing blow, then pivoted and swung its full weight at Wiley. He ducked, and it passed harmlessly over his head. Jackson and I pulled against the surging current and hauled up the choking, spluttering Wiley. We edged ashore, then collapsed with exhaustion. Our gear was intact.

We were within a day and a half of our second cache at the village of M Ngoi, which we were very anxious to reach. We were growing short of ammunition. Our uniforms and boots were decaying. Our bodies were worn out and cut about and bruised. M Ngoi was a safe village; we could rest there, bathe and repair our bodies. We pushed on through the night and the driving rain that soon started again.

M Ngoi was thirty miles due north of our river crossing, but we anticipated intense mercenary activity in the valleys between. Our intention was to march east for nine miles along the northern bank of the Suong, then strike north and drift back west to M Ngoi. But within an hour we were in vegetation so thick we had to chop our way through. In three hours we managed to cover less than a mile.

"We'll lose a day doing this," Toliver said. "I'd rather take my chances with the mercenaries." We turned back toward the river crossing. By the time we got there, the rain had stopped, and the ground water was quickly running off. We struck north on a direct bearing to M Ngoi.

We broke out of the dense vegetation onto a plain of shrub grasses and woods. The number of farms was increasing on the upper valley slopes, where the soil was better.

Morrosco took point a hundred yards ahead of the rest of us. He was breaking cover from a stand of trees when he let off a long burst of automatic fire. He had walked straight into the middle of a patrol of tribal mercenaries strung out in a line in the tall grass just beyond the trees. We quickly closed behind him in a V formation. He was exchanging fire with five men who had taken up prone positions in the grass. Five men bunched so tightly meant a very large patrol and a larger unit somewhere nearby. The two ends of the patrol, split by Morrosco's action, started closing on us. I counted eighteen or twenty altogether, but they were split into three groups.

Tribal mercenaries were impossible to second-guess. They had practically no access to field intelligence, knew nothing of tactical warfare, fought with any weapon—American, Czech, Russian, Chinese—that fell into their hands. They respected neither discipline, rank, nor fear. They roamed everywhere, fighting for the highest bidder, or for what they could loot. And they were ready to make every fire fight a shoot-out to the last man. They were forever getting themselves killed needlessly, but their spontaneity and unpredictability made them extremely dangerous. If we did not hit them hard enough, they would make it their business to track us down. For head money and for revenge.

Toliver gave no orders, because we all knew what to do. We were outnumbered, but we had greater fire power than any of the three parties facing us. We were running low on ammunition and could not sustain a long fire fight. We had tree cover for the moment, while the mercenaries were trapped in the open. We had to move fast, hitting one party at a time.

Morrosco's initial burst had killed one man and wounded another. The other mercenaries were joining the battle singly. Morrosco led us in a rush out of the trees. We over-ran and killed the four in front within seconds, then swung right to hit the stragglers caught in the open. We killed four more in a rolling action and drove the rest back. Before they could recover, we struck northeast on the run, fighting a fading action as we moved. We were almost out of range when Tan gave a short cry. I spun around. Tan was still moving steadily on his feet, but blood was pouring from a wound behind one ear.

"I'm all right," he yelled. "It's a ricochet or splinters."

Wiley dropped back with Jackson to lay down covering fire while Tan slapped a compress on his head. We kept running. The firing grew more distant, then stopped. The mercenaries would be regrouping, counting their dead, wondering how many of us they had come up against. We kept moving at the double until we gained the lower slopes of a jagged green hill. There Toliver took a new bearing to the north, and we moved off cautiously, working our way to higher contours. We marched all day and through the night, breaking once for two hours. We saw no one.

We arrived at M Ngoi just after noon the following day. Tan, Jackson, and Wiley circled the village to the north. The rest of us spread out through the trees on the south side.

Though we expected M Ngoi to be secure—Green Berets had been operating from there for more than a year—we watched and waited. Our cache served as a form of insurance. The Green Berets would have brought it in, then left it to the village elders to hide. If anything went missing, the Green Berets would punish the entire village, and if the Pathet Lao discovered the cache, they would kill every man, woman, and child and burn the village, so the villagers had selfish reasons for remaining loyal to us.

M Ngoi was not much larger than the hamlets we had been skirting in the hills. On three sides of a rectangle, stilted longhouses of bamboo and thatch faced a clearing, their backs to the jungle. The open side of the clearing held a few small sheds. We saw no signs of tension among the people. The men were smoking and talking on the upper side of the village. The women moved casually about their chores. But these villagers were masters of deceit, or they would not have survived thirty years of warfare. I looked for the children. They were playing about freely. If this was a setup, they would have been hidden away. I suddenly realized how much I wanted M Ngoi to be safe. How much we needed a civilized respite. Hot food. A bath. A shave. Undisturbed rest. We waited for three hours for that telltale clue that something was wrong. Finally, Toliver stepped out of the trees.

"Let's move," he said.

He whistled and waved to Jackson. We closed a net around the village, moving everyone toward the clearing with a wave of our weapons. There was no panic whatsoever. The women kept working until the diminishing circle caught them up, then they grabbed up the small children and nudged the older ones in front of them. The village men huddled quickly, then four younger ones came forward to meet Toliver; the old men hung back in the shadows of the houses. I felt good about the whole scene, though we still kept our weapons at the ready. Toliver went forward to meet the welcoming committee. They greeted him with a bow and a prayer sign. The oldest of the four, obviously the spokesman, must have been in his late forties, the other three ten years his junior; they were all young, I thought, to be village councillors. The spokesman welcomed Toliver in fluent English. Toliver was cool but not unfriendly.

"Where is the head man of the village?" Toliver asked.

"I am the head man," the man replied, smiling.

"The head man is well known to my people. He is very old and has been a friend to the Americans for many years," Toliver said.

"The old man was honored by our people too. Now he is dead, and we honor his memory. The people have chosen me as head man. Please accept the humble hospitality of our small village."

Toliver looked at Tan. Tan questioned the other three men sharply.

"They say he is telling the truth," Tan said.

"We accept your hospitality with pleasure," Toliver said. "Tell your people that no one must leave the village while we are here. Anyone attempting to do so will be shot. Even the children. If you obey my orders and treat my men well, you shall be rewarded. We wish you no harm."

The man spoke to the crowd that was gathered in the clearing. When he had finished, one woman grabbed up a small child and ran into the house. The rest remained impassive; they had heard the speech many times before. The crowd slowly broke up. The women dragged the smaller children to play around them while they carried on with the cooking and washing. The men and older boys hung about to watch us.

"What do you think, Gayle?" Toliver asked me.

"I think the village is secure."

"Tell me why," Toliver said.

"Three reasons. First the women. They're not afraid. There were not enough babies snatched up when you threatened them. The men can fool me with their smiles and bows. But if they were setting us up, the women would be frightened out of their wits. They don't look frightened. Secondly, if they were going to hit us, these young blokes hanging about looking at our gear would have been staked out waiting for us. They would have hit us before we could take the village."

"And thirdly?" Toliver asked.

"And thirdly, Tan's not complaining."

"I agree with you," Toliver said.

"Where is the Green Beret unit we expected here? Are you going to ask?" I said.

"No," Toliver replied, "and I want no mention of the cache until I'm completely satisfied. The men not standing guard can fall out but I don't want any weapons broken down yet."

Wiley and Jackson stood the first guard at opposite ends of the village. Toliver continued to question the head man while Tan talked with the others. After half an hour, Toliver called for food and hot water.

When Morrosco started tending the wound in Tan's scalp, a woman came and gently pushed him aside. He watched suspiciously as she probed the blood-caked gash, then let her get on with the job. The rest of us cleaned weapons a few at a time, always leaving some primed for action. A great wooden tub in a wash shed was filled with water heated over open fires. Two at a time, we soaked in the steaming water while the women scrubbed us with soapstone. After bathing, we wrapped clean loincloths about our waists and rested on a shaded balcony. The older boys, those still too young to be kidnaped into one army or another, questioned us timidly in broken English about our weapons, which we forbade them to touch. The children hung back at first, then came slowly forward.

They gathered about Morrosco, and he fed them gum and chocolate from the rations. I distrusted them as just more flotsam in the tides of war washing across Indochina. I had seen a five-year-old lob a grenade into a group of soldiers; I had seen two-year-olds running down the streets with their clothes on fire.

The women sewed the rents in our uniforms, then soaked and scrubbed them in hot soapy water. As they dried in the sun, the women worked the heavy canvas with their hands to keep it from going stiff.

We dressed when the evening grew chill. The men led us to the village longhouse. Rush mats decorated with flowers were laid upon the floor. Toliver and I sat side by side with the village councillors opposite us. Toliver questioned the head man about troop movement north of M Ngoi, particularly North Vietnamese units that regularly patrolled this far across the border. There was no unusual activity.

"Where is the Green Beret unit?" I asked Toliver.

The village men recognized "Green Beret" and immediately grew silent, looking from me to Toliver.

"I don't know," Toliver said. "I expected somebody to meet us. I'd like to know if there's any indication our pattern of movement has been picked up. If they're not here, there's a good reason, and we're not going to get it from these people. They may be out there in the trees watching us right now."

No one had spoken while Toliver was talking to me. When he stopped, they all burst into conversation at once. Several of the younger men spoke broken English and made an effort to talk with me, but they soon lost interest and fell into conversation among themselves.

"Tan," I called out.

Tan was seated at the far end of the room.

"What is it?" he asked.

"Come and sit next to me. I don't like people talking when I don't know what they are saying."

The women handed each of us a small wooden bowl, then carried in half a dozen cast-iron kettles. They ladled a blood-thickened meat stew into our bowls. One man broke up a large cornmeal patty and passed around great hunks which we dipped into the stew. When the rich juice was gone, we ate the tender meat with thumb and forefinger. The stew was followed by several rice dishes, some with bean shoots or potatoes, others with bits of fresh perch from the mountain stream. There was a delicious soft goat's milk cheese with pieces of pineapple cut up in it. I drank goat's milk through the meal, while the others drank milk wine made with potatoes and ground onions. The women cleared away all the dishes and brought guavas and sour grapes to end the meal.

"They are proud of that meal," I remarked.

"They ought to be. That was some feast," said Morrosco.

"It is their way of welcoming the foreigner into their home," Tan said.

After the fruit, we drank coffee and mint tea. Prather and Wiley offered tobacco to the village men; only the young ones accepted. Jackson pointed out that the coffee and bags of wheat flour we had seen stashed in a corner meant Green Berets had recently been in M Ngoi. The old men retired to the far end of the longhouse to "chase the dragon," catching in flared nostrils the wisps of smoke that rose from tiny putty-like balls of opium that smoldered at the end of thin wooden sticks they gripped delicately between their frail fingers.

After the meal, Toliver and I remained at the table to quiz the younger men with Tan's help. The older man was titular head of the village, but the trio of young men were the active leaders and likely liaison with the Green Berets.

Prather stayed a short while, then left to sleep. The

children attached themselves to Morrosco. They followed him like a Pied Piper around the village, and he encouraged them to teach him their games. To my surprise, Jackson had a warm regard for the villagers and showed a remarkable familiarity with their customs. He wandered aimlessly about, chatting in English to anyone who would listen. Wiley lay on a mat on the porch. The women washed him with cool rags and fed him herb tea to combat his fever. Finally, he slept.

After an hour of intense interrogation, Toliver decided we had learned all we could from the young men. Tan rose quietly and left the longhouse. I saw him stoop to pick up a rush mat from the porch. He carried it across the clearing and mounted the steps of another house, dark and silent. Carefully he spread the mat on the porch. With a slow, fluid motion, he sat cross-legged on the mat, then brought his body effortlessly into the lotus position. For a few seconds, he rocked his torso back and forth. Hands resting lightly in his lap, fingertips touching, he stared straight ahead.

Morrosco and Jackson managed to find two seemingly unattached young women; the village men raised no objection. They looked to Toliver for approval. He ignored them. We were pulling out in a few hours; if they wanted women rather than sleep, that was their affair. Morrosco looked at me for reassurance. I shrugged. The two men made pallets on the veranda and went to sleep.

I was sympathetic to the two. In a different way, I too had been seduced. In Western terms, there was nothing sophisticated about these people; they were peasants in a small village struggling to survive a war they did not understand. Yet there was a charm here I could not ignore. The village lived on the bitter fruits of war. Yet these people we held by force of arms welcomed us with feasting. The village was neat and tidy, the villagers freshly washed. In a way, theirs was a rich, fulfilling life; they were completely at one with an environment that provided clothes for their backs, a full stomach of fresh and delicious food. These were just simple mountain people, but they had much to admire and envy.

But nothing is quite that simple, I reminded myself, shaking off a false sense of security the bath and feast had brought on. There was not a weapon in sight except those we had brought with us. But these gentle people must have been armed to the teeth. And they could use those arms, otherwise M Ngoi would not be a Green Beret village. It was their guile that deceived me. It took more than arms to keep a village standing in Laos. A Pathet Lao unit could walk in tomorrow and get the same warm welcome, the fish and rice, the hot baths, the smiling women who tended to rent uniforms and battered bodies. The Pathet Lao were no more fooled than we were or the Green Berets. The Pathet Lao would not mess up M Ngoi so long as they could ignore it; that would alienate them from the peasants who fed them. And they courted no trouble with village mercenaries.

There was not a man to be seen here between fifteen and thirty-five. M Ngoi must have had a mercenary unit out at this moment. They might even be guarding the village, ready to burst in on us at the first sign of trouble. Meanwhile, the mercenaries and the Pathet Lao were maintaining an effective truce in order to fight their common enemy, the Laotian National Army. There was this strange bush diplomacy in these regions where even the Green Berets were left unmolested if possible.

It was all considerably more sophisticated than this gentle, friendly village would suggest. You had to know who your friends were. And you never could. Besides the Green Berets, M Ngoi might be in the pay of the national army or even the North Vietnamese. Or all three. Blokes like Morrosco and Jackson never worried about that sort of thing. But I felt myself drawn daily more closely to Toliver, to my role as second-in-command. I had seen no sign of jealousy or resentment in the unit over my rank, even after the fight with Jackson. The team accepted it, encouraged it now that

I had proved myself worthy. And Toliver was growing to depend on me more each day.

It came down to the difference between soldiers who were very good at their job and soldiers who looked at the situation in a wider concept. I had as much respect for the trio's touch for the bush and combat savvy as any soldiers I had ever known. But there were limits to how much they cared to get involved. That is where you get a separation in authority and leadership. A Green Beret private and a Green Beret officer were two of the best soldiers anywhere, but they had a different way of looking at a military situation. They made such a devastating team partly because both recognize that difference. In our unit, military order closely paralleled the natural order. It made life less complicated for all of us.

When Toliver finally stretched out to rest, I made a pallet and fell instantly into a deep, dreamless sleep.

"Rivers!" Toliver called and shook me awake. "Get them together. We're moving out." It was 0300 hours. The men moved sharply. The sleep and hot food had made us stronger. The bath, a shave, a clean uniform, a momentary respite from combat in which to breathe the air of humanity had lifted our spirits. Wiley was not well, but he was holding malaria at bay. As we left M Ngoi, the village women draped our shoulders with wicker baskets of fruit and boiled vegetables. The village head and the three younger men led us half a mile north through almost impenetrable foliage to the cache. It was enormous. This was the last friendly contact and resupply point until we reached M Ngoi on the return journey. The Green Berets operated north of here, but if a cache were discovered, it might expose our mission pattern to Hanoi or Peking. The conference was little more than a week away. The least sign of movement toward Ta shu tang would cancel the conference or change the venue in an instant. When we marched away from this cache, we had no further link-up, no further source of resupply, and no support. We were truly alone.

We immediately sorted out the ammunition.

"Rivers!" Jackson called out. "Your shotgun ammo."

He handed me two dobie bags I had forwarded from Bien Hoa. I also took a new Armalite to replace mine, which had been jamming. We all had fresh uniforms. Clothing was our armor against the environment; the longer a mission endured, the more important a man's uniform became. Tan and Prather changed into new shirts; despite the repairs at M Ngoi, theirs were little more than tattered rags. The rest of us saved ours. We all changed socks and stuffed our pockets with extra pairs. Socks were our best safeguard against blisters that would cipple a man hiking ten miles without rest, but they were worn out in three days. Toliver threw away his torn boots and struggled into a pair too small for feet swollen from a fortnight's marching. All our boots were falling apart, but only he chose to break in a new pair; the rest of us packed ours with the uniforms. The essentials sorted out, we dealt more leisurely with the rest of the cache.

"These people are one hundred per cent secure," Toliver said. "They didn't even break into the Red Cross packages."

What remained was a treasure trove of items unobtainable for these mountain peasants: cigarettes, chocolate, sewing kits, medicines. Morrosco sorted through the medical bags for more antimalaria pills now that Wiley was using them. We rifled through the rest, stuffing our pockets with glucose tablets and sugar cubes, cookies and dried fruit. There was enough to have supplied us five times over. This was done purposely so that we could leave a generous parting gift for the village.

Toliver had Tan call our escort from where they squatted quietly under a nearby tree. If we made it back from China, the survival of the unit could rest in the hands of these four. Toliver made a brief, almost formal speech in English which Tan translated, thanking the villagers for their hospitality. As a gift, he offered, with a deepest regret and humanity for its insignificance, all that remained. To the head man he presented a score of grenades and an M-3 with a dozen clips. The four men would parcel the goods to their advantage; the villagers would find use for every single item, down to the torn shirts and abandoned boots. Toliver and Tan shook hands with each of the four men. The rest of us gave them a farewell nod. They bowed and made a sign with their hands. They waited for us to leave.

"Let's go," Toliver said.

We started north. To North Vietnam. To China.

CHAPTER 9

I felt better than I had on the first day. I was broken into the trail, used to the twenty-four-hour pace. I was tougher and more enduring than I had ever been before. I was confident of myself, of Toliver, of the unit, and every man in it. We had proved ourselves unsurpassed in combat; after two and a half weeks in enemy territory, we were not carrying a single bullet wound. We were whole and healthy. Tan's scalp wound and Wiley's fever, the scraped elbows and knees, sore and twisted muscles were expected in this environment.

We came down from the hills around M Ngoi to follow a stream flowing to the northeast. We marched all night and the next day, stopping only for brief rests, radio transmission, and cold food. The route wove east, then west as we followed the natural contours of the landscape, but we were making steady progress north and fast approaching the North Vietnamese border.

At what was supposed to be an easy ford across the Nam Pa, we found a white-water river raging out of its banks from days of rain. We scouted for two hours before finding a spot where the river shallowed around a wide bend. Morrosco ventured out, probing in front with a long stick. The bottom was solid, and the waters never rose above his thighs for 150 yards. At the opposite bank, there was a five-yard stretch where the current, pierced by a huge boulder, cut a furious path. When Morrosco probed the chest-deep water with his stick, he was nearly swept off his feet.

"What do you think?" Toliver asked him.

"It's fast, but it's not that fast. We can make it."

We lashed the gear to driftwood as we had at the Nam Suong. With Toliver leading, we walked singly through the shallow waters. We stopped near the rapids and locked hand to wrist, then inched our way into the boiling stream. Two minutes later, Toliver grabbed a root on the opposite bank. He yelled at me at the other end of the chain to come across. I handed the raft over to Tan and worked my way across the river by holding on to the men's shirts, then quickly scrambled up the bank. Tan passed the raft over. I held the raft with one hand and unloaded it with the other, then let it drift away. Tan then began working his way along the line. He was holding Toliver by the belt and reaching up toward my outstretched hand when a log shot around the boulder and hit him squarely in the back. Tan sank like a rock between Jackson and Toliver. Toliver grabbed Tan's shirt, but the force of the current tore the limp body from his hand. Jackson reached for Tan's hand but grabbed the barrel of his M-3 instead. The weapon slipped off Tan's shoulder. He started on a rolling, tumbling course down the river. He was half conscious and trying to swim, but his pack made him top-heavy. Toliver grabbed Jackson, who pulled the others across behind him. I helped Toliver up the bank, then sprinted after Tan, who was already thirty yards downstream. As I swung around an overhanging limb, I saw Tan fly backward against a boulder. His head snapped back and hit the rock with crushing force. For an instant he lay poised on the top, then the current swept him away. The pack was torn from his back and bobbed like a cork on the water. Tan rolled and turned in the rushing current. I ran for another ten yards until the jungle closed in on the bank. I leapt in the river and paddled frantically toward Tan. Tan's shirt caught on an uprooted tree, and I grabbed him as I swept past. Holding him with my left hand, I reached out at passing rocks and branches with my right. I was losing my grip on Tan's shirt when we washed up on an egg-shaped boulder. I pulled him up on the rock, then fell back exhausted.

Within five minutes, the others had cut their way along the bank and stood opposite us. Morrosco stripped a long tree limb with his machete. I rolled Tan on his back.

"He's alive!" I shouted.

The back of Tan's head was swollen where he had banged it on the rocks. He was unconscious. His shirt was torn in several places, and he had lost half a dozen grenades.

"Wiley," Toliver ordered, "go after the pack."

The pack had disappeared downstream. And with it the radio. Morrosco swung the stripped limb out across the water like a fishing pole. I wrapped my right arm around the limb and tucked it under my armpit. I slipped my left hand through Tan's belt and grabbed it from the underside. Pulling him behind me, I edged my way into the current. I scrambled quickly back onto the rock.

"We won't make it," I shouted over the roar of the water. "The current's too strong."

"Tie him to the pole," Toliver yelled back.

I tied Tan to the limb with his belt, then eased him into the current. Tan went straight under the water, but Toliver and Morrosco hauled him ashore within seconds. They pulled me across in the same way. While Prather and Jackson stripped Tan, Morrosco was dressing his head. Wiley came running back.

"It was washed up onshore," he said, waving Tan's pack.

Toliver jumped up and grabbed the pack from Wiley's hand. He ripped it open and fished about until he brought up the radio. Water cascaded from the set when he snapped open the back of the small aluminum casing. Toliver tore his dog rag from his neck and mopped furiously.

"How bad?" I asked.

"I imagine it's ruined," he replied.

"We're not likely to get an abort signal on a bloody broken radio," I said.

Toliver was grinning.

"Not bloody likely, old chap," he said, "so we'll bloody well get on with the bloody job." Toliver shook out a few more drops, then leaned the radio against a rock so that the innards could catch the sun. We turned to Tan.

"How is he?" Toliver asked Morrosco.

"He doesn't seem to be broke up anywhere."

"What about his head?"

"There's no way for me to know how bad it is," said Morrosco.

"So we wait," said Toliver.

Within minutes, Tan had regained consciousness. He needed rest before he could walk. Toliver looked at his watch.

"Radio transmission in less than an hour. We'll sit it out here."

As we stripped and dried our gear and weapons, I thought about the one incalculable factor in combat. Luck. Fate. The odds. Whatever it was called, I hated it. Because I had no control over it. One more time now it had run in our favor. If the log had hit the driftwood raft instead of Tan, we would have lost the explosives and half our supplies. As it was, both Tan and I could have drowned. The crossing was a tough situation that had gotten away from us, yet we survived it with a bumped head and a few lost grenades. Luck. Where do you enter it on the accounts ledger?

The radio was another matter. At 1515 hours Toliver tried and failed to raise a carrier wave. I felt divided. Every time my exhausted legs crested a hill, every time I fired my weapon or hacked a path through the jungle, my determination to carry out the mission had redoubled. At Bien Hoa the odds had seemed so enormous as to be preposterous: a seven-man team pitted against half the armies in southern Asia. But in the confines of the air base, that remained hypothesis. Here in the field, it had become reality. And the team was so good, it was not only surviving, it was advancing. We were on schedule and only a week from the mission site. A day's march from North Vietnam. Tomorrow was the last chance to call us back. Part of me wanted to see Toliver grab up the useless radio and throw it into the bush. Another part of me did not want to turn loose from that last fragile contact with a friendly world.

At 1545 hours, Toliver switched off the radio and handed it back to Tan, who was sitting up and cleaning his weapons.

"Can you walk?" Toliver asked.

"I'm all right," he said.

Tan tried to stand but fell back into a sitting position. Morrosco gave him a glucose bar. Within minutes he was on his feet, and we were back on the trail. Tan was unsteady, hardly fit for combat, so Toliver slowed the pace for the rest of the day.

We moved very cautiously now. This area was heavy with NVA patrols which protected Highway 19 to the north and a bulge in the North Vietnamese border, which at one point was only ten miles east of us. We traveled up the Nam Luang Valley, crossing it first to skirt the village of Pak Luong, then again to follow a branch when the mainstream turned east into North Vietnam. We were in a stand of trees just below the village of Kung Sala when Jackson, at point, dropped to the ground. We broke for cover and waited. After five minutes, Jackson crawled back to Toliver. I crawled forward to join them.

"NVA patrol," Jackson asid.

"How many?" Toliver asked.

"Five," he answered. "In the tall grass beyond the trees. Headed right at us. But they ain't looking for us. They're moving too careless."

"How are they spread?" Toliver asked.

"Hundred yards front to back. In a file."

"How much time we got?"

"Six, seven minutes."

"Five scouts. That means a minimum party of twenty. We have to take them. Otherwise we could get caught out between two parties, if either one sees us."

Discretion was vital. One burst from an automatic weapon could call down twenty men on us. We would have to take five men silently. That meant taking them simultaneously.

I pulled my machete and showed it to the men behind, then held up five fingers. Prather inched his way forward to join the three of us.

"Tan's in no condition for combat," he said.

"Take him to the rear, Lew," Toliver said, "and cover us. Rivers, you stay here with Wiley. I'll go forward two hundred yards with Jackson and Morrosco. We'll let them walk through, then pick up the last three. We'll wait for you and Wiley to make the first move."

I lay in wait in knee-high grass behind a large tree. I did not strip off my pack or unsling my two weapons. If things went right, I would never feel their weight; a man taken by surprise can be curiously slow to react. I should have time to come up off the ground and slash the man's throat open before he could fire with a weapon already in his hand. When a man has the edge, a thirty-five-pound pack is as much an integral part of his body as arms and legs. When he loses that edge, thirty-five pounds is a bastard. But if we had to run, my gear was going with me.

The NVA scouts advanced into the trees with the carelessness of a patrol that was a week's march from the nearest battlefield. I caught occasional glimpses of Morrosco, Jackson, and Toliver moving in behind them. When the lead man was ten yards in front of me, I heard a crash. I glanced up and saw Morrosco sunk to his waist in a pile of rotten foliage. The man Morrosco was stalking whirled around, shouted, fired his weapon, and started to run. Suddenly there was confusion everywhere.

While the NVA were yelling back and forth, trying to sort us out, I jumped up. My target spotted me immediately and tore off through the bush. I ran after him. My gear weighed a hundred pounds now. If I did not catch him in thirty yards, he was gone. I heard two short bursts from an AK-47. We've sprung it, I told myself. I kept running, expecting the bushes to part and reveal half the North Vietnamese Army.

The man was pulling away from me when he caught his foot on a vine and went sprawling. I tackled him as he scrambled to his feet. He twisted and fell on his back. Before he could recover, I straddled him. I raised my machete and brought it down on his head. He caught the blow with the stock of his rifle. I jerked the machete up to chop again, but it was embedded in the wood. I let it go and grabbed the rifle by both ends and forced it down. The weapon hovered, then slowly descended across the man's neck. I threw my full body weight against the weapon.

When the rifle reached his throat, the man let go one hand and grabbed at my face. He tore frantically at the flesh, groping for my eyes. I grabbed his index finger in my teeth and hung on. His face swelled purple, and froth spilled from the corners of his mouth. His fingers fluttered briefly against my face. His body gave one convulsive heave, then stopped.

I was appalled. This was not calculated combat; it was a free-for-all in the jungle. Amateur stuff. Heroics. I did not want any part of heroics, because I was not ready to die. Special forces were not trained for this nonsense. I had survived a dangerous, untidy fight only because I was the better man. While I had been killing one man in the ugliest way possible, I was totally exposed. I could have been blown away at any moment.

I slit the man's throat, then jumped up. I heard yelling and fighting at every quarter, but I could see no one. I sprinted toward the sound of a scuffle nearby. At that moment, a man broke out of the bush ten feet in front of me, running at full stride. Before I could change course, the man slammed his rifle into the side of my head. My legs turned to rubber, and I dropped in my tracks without losing consciousness. I tried to jump up, but my body had stopped functioning. I lay on my back and watched the man dive on top of me. My brain struggled, but my muscles would not respond. The man raised his rifle overhead to smash my skull in. At that instant, Toliver appeared from nowhere; he chopped the man's arm off with a savage swing of his machete. The blade carried on, bouncing off the man's head and severing one ear. The weapon and the arm holding it fell across my chest. Toliver chopped again, splitting the man's throat like a slaughtered pig. A fountain of blood burst in my face. The man fell on top of me. Toliver shoved the dead man aside, then looked me over quickly to confirm that the blood that drenched me was not my own.

"Get up," he shouted.

I tried to answer, but no words came out. Toliver grabbed me by the shirt and dragged me through the forest. My left eye was completely closed; through a film of blood that covered the right eye, I watched the jungle floor creep by. Toliver was not hurrying. The sounds of fighting had ceased. I realized that all the patrol must have been killed. But how badly were we hit? That was one fuck of a way to ambush somebody, I told myself. Suddenly the numbness gave way to exploding pain in my head. I must have convulsed, because Toliver stopped and leaned over me.

"Hang on, Kiwi," he said, leaning close to my face. "You'll be all right in five minutes."

He laid me on my back with a pack under my head. Then he sounded off, and the others drifted in one by one.

"Anybody hurt?" Toliver said.

"Morrosco," Tan said, as he began to dress an ugly flesh wound in Morrosco's forearm.

"I'm all right," Morrosco said, though he appeared to be in considerable pain. "When I stepped in that hole, that guy hit me immediately. I don't know why he ran. He could have finished me."

"You'll be all right," Toliver said.

"I know that," Morrosco replied. "What about him?"

"He got hit in the head. He'll be okay."

My head was clear, but it was pounding with pain. I listened as they described what had happened. Morrosco's fall had blown the ambush. The man he was stalking hit him with the first machine-gun burst, then missed Toliver with the second. Then all five scouts took to the bush. After that, it was happening everywhere, like a running fight on a crowded tube platform, where the crowd parts and one gang does the other gang, and when the noise dies down, the crowd closes in again, and it is all over.

But ten minutes had destroyed the myth of our invincibility. The greenest soldiers in the field could have done as well. The shouting and automatic weapons would have been heard over a great distance. We had no idea where or how big the main NVA party was. And Morrosco was wounded.

I tried to stand. My knees gave way beneath me. Five minutes later, I was on my feet. We moved out as quickly as I could walk. We badly needed time and distance between us and this messy business.

Toliver kept the pace slow; Tan had recovered from his ducking and was carrying Morrosco's weapon, but my stride was unsteady for several hours.

It was well into the night when we joined a branch of the Nam Pa at a point where a main trail to Highway 19 followed its northern bank. We had swung sharply east to circumvent the area where the patrol had come from, then turned northwest to get back on our original course.

A dirt and timber bridge spanned a shallow stretch of water, joining a smaller jungle trail on our side to the larger one on the far shore. We waded the river below the bridge, then grouped on the north shore. Silently we mounted the mud embankment that led to the trail ten feet above.

We spread out along the edge of the trail, which was little more than a dirt track fifty feet wide at this point. On the far side, the bank dropped sharply where the jungle grew up almost to its edge. Toliver waved Jackson across. He jumped to his feet and dashed over the road and down the slope on the opposite side, disappearing into the underbush.

Toliver waved me over. As I rose to a crouch and started to run, we heard a shout in Vietnamese, then a blast from Jackson's M-16, answered immediately by half a dozen AK-47s. Then a lot of shouting from our left. In all, we must have heard ten or fifteen voices. A party of twenty men, assuming they were not all yelling.

A lot of lead was being thrown at Jackson. He returned it sparingly with his weapon on semiautomatic fire. I signaled to Toliver that Tan and I would go across to relieve Jackson, but he waved us down and motioned for us all to remain silent.

We were most likely facing the NVA unit whose scouts we ambushed. They had found the bodies and tracked us through the night. But they had moved faster than we, and we had passed in the night without bumping into each other. They assumed we had crossed the Nam Pa and were searching both sides of the trail for us. Jackson must have run right into the middle of one party. When Toliver refused to let us relieve him, I immediately guessed why.

Within a minute, half a dozen NVA came out of the trees on our side of the trail, fifty yards to our left. They thought everything was happening on the other side. They bunched at the edge of the track and dashed across together. They were perfect targets, sky-lined in silhouette above the road. Toliver held our fire until the NVA were in the middle of the road, then all six of us fired together. Bodies flew everywhere. We killed four outright. Two more were knocked down by their comrades, but they jumped up and scampered over the edge of the road. The two NVA parties were now separated and thought they were surrounded. I decided to move before they could recover from their panic. I sprinted for the spot where the two survivors had ducked out of sight. Tan was right at my heels. The two NVA did exactly what I expected. When the firing stopped, they climbed back up the road to see if they could spot us. When they stood up together to look over the edge of the road, I was fifteen feet from them, running full out with my shotgun at the ready.

In less than three seconds, I blew them both out of my path. But I was running too fast, and the steep slope took me by surprise. I raced down out of control, my legs trying to keep up with my body. I stumbled, regained my footing, and ran smack into the middle of six men. Before I could fire, Tan ran into me from behind, knocking us both off our feet. We jumped up and everybody started firing. Bullets went everywhere. One of the NVA was cut down by a wild burst from the man standing next to him.

I took a crushing blow on the shoulder and went to my knees. I'm back-shot, I told myself, expecting the warm blood to start washing over me. When I tried to jump up, my pack was entangled in an enormous branch that had been shot off a tree above me. I wriggled free just as the NVA closed on the two of us for hand-to-hand combat.

"I'm coming!" Toliver shouted.

He came bowling over the edge of the road. A man lunged at me with a knife. I parried the thrust with the shotgun and smashed his head in with the butt. Tan fired from the hip, putting another one down. I caught a glimpse of a man leveling his AK-47 at Tan. I whirled and blew his chest open with the shotgun. The man jackknifed and flew backward, his weapon firing a short burst skyward, then a longer burst into the ground. A hand reached from nowhere and grabbed the barrel of my shotgun. I hit the man a wild swinging blow with my left fist. A second man tackled me from my blind side. I fell straight over backward down the slope, still clutching my shotgun. The man leapt at me with a knife in his hand. I whipped the shotgun upward and he fell onto the end of the barrel. I pulled the trigger. Flesh and bone and gristle exploded in my face, bits and pieces cut and tore into my skin. I rolled and leapt to my feet. I slammed fresh rounds into the Greener, then turned toward the sound of the nearest fighting. I stared straight into the barrel of an AK-47. As I jumped to beat the bullet I could not outrun, I saw the top of the man's head torn off in a vapor cloud of disintegrating skull. Tan had drilled the man through the ear with his M-3. After that it was scrambling, running, yelling, fighting with bullets and knives and gun butts and fingernails. The momentum of the battle mounted to a raging snowball of death that hurtled downward out of control, faster and faster, people killing people until there would be no more to die.

I saw a man coming at Tan's blind side with a bayonet. I could not use the shotgun without hitting Tan.

"Behind you, Tan!" I yelled.

Tan looked frantically around, but he was too late to protect himself. As the man lunged, Toliver shot him with his Armalite from fifty feet. When the man fell, he left Tan and me exposed to two more NVA. Tan did not see them, so I grabbed him by the shirt and pulled us both over. Bullets tore the underbrush apart where we had been standing. Toliver killed the two with one long automatic burst.

I heard the surviving NVA break off the action from where Jackson was pinned down, yelling to one another and fading away. Then there was a lot of Armalite and M-3 fire moving toward us, with no returning fire; someone was being chased in our direction. Three NVA burst upon us out of the bush. Tan instantly killed one and Toliver the other two. We heard the rest running through the jungle.

"Let them go!" Toliver yelled as I started after them. "We'll never get them all."

The three of us quickly and silently inspected one another. Tan had cut the back of his head once more in a fall, but none of us was wounded. We ran back to the others. They too were unscratched. Jackson was standing beside the fallen log he had used for cover. Beside him, two small trees lay bent to the ground, their trunks ripped apart by machine-gun bullets. Every tree within twenty feet had been shaved clean of bark, and fallen limbs cluttered the landscape. Hundreds of bullets had whistled around Jackson without one touching him. We stared at the bizarre scene.

"Knock on wood," said Morrosco.

"There's not much of it left," Jackson replied.

We regrouped smartly, prepared for a counterattack. There was no backslapping, no mood of jubilation. By all rights, Jackson should have been dead. Half of us would have been blown away if we had charged across the road. But one fire fight forebode nothing of the next. Every one of us had led units that had survived the most ferocious fire fights unscratched, only to see half the unit decimated in a minor skirmish.

The adrenaline was still racing through my veins; my heart was pounding as if it was about to explode. We all wanted to get out of there. Toliver took a bearing, and we struck north through the waning darkness, moving in a silent route march. No one wanted to talk about the events of the last hour. As we double-timed through the night, I picked off pieces of a human being that had dried on my face. My dog rag was caked in dried blood. Bone and scraps of canvas and leather clung to my fatigues and the backs of my hands. I found a stub of intestine moving around inside my shirt; I dug it out and threw it down in disgust. I desperately wanted a river to plunge into.

As we pushed on, I thought about the fight at the bridge. It can all go wrong so quickly when the odds are initially in your favor. The NVA had been fresh and heavily armed and tracking a unit a third its size. It should have wiped us out to a man. But confusion and the stupid dash across the road had eliminated half their fire power before they knew they were in a fire fight. If they had observed the fundamental rules of combat, if they had found the enemy before attacking, if they had walked another hundred feet down the trail before breaking out, they would have pinned us down, an inferior force with no cover and our back to a river. Blind circumstance, impetuosity, and panic had turned the odds around, and the patrol had been blown off the face of the earth.

But the intense ferocity of this particular action had almost frightened me. The punch, the impact had been like a train running at full speed and piling into a bus at a railroad crossing. Lives were scattered all over the jungle.

When it started, my blood had turned to ice. In combat, my nervous system seemed to disengage from every unnecessary function. My senses responded only to an instinct for survival that was almost eerie. When I took off across the road, it was almost *déjà vu*. I *knew* when the two NVA scouts would pop up for a look. If they had moved ten seconds sooner, I was dead. But I *knew*. Anyone watching would have thought I was a madman. I had responded to an automatic function, a combat instinct that had to be right.

I became strangely detached from my body during a fight. When the man had tackled me, I did not experience the physical presence of another man with his hands all over my body. The man became a thing I had bumped into in the night, and the thing was a man who had probably overextended himself, who had overrun his target and was as off balance as I was. And more frightened. So I had set about killing that thing, that man, because otherwise that man was going to kill me.

My thoughts returned to the mission. We all knew that as we drew closer to China, the combat alternatives were shrinking. Seven men operating alone this far into enemy territory with a target date and site could no longer afford the luxury of a withdrawal action. We had no time to go on the run with people tracking us. Now every enemy had to be destroyed for our own survival. This was a different priority from just staying alive. The only solution was to move into the worst of it, and when the noise and the fighting stopped, to find ourselves among the living.

We walked and ran, sweeping aside the thick jungle, for an hour until we broke out of a tree line near a river. We stopped for water and rest just as the sun rose up through a crack in the chain of mountains to the east. I studied the others. They looked like men who had journeyed through hell. One side of Tan's face was covered with another man's blood. His own blood, mixed with dirt, caked the back of his swollen head. Toliver's shirt was soaked stiff and unyielding with blood. All of us were scratched and bruised and caked in mud. Morrosco's wound had bled through the gauze, and the bandage was covered with leaves and dirt. Morrosco caught me staring at him.

"You're looking wonderful, Kiwi," he said, smiling.

I looked down at my clothing. Bits of flesh and fecal matter clung to my shirt. Both my hands were brown with dried blood. My neck and face were sticky with blood and covered with little pieces of body matter like grains of sand. I gingerly probed a deep abrasion in my scalp. An elbow showed through a torn sleeve, and my knees were swollen from rolling around on the ground. We must look like madmen, a maniac band of killers, I thought. Wild animals, stopped to lick their wounds.

"We'll wash, then move out," Toliver said.

We stripped and waded into the river. We washed our shirts, flailing them against the rocks, and scrubbed our torsos with sand. I ducked beneath the water and shook my matted hair with both hands. The water calmed me, washing away the ugly stains of fear and rage. We rested on the bank while the morning sun dried us. Prather shared his tobacco with Morrosco. Wiley and Morrosco bantered lightly; it was their way of recomposing themselves. I stayed aloof from the chatter. I was not impressed with being alive. Yet the sight of the others in the morning light had startled me. It had been a very ugly business. Very close. I stared at the sun's reflection on the river as it rose in the morning sky.

Tan had not spoken since we left the battle scene. He had marched in silence and now sat staring blankly at Wiley's attempts to be humorous. Suddenly he stood up from a rock and walked toward me. He extended his right hand. When I offered mine, he closed both hands over it and held it tightly.

"Good morning, Gayle," he said. "I am glad to see you. It is a beautiful morning."

Still clinging to my hand, Tan stared beyond me at the sunrise, then turned to look at the distant mountains as they woke up to the morning light. The others stopped talking. Abruptly Tan dropped my hand and walked to Prather, who lay with his back against a rock, his pipe between his teeth.

"Good morning, Lew," Tan said, once again offering his hand.

Prather stood, took Tan's extended hand, and touched him lightly on the shoulder. Tan went to each man in turn, spoke his name and shook his hand in a formal manner, then held each of their hands in his own for several seconds. We remained silent until Tan had made a circle of the unit. When he had finished, he squatted on his haunches and waited. No one moved for several seconds. Wiley leaned across and hit Jackson lightly on the shoulder with the knuckles of a half-closed fist.

"You son-of-a-gun, you really stuck us in it," he said softly.

"Vic," I said to Toliver, "it was close."

He was bent over the mapping case, studying the route ahead. He looked up sharply. He stared at me without replying. He folded the maps and replaced them in the case, then rose stiffly to his feet. He looked around at the group. All eyes were on him.

"Let's move out," he said.

CHAPTER 10

Toliver wanted to move us before the adrenaline stopped pumping and fatigue set in. By going out now, he could refocus our attention on the mission ahead. Draw the mission purpose close again. Leave the rest behind as past history. We were still on edge. Every time a leaf rippled, we were ready to blow the jungle apart. We needed to cover miles, restore our motivation for being there. Then we could take a rest.

We helped one another into our gear, exchanging fleeting touches on the arm or shoulder. Then we moved off sharply.

We followed the river until it joined the Nam Pa, then along the Nam Pa toward its junction with the Nam Meuk. We stopped on a hill overlooking the Nam Pa Valley south of the village of Pong Nang.

We pitched camp at a calculated, steady pace; we were all at the outer edge of nervous exhaustion. I felt that if I did not ease into relaxing, I would collapse. Jackson built a small fire and reheated some of the cold vegetables. Prather and Wiley lashed boughs together and tossed their groundsheets over them to make a rough lean-to where we could sleep out of the sun. Morrosco fussed about like a grandmother, treating our minor wounds. Tan tested the radio and managed to raise a signal; the water had not reached the batteries. I joined Toliver to study the route ahead.

"How long are we going to stay here?" I asked him.

"I know we're behind schedule," he answered. "But we all need the rest. That last business was careless. Sloppy. We've got to get back on an even keel. We'll stay here the rest of the day. Get a good sleep."

We ate, then spread our gear about and helped one another clean it. The monotony of the task and the peaceful campsite helped us unwind. I walked to the edge of the camp and gazed down at the panorama spread beneath us. The river ran through a wide mountain valley, the floor of which was covered in waves of small green hills. To the east, the hills rose in an unending chain of lush mountains that climbed into North Vietnam. Between the hills a series of small streams twisted their fingers into the Meuk like the roots of a mangrove tree reaching for the ground.

I closed my eyes. Instantly, I was back in the bush, choking the life out of a man, waiting for the bullet that never came. I opened my eyes. I could see the hills and rivers again.

I never unwound after combat until I had relived it in my mind's eye: every option, every mistake I or someone else had made; analyzed it, and filed it in that corner of my memory labeled "survival." My thoughts turned to the team. Tan's strange behavior at the river had emphasized the bond, almost of love, that was growing among us.

Rarely in my life had I experienced what I considered love, and each time it had been equated with pain. Shallow love was a false emotion; I was too pragmatic to succumb to that again. And real love had always been the forerunner of sorrow. But I could not help myself. I felt some of what Tan had shown that morning. Every time we went into combat and emerged alive, a unique experience was binding me closer to the others. I feared this as a dangerous weakness yet felt powerless to halt it.

I thought of what I had once told a young Marine whose best friend had just been blown apart by a mortar shell. If you see enough death and cause enough death, you never take it for granted. You just do your damndest to stay alive. I recalled my father in New Zealand, pushing a plow all year around to get the finest crop he had ever had, and at the last minute the wind would blow the whole damn lot away. This team worked at staying alive. It was the best I had ever seen. And we could all be blown away in a sudden storm.

It was the preoccupation with staying alive that kept us sharp. Yet ultimately the choice was not ours. I never forgot that a bullet through my own head was any different than my bullet through another man. We simply had to keep trying.

"I don't know how you kept from being hit back at the bridge," Morrosco said to Jackson.

"Bitin' dirt, son. I dug me a trench with my teeth."

"What happened?"

"I'm not sure. I jumped off that road, right into the middle of those motherfuckers. They was yelling and blazing away, and I couldn't even see them. So I went to ground and returned fire to the flashes. Bullets were flying everywhere. I got down to about snake height. I'll be spitting out rock for two weeks."

"Next time, be sure you know where you're going before you go," Toliver told Jackson.

Jackson did not resent Toliver's remark. We all knew what Jackson had done was unavoidable; Toliver was reminding us all to maintain maximum vigilance. A word of reprimand from the commanding officer gets things back on an even keel.

"Well, boss," Jackson said, "you go first next time

and I'll be right behind you. I heard your pop gun, Kiwi. How'd you do?"

"Four rounds. A body count of four," said Prather with some awe.

My shotgun was drawing considerable attention. In a fire fight with automatic weapons, you could not tell how effective you had been until after the event. But my shotgun made a distinctive noise. There was always a stark realization of what it was doing. I allowed myself absolutely no human reaction, because it was total devastation. When I hit a body in bone such as the rib cage, there was little to hold it together. If I thought about that for half a second, there was a bullet on its way to me.

Gradually, the conversation turned away from the battlefield. We talked about the countryside and admired the landscape around us. The rest of us grew quiet when Wiley and Morrosco talked about girls they had known a long time ago. In a unit like ours, people did not dwell on the future. We never got the expanded dream talk regular soldiers indulged in, because we recognized the reality of our environment. Once we had crossed the Mekong, I never thought about the outcome. I knew the mission purpose, and I knew it would be carried out. After that, what happened . . . happened.

Their conversation stirred my loins. All the marching and fighting and trying to save lives could not overcome the sex drive completely. On the early days of a mission, it would dig at me until finally I would get fed up and fit it into the back of my mind. When we were well fed and rested, it could come rushing back. When the conversation stopped, I knew everyone's thoughts were drifting in the same direction.

We each had our own interpretation of what we wanted, and we kept these to ourselves. Prather would be thinking about his wife and children and the farm in Devon. I could never tell about Toliver or Tan. The others were more obvious. I never thought about Sai Pei or the women I had known in Saigon. I thought about someone many years in the past. For one moment, I was overcome by sadness that it was finished, and I was here in the jungle. The sadness turned to bitterness, then to anger that I was allowing my sex drive to dominate me. The memory faded into the past.

Barry did not have the same control. He took out the picture of the girl he had found in the dead man's wallet, stared at it for a moment, then got up and walked into the bush. He needed release, in the only way he would get it.

Rape was commonplace in Indochina, but I did not expect it in our unit. It happened more than once in units I was leading; if I was around, I would stop it; if it happened prior to my arrival, I just did not give a damn. I rejected the entire Oriental theater; the civilians meant nothing to me. The girls were raped three days in a week by troops going in different directions. I would never take part in a rape. I never actually saw one of my men commit rape, though once I saw the aftereffects. It was in the northern part of South Vietnam, where the people had been pillaged for years. The girl was not young; she must have been in her twenties. She had been raped, not by one guy but several. She walked to an older woman who took her away. She was not crying, just empty. She looked beyond emotion. There was nothing left of importance in the lives of these women except their children. Sexual fulfillment for them was gone forever, not unlike certain women in our Western society who just get screwed silly. It was as empty as that, a mechanical thing, void of all feeling.

I interrupted a mass rape by a Pathet Lao unit which was a very different, very ugly scene. It was strange; when an American raped a woman, it was not really rape. He would take her, and she would put up some resistance, but he would get into her. And then there was an animalistic release, and it was over. He would go one way looking pleased with himself, and she another. That was rape, sure. Until you had seen the other thing.

We were a party of twenty-two. Nine of us were special forces, the rest what was left of an American unit that had been trapped in a village. We had freed the unit and were walking to a pickup point when we came on a village that was held by fifteen Pathet Lao guerrillas. They had herded the villagers out into the clearing and were making them watch a mass rape. This village was no more friendly toward us than they would be to the Pathet Lao, but they just wanted to do this thing. They had four women. One was a girl of fifteen or so. The others must have been in their twenties. The rest of the villagers were herded in a circle around them, guarded by four men. We quietly surrounded the village, but the peasants were between us and the Pathet Lao. We could not hit them without wiping out the entire village. So we had to sit and wait.

They stripped the young girl and bent her backward over the bonnet of an old vehicle, and the guys jumped her from every direction. One was fucking her and another jammed his rifle barrel up her ass, and another one was beating her teeth out with a belt buckle. They just tore her apart, and when they finished with her, they threw her aside like a sack of potatoes and grabbed another one.

The guys with us, the regular soldiers, were going crazy. Some were vomiting, others were priming their weapons and begging us to go in. We split the party up with one special forces man covering a couple of regulars. We sat there and waited until those four girls were finished and the villagers had been moved around.

We hit the Pathet Lao unit. Not one escaped, and few died quickly. I really enjoyed killing that day. I shot one guy to pieces, a little at a time; he had been ramming his rifle up the girls and ripping them open.

When it stopped, the young girl was still alive, but blood was pouring from her mouth and ears, so one of the Americans shot her. The villagers stood around with their eyes to the ground.

When we cleaned the village up, we found five children lashed to one of the huts. They were dead. They had all been tortured. A tiny girl of nine or so had been raped. A man can do a lot of damage to a child. In the end, that nine-year-old was no longer a child, she was a woman. That was how ridiculous it could get.

We rested for five hours, then struck north toward Highway 19. We were walking mid-contours on the hills, from which we could spot activity in the valley floor. We crossed the highway in daylight between two enemy outposts without making contact. We headed for a trail that would put a range between us and the Vietnamese border, which swung dramatically toward us north of the highway. We ran into a unit of North Vietnamese regulars, whom we avoided by going to ground. They forced us to strike east of the range and push north into very rugged terrain. This area was well patrolled by Pathet Lao and North Vietnamese units. We stayed high on the hillside for better observation.

We followed the Nam Pa toward its junction with a branch of the Nam Meuk. We were entering dangerous territory; there was a road near the junction of the two rivers that carried a lot of military traffic over the border.

Near Sop Nhom, we started bumping into patrols. We kept moving closer to the river to avoid them; finally we were forced onto the riverbed for cover. We knew there was an outpost where the two rivers met, so Toliver decided we would cross the Pa where the road forded it in shallow water.

We arrived at the ford at dusk. Before we could move, two NVA patrols went across. We decided to wait until dark. Time was pressing at our backs; we could not stay here indefinitely.

The riverbed was wide and flat, surfaced with sand

and shingle. We waited until two hours after nightfall, then started across. When we were well into the river, four vehicles came down the road on the far bank and stopped at the river's edge. We went to ground where we stood. Fifteen or sixteen men got out and disappeared into the jungle beyond the riverbank.

"Do we go back?" Jackson asked.

"Hang on," Toliver said. "Let's see what they do."

For an hour, we watched them move along the shore. They appeared to be reconnoitering to set up a machine gun or a campsite. Finally they all came back to the jeeps. Half drove away, leaving eight men and two vehicles behind. They started to lounge around the vehicles, their vigilance lax. Toliver waved for Tan to crawl up beside him.

"Go see if you can hear what they're saying."

Tan inched his way to within fifty feet of the men and listened for a quarter of an hour. Then he crawled back.

"There are more people coming back," he said. "They are going to pitch camp right there."

We had to get out of there before the others returned, and there was no way to do it except to take these people. We could not work a fire fight this close to the border. It had to be done quietly. For the first time, I felt we were outnumbered; just that one extra man made me uneasy.

Toliver and Wiley crawled forward until they were almost to the bank. Tan, Morrosco, and Prather crawled out to our far left flank. Jackson and I stayed put. We were the only ones to retain arms; the others dropped all their gear in the riverbed.

Tan and Morrosco stood up and started walking toward the eight men, with Prather, because of his height, several yards behind them. Tan chatted in Cantonese in a loud voice, and the other two nodded and mumbled. The NVA were puzzled but did not show the slightest alarm. Three of them came forward to see who it was. As luck would have it, they did not bother to fetch their rifles, which were in the jeeps. The only weapons they carried were the long North Vietnamese bayonets they all wore on their sides. They walked past Toliver and Wiley without seeing them. When they were well clear and closing on Tan, Toliver came off the ground and barked orders at the other five in very authoritative Vietnamese. Unfortunately only three of the five came forward; the other two stayed in the jeep.

Wiley and Toliver jumped the latter three with machetes. They both hit the first man simultaneously and killed him instantly. Wiley swung his blade at the second man and missed. Toliver killed the third before he could unsheath his bayonet. The man Wiley had missed shouted and ran for the jeeps. The other three turned and, whipping out their bayonets, went for Toliver and Wiley. Tan, Prather, and Morrosco moved in behind them, and a wild fight broke out, bayonet against knives and machetes. There was a lot of shouting and the eerie clattering of boots on shingles.

Jackson and I charged right through the fight toward the last two in the jeep. When we got close, I saw that one was drawing a bead with his rifle, so I bowled him over with my shotgun. The guy Wiley had missed beat me to the jeep, grabbed a weapon, and at the same time threw on the headlights just as Wiley and Jackson arrived behind him. I was completely blinded but kept running. Wiley climbed over the front of the jeep and got into one of the two, and Jackson got into the other. Jackson disarmed his man and threw him, but fell down himself. He had the man around the waist and was getting nowhere, so I jumped in and was trying to pin the man for Jackson when I heard Wiley scream. I came off the ground and saw the other guy about to drive his bayonet into Wiley. I drove my knife into the back of his neck, then stabbed him twice more before he died. Jackson had recovered and killed his man. He and I jumped up. Toliver was the last man fighting. Before we could reach him, he tore the throat out of the man he had thrown to the ground. Then he ran forward and kicked out the jeep headlights, throwing the scene into darkness.

"Sound off!" Toliver shouted.

Everyone answered.

"Who's hurt?"

"Wiley." It was Jackson.

We all ran to where Wiley lay on the ground.

"I was dodging the bayonet," he said. "The tip caught in my shirt."

"How bad is he?" Toliver asked Morrosco, who was examining the wound near Wiley's waist.

"I don't think it hit any organs. It looks like it hit a rib and was deflected. He's got some muscle damage and a lot of torn flesh. He's going to be in pain, but he'll be all right."

"What are you doing?" Toliver had turned to Prather, who was wrapping a compress around his left hand.

"I grabbed for the bloke's wrist and caught his bayonet blade. He withdrew it and split my hand open. Nothing serious, Vic."

"Let's clean up and get out of here."

We ran back to the river, strapped on our gear, and tore back to the vehicles. We grabbed all the weapons in sight and faded into the bush. We hoped the theft would make it look like work of bandits.

We hit rugged terrain immediately but pushed on at a hard pace for half an hour until Morrosco noticed that Wiley's wound was bleeding profusely. He had said nothing because he did not want to slow us down. We bound his side tightly and moved on more slowly. Our route called for us to take a trail to the northeast, but that was the direction in which the two jeeps had departed, so we went due north into the wildest country we had seen. What looked from an elevated position to be rolling hills proved to be a landscape of sheer cliffs, deep ravines, and broken rock faces with heavy jungle vegetation growing straight out of the cliffs. From above, the trees made a smooth blanket of green, because they had all grown to the same height to share the sunlight; in reality, some were forty feet high, some were ten feet.

We stopped at a riverhead an hour before dawn. The border lay on the far side of the range facing us. We had walked all night, stopping when Wiley could not maintain the pace, despite the morphine Morrosco had given him every hour.

We rested in a sheltered area overlooking the valley. There was no one for miles around. Toliver decided to make camp for the day to give Wiley time to recover. We would cross the border that night.

During our respite, the realization grew in my mind that a chunk had been taken out of our armor. Wiley was still bleeding and growing weaker; Morrosco stayed in constant attendance on him and finally stemmed the bleeding. Prather was in pain, though not badly hurt. There was little he could do for his hand. He wrapped it tightly, leaving the fingers exposed; it was one of those superficial wounds that would open and close for days. We were all banged about sufficiently—torn elbows and knees, scratched faces—to be that fraction slower. For some reason, the inside of my ear was bleeding.

We got a reasonable amount of semi-sleep. We were weary, but by no means exhausted. But there followed a lull after a piece of action like our last, which had come so close to going wrong, when people's energies dissipated and needed time to be recharged.

Wiley felt bad about slowing us down and kept insisting he was all right. We ignored that; we would draw our own conclusions about his condition. But this was the man coming out in him. His only concern was about hindering the mission.

I thought his fever might slow him. But we were strong people, and we were up in the highlands where it was cooler, where we had no jungle environment to contend with. Still, there was a feeling that we had gone a long way, mentally perhaps more than physically. We had to consider how we had been doing things for the last few days, because we were on a mission of the utmost discretion, and yet we had gotten ourselves in half a dozen furors.

We had reached that psychological moment that comes in every mission when we looked at one another and saw that we had all survived and everybody was more or less healthy, and we had this feeling that the thing would work. This was a gradual transformation that came after an initial rejection of the environment. I had come out of Osaka and then a base camp and finally a forward camp into the stark reality of jungle warfare. I had not liked it, and I saw my sentiments reciprocated in the other men. But a couple of weeks had formed a mental graft over the comforts of life, and as the memory of those receded, we settled down to playing soldier in the jungle. From the beginning, I had shared a strong sense of purpose for the mission with Tan and Toliver, and to a certain extent we had been pulling the others along. Now we stood at the point of no return. We were right on schedule; this was the day we were expected to reach the North Vietnamese border. The signal was due now or never.

Our instructions were to maintain watch right up to the last day. There had been allusions in the briefings to the mission being aborted because of the sheer impact of going into China. We had been briefed that if we received the abort prior to North Vietnam, we could look upon it as a mission complete; the whole thing had been forgotten, written off. We could turn around and come back home, our job done.

In briefing, we had been promised repeatedly there would be no abort after Laos. And every time, the briefer had hedged with half a dozen exceptions. Abort after today would mean a panic situation. Someone had had a drastic change of mind; or the conference had been canceled; or we had been observed, and political pressure was being applied.

No one spoke when Tan switched on the radio. If we went in, the chances were strong that we would not survive. This feeling had been heightened by the fury of our recent combat. From where we sat, we could look into this land that was totally alien, totally hostile to us. We were really going behind the lines now, absolutely universes away from safety. We were walking into a coliseum with the lions, and the gates would be closed behind us. We could survive only by killing the lions.

I accepted that challenge. Suddenly I was thinking about Giap again, thinking how much I wanted to get the man. I started functioning again as that type of operative, making connections with that side of my character. And I got a positive rush, as if someone had shot me full of Benzedrine. I started to flex my muscles again. I would climb the mountain to its highest peak. And I would survive the bitter winds to come back down again. I would get the man, and I would beat the game. I would get away. No one could stop me. Not even Toliver. If the abort came now, I would take off on my own. The others may not have shared my excitement. I sensed a certain mood—or it was something I saw in their eyes—as if some might have been thinking a bit too much about living.

"You know," said Wiley, "it's a hell of a thing we're getting ready to do."

"Not many guys get a chance to change history," said Morrosco.

"Make history," said Prather, "not change it. History has no life of its own. It's made by the men who control its destiny."

"Well, we're getting the chance to stop a war," said Morrosco.

"Or start one," answered Prather. "We're making a clear parallax with world opinion."

"What does that mean?" asked Jackson.

"Assassination is frowned on everywhere. Who knows what the reaction will be?"

"The people that sent us in know what they're doing," said Jackson.

"I hope so," said Wiley.

I looked at Toliver. He showed no sign of having

heard. He looked at his maps, then into North Vietnam. Each of us was reacting in his own way to the realization that the real mission was about to begin. Everything to date had been just getting us this far, and we had become slightly detuned from the mission purpose because of our involvement in the normal en route conflicts. Now that the mission was upon us again, people were having very real, very human doubts. The best way to overcome those doubts was to become totally preoccupied with the soldiery of it all. Jackson inspected his rockets. Tan nursed the radio like a baby on mother's milk. I made contact with the Sahka. I detached myself slightly from the others and cleaned my weapon slowly and carefully. I assembled it, then broke it down and put it away; it was an act of reassurance that I was maintaining my deadly application to the job.

"Fifteen forty-five," said Toliver, looking at his watch. "That's it. That's time, Tan."

Toliver walked to where Wiley lay resting.

"How are you?"

"I'm fine. The bleeding has stopped, I won't slow you down."

"Does anybody have a reason we shouldn't push out now rather than in the morning?"

We grabbed our gear and moved out.

CHAPTER 11

We traveled fast, because we wanted to be in the highlands by midday. Our early departure had been an immediate positive action at a moment of great psychological stress. We climbed a long land corridor that jutted into North Vietnam and followed a river toward its source. The river began at a series of sharp hills; when we left it behind, we were in North Vietnam. We passed four hamlets without incident, moving with great caution because we were approaching Lai Chau, a township that radiated considerable military activity. To avoid the increasingly frequent farms, we climbed farther up the hillside, which soon grew into four-thousand-foot mountains. The terrain was rocky, with little cover, but we were out of sight of people moving in the valleys below.

We crossed two highways in the next two days without being observed, but we were edgy because we could hear traffic closing on us constantly. We forded the Nam Po at night without seeing anyone, though it was a busy river.

We were still in the highlands, and the population was increasing below us. Above Tao Vai, we had another river to negotiate, and when we stopped on high ground to reconnoiter it, we could not see the river because of the dense vegetation below us. We would have to approach it blindly.

We fanned out over the hillside and moved with extreme caution. The river was a mile below us, down a steep grade. Jackson moved out ahead, with Tan and me following, and the others farther behind.

It was refreshing to come down out of the barren landscape of the hills into these river valleys. Vegetation, dense and moist, suddenly thrust itself around us. The sounds of birds and insects intensified. What had all been pale and gray was now awash in yellows, reds, and many shades of green. The shading of the bark on the trees changed every few feet because of the moisture at different heights up and down their growth. The bush turned to jungle vegetation so thick that it was total darkness below the treetops, and then all of a sudden we would break out into brilliant sunshine.

Tan and I were a hundred yards short of the river when I saw Jackson slip out of sight over its edge. Immediately I heard a man shouting excitedly in Vietnamese, followed by abrupt silence, then a lot of splashing and the sounds of a struggle. I waved the others down, and Tan and I ran toward the river. Before we reached it, I heard two or three more excited voices.

We broke out on the bank to see Jackson attacking a peasant with his knife. He brought the man down on rocks near the middle of the river; the man must have spotted him and tried to run. Though the man was down, Jackson was having trouble putting him away. Then suddenly he was dead. The man must have been with companions whom Jackson had not seen, because as we reached the riverbank, three more men set into Jackson from behind with rocks. At that moment, Toliver broke out alongside us.

"For Christ's sake, get them!" he shouted.

Jackson was just holding his own. Tan and I charged off the bank into the river.

Sometimes it would be funny to watch a totally frightened, totally helpless human being fighting for his life when he had no chance to save himself. I had seen it so many times, and it was always the same. Jackson and the man would have seen one another simultaneously.

The man started running. He was chased by a man who looked the part he was playing; he was a soldier, he had guns, he had knives, he was chasing a guy who wanted desperately to get away. The guy was running and falling down and yelling all sorts of things, trying to get away, like a little boy running from his father. He was brought down, and he struggled like he had never struggled before. It was funny. He was biting and kicking and gouging at eyes, and he never had a chance. And then he was dead.

But the other three were giving Jackson a bad time. When we got close, Tan tried to jump a pool and went in up to his chest. The three heard us behind them and came off Jackson to take us on. Two went for me, and one jumped in the water after Tan. And we had a hell of a free-for-all.

The North Vietnamese peasants were far more spirited than the people we had been up against so far; they were not the whipped dogs south and west of here who just wanted to be left alone. They were more like us. More their own people. Because they were part of a unified culture. They were communists in a communist country; they were making a living out of the land, and I guess they were proud to be what they were. Communism had given their nation solidarity. If these peasants had any political inclinations, it would be to unite all of Vietnam under communism. We were facing a different attitude now; we would not be pushing anybody around. We were up against men, not subservient human beings.

Tan was struggling in the water with the man who

had jumped on top of him. Another had put Jackson down with a rock and was doing him, though Jackson was putting up a good fight. The third man turned to me, and we squared off. I had my knife. He held a rock in his left hand and a short ax handle in his right.

Twice I moved in, protecting my head with my left hand, and he hit me two whacking blows in the ribs with the ax handle. The third time I turned and caught the blow on my pack. I grabbed the handle under my armpit and gave a great shove upward, bringing the man to me. He lost the ax handle, but before I could use my knife, we both fell. We were on our feet instantly. He swung at me with the rock. I went under the arc and drove the knife into his rib cage. He did not die instantly, but he was finished, and he was out of the fight.

The other guy came off Jackson, kicked him in the head, and turned toward me to protect his rear. Jackson jumped to his feet behind him. The guy came at me, nervous as hell and determined to come off better than his mates and wondering what the hell he had gotten himself involved in. We were circling, our eyes darting all over the place. I threw my empty hand up a couple of times to open him up for my knife. I was just coming in to make contact, when Jackson drove his own knife into the man's kidneys. He was dead instantly. We turned quickly, but Tan had killed his man as well. The others came from the shore, where they had been covering us; they would have fired if we had been in real danger. We dragged the dead men into the jungle and pushed off. Decomposition or animals would take care of the bodies within a few days.

We moved on quickly in the early morning light. Jackson was groggy and had a gashed head, which Morrosco treated as we moved. There had been a lot of shouting during the fight, which could have been overheard. We were really in the soup now if we were spotted, so we maintained the minimum profile, crawling around exposed outcrops to retain cover. There were people about everywhere. We could see them below us. A man cycling on the road with a load of sacks over his bike. People moving down to the rice fields in the flats. It would have taken only one pair of eyes to land on us and the entire countryside would have been on our trail.

We stayed well west of Lai Chau, which meant circling a fifty-five-hundred-foot peak on which the undergrowth petered out to nothing; we stayed low, within the vegetated area. We made the upper regions of the same range and rested for a couple of hours, then climbed to the top of the range, where we could look down on Highway 4. The last pull up the mountain had been hard. As night was falling, we struck camp.

Our bivouacs were very primitive now. We made no fire and ate what we had gathered on the march. We slept in our clothes, not even stripping off our boots. We were rough men, living on the move. Very different men from the hapless young GIs in South Vietnam who flailed at the Viet Cong like a battered, half-blinded heavyweight trying to catch an opponent who could only jab and run. They were dying because no one had taught them how to stay alive.

It was my second year in Vietnam. I had only recently been attached to the Yanks as adviser. I was leading several sections of American infantry against a Viet Cong unit that had wasted a village. We were setting an ambush. When I went to check out one section, I saw a soldier with the earplug from a transistor radio in his ear. He was listening to the radio in the middle of a combat zone. I told the sergeant to tell the guy to put away the radio and do things properly. The sergeant walked over to the guy, and I turned away to tend to something else.

The next thing I heard was music. In complete contempt for his sergeant, the guy had torn the earphone jack out of the transistor. The guy's contempt for his sergeant was inadvertently reflected on me. But that did not enter into the situation. He was such a low priority to what we were doing, he just did not matter. Except that now he had become a nuisance. I called the sergeant forward.

"Go tell the son-of-a-bitch to turn off his radio within one second of your arrival," I said. "Or I will shoot him."

I watched the sergeant walk back to the boy. The boy jumped, looked at me—I gave him an extra half second—and threw the radio into the bush. He never spoke again on the mission.

I would have killed him in a totally depersonalized way. In combat, surrounded by Viet Cong, we survived largely by our discretion. This boy was risking the lives of a score of men. I gave no thought to who, what, or where he belonged. He would have gone.

This boy just totally misunderstood what he was involved in. This was the immaturity in America coming out. A sort of immaturity where he believed there would always be someone there to help him out.

Highway 4 was a major tar-sealed road. The traffic we saw was unnerving: push-bikes, cars, even buses. But when it was well dark, we fell down to the highway and crossed without incident, skirting two military outposts on the way. East of the highway, we came quickly out of the hills into low-lying ground.

There we moved into a mangrove swamp which, as we marched toward China, became thicker and wetter and muddier and stinking hot. Our progress came to a standstill; in two days we made twenty miles. The mangroves were growing directly out of the water with roots and branches six inches thick entwined like balls of string. We had to hack our way through, walking on bearings because we could see no landmarks. We were on constant alert against snakes; there were two species of constrictor here large enough to drag a man into the water and drown him. There was a ming blue spider, deadly poisonous, that spun a web tough enough to catch small birds. I spotted their webs on two occasions.

Leeches dropped on us like rain water; within an hour they had pinned my shirt to my arm, biting into the flesh through the heavy canvas. I watched their bellies fill with my blood. We were all too busy to have the privilege of burning them off, so I had to leave them or dig them out with my knife. I was desperate . . . the constant nauseating sucking and swelling . . . the feeling that they were spreading malaria through my body.

Wiley let out a scream, then a series of ugly grunts as he hacked to pieces a snake entwined about his M-3. Prather's face puffed from the unceasing stream of mosquito bites until his eyes were slits. The mosquitoes went in through a rip in Morrosco's shirt and bit his arm until the swelling filled his sleeve. We smeared ourselves with a stinking yellow repellent that the insects ignored.

It was useless to stop, impossible to rest. We walked for two days with only the stale water in our canteens to quench our thirst. We listened for radio transmission on the march; the receiver refused to transmit a carrier wave. I assumed the radio was finished. Morrosco tied Wiley in a tree and changed his bandage. The night was worse than the day. Our nerves were screaming. Everything that moved was a poisonous snake. We plunged into waist-deep bogs and thought we were drowning in quicksand.

We broke out of the mangroves in midmorning onto a grassy plain. We were all sick and exhausted, but we had to force ourselves on another five miles to better cover before we could rest. We moved across a high, wind-blown plateau through ankle-deep water from which sprung a flax-like grass taller than a man's head. We took our bearings off Fan Si Pan, a vast mountain that dominated the horizon, and pushed toward Highway 132.

We crossed the plateau in the heat of the day, because we wanted to reach Highway 132 before nightfall; it was a busy road, and we needed daylight to cut it safely. We were moving toward wild mountainous country now. Below lay a flat valley with ample cover, but we could not go down there because the Kun Ming railway line ran its length.

We moved at a staggering lope, covering the ground quickly. But we were pushing up against exhaustion. It took all our strength now to maintain schedule and the personal application we needed to stay alive . . . hell, we had been twenty-five days on the march.

We were all overtired, drawing on fast-dwindling reserves of strength. Wiley's wound grew pussy and burst open every few hours, but he would not let it slow him down. Morrosco stayed with him and worked to keep the infection under control.

Three miles short of Highway 132, our route was cut by a secondary road, a very narrow dirt path. As we approached it, we heard voices closing on us. We went to ground. A dozen North Vietnamese regulars came down the path on bicycles. We gave them a few minutes to clear, then struck off across the road in pairs, with Wiley and Morrosco in the lead. Halfway across, the two got their legs tangled and fell over. The others raced past them to take up positions in the trees, while Tan and I ran to jerk them to their feet. At that moment, two more guys came cycling down the road. They spotted us and started yelling. We ran into the undergrowth.

They must have thought there were only four of us, two wounded, because of the way we had been staggering around on the road. They took out after us, firing and yelling. We kept moving without returning their fire. Then I heard a lot more voices behind us. The first lot had heard the firing and come back. A hunt began.

They broke into the bush behind us, and we started to run. Somehow Wiley managed to keep the pace. We had a fifteen-minute lead and good cover, so there was a chance that we might slip away.

"Toliver!" Prather yelled out. "We're taking them to the road!"

Highway 132 was only half an hour ahead. If there was anybody there, we could be caught between two groups. Our pursuers were closing on us fast because Wiley could not run. Every few minutes, we heard them firing off rounds when they thought they had found us. We broke out of the trees into a small clearing. Beyond the clearing the jungle thinned toward the highway. Beyond the highway lay a range of hills. When we crested those hills, we were looking into China. We were right on the doorstep. And so close to being stopped.

"We'll take them," Toliver shouted. "Morrosco and Wiley go forward."

The two went a hundred yards down a steep slope just ahead of us. I heard the NVA pick up their pace; they were expecting to find four wounded men running down that hill ahead of them. We fanned out, with Toliver and me in front and Jackson, Prather, and Tan in a semicircle to our rear. The NVA came loping into the clearing in a tight group and ran past Toliver and me. The lead men were right on top of Tan when we all cut loose. We killed five outright before they broke out and a general fire fight started. Four rushed down the hill in a group, and Morrosco and Wiley killed them with grenades. The rest sought cover behind trees. The setup and initial impact were the only static moments in the fight; after that, we broke from cover to cover, stalking, outflanking one man, intercepting another.

When the firing started, there were three blokes moving straight on to me. One broke to my right as I was drawing a bead on him, and the others turned off to my left. I killed the first, but the other two, instead of seeking cover, circled and rushed me on my blind side. I heard movement and spun around to find one coming down on me. Lying on my back, I stuck the barrel of my Armalite at him and fired.

He was four feet from me when the round carried him away. The second man was standing directly over me now. He leapt at me. I fired and missed. He grabbed the barrel of the carbine and twisted it out of my hands, then rolled to his side. Before I could recover, he drew a bead on me with his weapon. At that moment, Toliver came over the top of me. The man raised his barrel and shot Toliver through the stomach.

Toliver fell on top of the man. I grabbed my weapon and killed him by sticking the barrel up under his chin and blowing his head away. I glanced around for another target. I saw Wiley in the distance strangling a man with his hands. I jumped up to help Toliver. A bullet slammed into my hip and bowled me over. I went down, but kept shooting. Bullets were flying everywhere. I knew I was hit, but I felt no pain, just an enormous amount of strength. I felt I could do anything at that moment, like a man running from a bull who would vault a wall he normally could not climb. Adrenaline was racing through me. My gun was jumping around in my hands and firing at targets faster than I could recognize them. I saw two break for Prather. Tan brought one down, but the second put a bullet into Tan that knocked him over backward. The man kept running, and I lost sight of him. There was total confusion: bullets flying, people fighting everywhere with guns and knives. Gradually the noise abated. We had killed the lot.

I examined my wound. The bullet had entered from the front, bounced off my pelvis, and exited out the back. It had stayed near the surface and ripped a trench of flesh as it moved across my body. I was bleeding profusely but still feeling no pain. I stood gingerly on my feet. I could walk, so my pelvis was intact.

I turned to Toliver. When I saw him, the pain hit me like a searing iron. I left him and ran toward where the others were gathering. At that moment, a guy came up off the ground and threw himself on Prather. The two fell, locked in each other's arms. The guy was full of holes, a dead man, but he would not give himself up to death. The man grabbed Prather's throat, then tore at his face. He twisted one hand in Prather's hair and pulled his head back. Prather managed to get his weapon up between them and blew the man off him. It was a gruesome end to a scene of tremendous violence. Tan sat slumped on the ground, his right arm hanging at his side. No one was moving.

"Sound off!" I shouted.

All answered but Toliver. I ran back to where he had been lying. He was gone.

"Vic! Vic!" I shouted.

"He's here!" I heard Wiley reply.

He had managed to walk down the hill to Wiley and Morrosco before collapsing. I ran to join them.

Toliver had been so close when he took the round that his body had muffled the roar of the weapon. One look told me he was dying. His stomach had been blown open; half of it was hanging out the back. My knees gave way. Suddenly I knew how much I wanted him to live. And it had to happen like this. I had been staring at the bullet that would have killed me, and Toliver had taken that bullet.

He was conscious and writhing in agony. Morrosco filled him with morphine and stuffed the entrance wound with gauze pads. There was no way to avoid infection with the exit wound; Morrosco shoved Toliver's entrails back inside him and bound his back with gauze and tape. We put half a dozen penicillin tablets under his tongue. The morphine took effect quickly, and Toliver's ugly cries subsided to soft moaning. I turned to the others.

We were a ghastly sight. Tan's right shoulder was a mess. A bullet had entered just above the collar bone and exited through the shoulder blade, shattering it. He was suffering great pain with stoic detachment. Prather's back was covered in blood where a ricochet had split the skin open from waist to shoulder. It was more messy than serious, however. Morrosco bound my hip. The pain was increasing by the second, but I would still walk. Wiley's wound was forgotten. He was one of the whole ones now.

"We've got to get out of here," Toliver mumbled.

"What are you talking about?" Wiley said. "You can't move."

"Don't worry," Toliver said. "I'll move. Let's get in those hills."

Morrosco finished his rushed repairs, and we started off with Jackson carrying Toliver on his back. We had not moved fifty feet before Toliver began screaming; he could not stand the pressure against his body. We chopped two limbs and thrust them under his arms. We started running off down the hill with Jackson and Morrosco on the poles. Toliver dragged his feet behind him.

We were like a wolf running from a pack of dogs. We knew instinctively that safety lay in the solitude of the hills ahead. We crossed the highway quickly but not carelessly. Our cover had been blown; we no longer had the luxury of going around people. We were prepared to shoot our way through anything that stood in our path.

We had suffered total exposure. Not our identity, because we left no one alive. But we were exposed sufficiently not to bother with regaining our cover. We had to hope there would be no intelligence interpretation at a regional level of our destination and purpose. With a little luck, the reports might go no higher than an area commander who would take us for a Green Beret insurgency unit or downed pilots. The last thing he would expect would be that we were going to China. He would not know about the conference anyway. He would be aware of increased security; nothing more. So we told ourselves.

Toliver went in and out of consciousness as we moved. He was bleeding internally and losing a lot of blood from his nose. Death had its impact when it was this close. We had been a unit for so long. A feeling of great despair swept through us that one of us was going to go. We knew that Toliver would die soon. No one said so. But we knew. And he knew.

We were moving very fast, and Toliver was in tremendous pain. I was not feeling my wound, even when my boots filled with my blood. Tan too seemed to be feeling no pain, though his arm hung useless at his side; we had not had time to strap it up. We were in a hell of a state . . . seven guys, half carrying, half pushing one another alone . . . parts of us hanging off . . . a lot of blood . . . a lot of bone.

We went into a river and walked straight into a five-man patrol. Prather and Wiley ran in among them, firing from the hip, and killed them all in seconds. Wiley took out two with one third of a clip. With his M-3 on automatic, he had the presence of mind to regulate his fire. They were both dead in a second and a half. We dragged the bodies into the bush and stripped them of two AK-47s with ample ammunition. We were running short of automatic fire, though I had plenty of ammunition for my shotgun. The AK-47 was a good weapon, light and rapid-firing. We all knew how to use it.

We pushed into the hills up a riverbed with high cliffs on both sides. The cliffs leveled out, and we found ourselves on a flat plain rising to the north. We turned to look where we had come from. It was a fantastic sight. The road was now far below us. We could see a river in the distance where it cut a sharp line through the jungle foliage. Far off to our left, the three peaks of Fan Si Pan hovered over the landscape.

We forced-marched up the plateau for another three hours until we had passed the village of Yang Ma Sin Tiay, then rested for a quarter of an hour. It was growing late in the day, but we were not yet safe. We had to push on as quickly as possible. Wiley and Morrosco worked feverishly over Toliver. It was hopeless. But, hell, you don't stop saving a man's life until he is dead. I watched silently, then walked away from the others and gazed at the mountains ahead.

When I saw the two men, exhausted and ragged, trying desperately to push life back into Toliver's depleted body, it hit me like the bullet that had slammed into my side. For once in my life, I felt love for a man. A very courageous man, a good man who had almost made brothers of us all. And now he was going to die because he had saved my life.

The mission purpose was sorely diminished to my mind, if it was going to cost the lives of men like Toliver. I would be in charge when he died, and maybe there was nothing more important than getting these men back alive.

But I was still a soldier. And I was in command now. We were a military unit, the best around. We had a purpose, a mission which must be accomplished at the price of any of us. Or all of us. Toliver was going to die. I had to think beyond that. I called Prather over to me, more sharply than I intended.

"We've got to change the firing line, Lew," I said.

"I don't think Tan will be up to it," he said. "We've got a lot of reorganizing to do."

"We'll go through the entire thing with the unit when we break for the night," I said.

"Gayle," said Prather, "you know what Toliver means to Tan. And his target. When he finds out he's out of the firing line, he may wipe himself out up there."

"We need him," I said. "I'll talk to him."

We were joined by Jackson.

"Toliver is almost dead," he said. "He doesn't have much time."

We pushed on at once, climbing for an hour until we found a protected spot. We lay Toliver on his groundsheet and waited. His eyes were open, but he could not see us unless we bent near his face. His mind floated on a cloud of pain, morphine, and approaching death.

"Lew," he said.

Prather knelt beside him.

"I have a son. He doesn't know I'm going to die

on a hillside in North Vietnam. I hope he gets more out of life than this. There's got to be more. There must be. Hold me, Gayle."

I put his head in my lap and cradled him in my arm. He tried to speak, but coughed and convulsed, and blood spilled from the corner of his mouth. Morrosco was crying and trembling.

"You're not dying, Vic," he said. "I won't let you die. We need you."

There was only ten years between them, but Toliver had become the father Morrosco had always wanted, and now he was losing him. The daddy of us all, perhaps. Morrosco sounded like a small boy when he tried to speak. Jackson found himself driven away; he would come and stand by Toliver for a few moments, then drift to the edge of the clearing, then come back again. Tan sat quietly watching. Prather spoke softly, humoring the dying man, pretending he would live. Wiley was in despair.

I felt sick of the whole damn thing. It seemed almost unnatural. One man dying in a unit like this, where we had all seen so much death, where any one of us could have died, and we were breaking up. But Toliver was just the wrong man to die. We had all been damned good soldiers on the first day, and we knew it. But he had brought us together and made us close, led us and fought alongside us and made us into a body of men who belonged together.

Then something very strange happened. Toliver wanted to tell me something. He would start to speak, then a look of despair, of total frustration would pass across his face. He would stop himself by grabbing my hair and clutching at my hand. A minute passed in silence, and he began to talk about the outside world. After so many days on the march, we had forgotten there was an outside world. He reminded us that it still existed, and that it was worth staying alive for.

For one moment, he became a soldier again. He broke orders, passing the command to me, naming Prather as second-in-command. He tried to talk about

China, but he did not have the strength. He convulsed again, and his mouth filled with blood. I tilted his head to let the blood run away.

"Win the game . . . game . . . Pat . . . Pat, I'm here, sweetheart . . . get Giap no matter what . . . you're a good boy, Gayle . . . don't let it get to you . . . don't forget there's an outside . . . why did it have to be you? . . . oh, yes . . . go home . . . let's all go home . . . get my bag, Pat . . . I love you all . . . don't let it make you hate . . . I'm coming, Pat . . . where are the tickets? . . . give me the tickets . . ."

He raised his head and reached out with his hand. And he died.

CHAPTER 12

It took me five minutes to accept that Toliver was dead. Then I set about doing the things that had to be done. It was very dehumanizing, having to bury him as we did. He would not have a grave, just a hole in the ground on an unnamed hill in Vietnam.

We tore some gorse loose from the soil, then worked in shifts for two hours, digging with our hands and rifle butts. Prather clipped Toliver's dog rag to his beret. He laid the beret beneath his chin and spread the cloth over his face. We wrapped the body in a groundsheet and lowered it into the ground. We pushed the soil and rocks back and covered the raw earth with shrubbery. Tan knelt beside the grave. He rocked from side to side and sang softly in Korean. Morrosco sobbed tearlessly. The rest of us waited in silence.

An hour later, we snapped back to reality. We had allowed ourselves that indulgence, and now it was time to stop. The loss of Toliver only a day from China could not have come at a worse psychological moment.

We put our emotions and anxieties into cold storage and went back to work.

There was an immediate transition of command without a hitch. Toliver's leadership had been very diplomatic, almost democratic. It would stay that way; we would function as a co-operative, but no one doubted I was chairman of the board.

I turned my attention to Tan, whose arm was in a terrible mess. He insisted he could still hit his primary target, firing with his one good arm, but that was out of the question. Prather and I walked a short distance from the others and worked out a new plan for the hit. We would attempt to strap Tan's arm so that he could hold a weapon. Tan stayed in the firing line, but I took his primary target. Prather took Toliver's primary targets. Tan, Prather, and I would then get as many secondary targets as we could. It was not satisfactory, but short two men, the best I could do.

Morrosco did a quick but effective patch-up of Tan's shoulder, strapping the upper arm tightly to his chest but leaving the forearm free. While he tended to other various wounds, we redistributed the gear. I took the mapping case and Toliver's carbine and night scope; Prather took Tan's adapted M-3 and gave Tan his own. This gave Prather a better sniping weapon, and Tan could hip-shoot. We spread the balance of Toliver's and Tan's gear across the unit. Jackson and Wiley carried the AK-47s. We were overloaded with weapons, but we would need everything we could carry. We broke camp quickly and headed for the border. Dawn was approaching.

We listened for the abort signal en route the previous afternoon. Radio failure in the swamps must have been due to atmospheric condition, because we were now able to raise a carrier wave. No abort had been transmitted. As we were a day behind schedule, our command would place us in China, reconnoitering the hit zone from our final campsite. The conference was scheduled to open on the next morning.

We came down a steep incline, slipping and sliding in the darkness toward a tributary stream we knew would carry us to the border at the Red River. We moved through dense jungle; strange trees grew out of the sides of the cliffs and then shot upward into mushrooms of foliage. In places the decline became so steep that we had to lower the gear by hand. Storm clouds choking the valley below dissipated as we descended. We reached the tributary stream about twelve miles from its junction with the Red River. We eased off the bank and waded downstream in waist-deep water. A land route would have been less demanding, but the steep riverbanks gave us some cover from aerial surveillance. We walked all day without seeing anyone and reached the Red River in late afternoon. We went into hiding and waited for nightfall.

Though we stood on the threshold of China—the river was the dividing line between China and North Vietnam—we had a difficult march ahead before we touched Chinese soil. Our route at the Red River was like a half of a swastika; we had joined the river from the south by a tributary stream; now we would turn northwest along its bank for five miles before crossing over and leaving the river via another tributary that joined the far shore. Our crossing point would be a shallow stretch at approximately twenty-two degrees, forty minutes north by one hundred and three degrees, forty minutes east. Ta shu tang lay fifteen miles to the north.

Night fell, and we moved into the river. We had two small villages to pass—Coc My on the Vietnamese side of the river and Po Dai on the opposite shore—both very small but centers for patrol activity along the border. Running the length of the Chinese bank of the river was a major tar-sealed highway which was our last geographical barrier before the railway line at Ta shu tang. We saw lights and cooking fires in both villages but slipped past in the darkness without incident.

We moved with extreme caution, traveling by signal and a minimum of whispered commands. I felt as if China could pluck us out of the river and destroy us at any moment. We had to traverse some rough vegetation; when we slipped or banged our weapons, the sound seemed to carry for miles. We saw people on the road; we went to ground half expecting them to start shouting. A frogman had once talked to me of planting limpet mines on enemy ships. It was impossible that he had not been seen; there must have been so many eyes watching the water, it was impossible that he could escape observation. Yet somehow, he got away with it. I felt the same now; how dare we walk the Chinese border with such impunity?

A feeling almost of devilment came over me. We were a wee flea on the back of the giant, and the giant could not find us. The initial fear—if it was fear; I am not quite sure how to define fear, because I am not sure I have experienced it—our original anxiety was mingled with mounting excitement. I was suddenly feeling very clever. Cheeky. We were sneaking into China. We had worked so hard to get here that our accomplishment had a slight sense of unreality about it. When we got safely past the Chinese village, we relaxed a bit.

"You know," said Wiley, "we've been so long on the road, the whole world may have been blown up by now, and we'd know nothing about it."

"If that has happened, our little pin prick ain't worth much," said Jackson.

China, just three hundred yards across a muddy river, brought the uniqueness of our accomplishment into dramatic focus. Our isolation was complete. Absolute. We had all been behind the lines many times, but this was something different. We were in the lion's mouth now.

It took us all night to cover the five miles in the river. People wandered along the shore, came down to the river, pushing us against the bank in water up to our waists. We struggled over fallen trees, hid from the occasional fishing boat.

At last we came opposite the tributary stream on the far shore that would lead us into the mountains. We crossed over quickly before dawn and struck north after passing under a road bridge. We left the stream at a meander, rejoining it a mile farther on. The sun was just rising. We were in China. We had only to scale the mountain before us to look down upon our target. We were thirty hours behind schedule. The conference would open in twenty-four hours.

By the time we rejoined the stream, we were beginning to feel secure. We stopped instinctively and looked behind us. We were on a gently rising plateau, with Vietnam spread beneath us reaching out to the horizon; I had the feeling I could see all the way to Hanoi. Ahead lay a string of mountains, behind those a second string capped in snow. Around us the landscape was lit by the morning sun into a hundred shades of brilliant green severed by the white chalk of the riverbed.

"We'll break here," I said.

We stripped off our gear and lay it on the ground. For a long time, we just stared at one another.

"This is it, pal," Morrosco said. "This is the big C."

I picked up a stone, juggled it in my hand, and threw it as hard as I could into the water. It was all I could think to do. I was heaving with emotions I could not identify. Most of all I felt a sense of achievement. One by one, I saw the men's faces break into grins. Only Tan remained composed. I grinned with them and threw another stone. Jackson let out a whoop and jumped on a pile of loose boulders. They collapsed under him. He picked himself up, laughing.

"I always figured I'd end up breaking rocks in China," he said.

"If we muff it tomorrow," said Morrosco, "half of America will be here breaking rocks."

"Shut up and give me a ride," Wiley shouted. He

leapt up on Morrosco's back. Using his hand as a whip, he drove Morrosco across the river. On the far shore, he jumped down.

"I've always wanted to ride an ass into China," he shouted.

Morrosco threw a rock at Wiley. I was skipping stones on the water when I heard Prather behind me. I turned to look. He was standing on a huge boulder, his arms outstretched, his face toward China.

"A soldier told Pelopidas," he recited, " 'We are fallen among the enemies.' Said he, 'How are we fallen among them more than they among us?' " Prather bowed and, with a flourish, offered Morrosco his perch. Morrosco scrambled up alongside the older man.

"Confucius say, 'Woman who puts carrots and pees in same pot very unsanitary.' "

We were making too much noise, but I did not care. Our bodies were physically rejecting stress that had been accumulating since we pushed off from Thailand. The tension dammed up in us all had reached a bursting point with Toliver's death; now we were sluicing them off in a childish, almost hysterical way. We must have looked half mad, but it was harmless fun, so I let it go. I felt like banging my head against a rock, I wanted so desperately to release all the feelings bottled up inside me. My mind was racing. What the hell were we doing here? How could we expect to get away with it? How much more can we take? But we had gotten away with it. Here we were in China. Mission conclusion was a day away. I had almost a panicky feeling. I had so much to say and no way to express it. I let them play. We laughed and wrestled and jabbered away. And nothing was said.

Only Tan showed no sign of jubilation. He had not spoken since we crossed the border. His actions seemed to say that what we had accomplished in the past three and a half weeks was nothing; success could be measured only by tomorrow's results. Two months earlier, a mission such as ours would have been more fantasy than Tan's pragmatic nature could allow itself. Now he stood a day away from the crowning achievement of a lifetime. Until it happened, Tan would hold on to the suspicions and distrust that were the essence of the man's character. I knelt beside the solemn Korean. We waited quietly.

The others clowned about for fifteen minutes, then grew quiet again, looking slightly sheepish for the way they had carried on. They waited for marching orders.

"Let's go, guys," I said.

We headed out overland and climbed toward our final campsite; from there we would move to the impact zone the following morning for mission-complete. Had we reached our final rendezvous on schedule, we would have had thirty-six hours to rest, reconnoiter, and prepare our gear for the hit. Now we were being given half a day; we would push out during the night to cross the rail line and penetrate the outer security ring in darkness. By sunup we would be in position. We could not scout the impact zone in advance because of the risk of exposure.

We climbed all day without seeing the security patrols we had anticipated. We were often moving over open land, totally exposed to observer aircraft, but we never saw a single plane. If a plane had gone overhead, we would have scrambled for cover, but it would have been little more than a formality; there was no hiding from the camera. Infrared film would have picked up our body heat.

We crested the range in midafternoon. On the far side, we all pushed forward to the edge of a narrow cliff that dropped sharply away beneath us. For days we had been moving through a landscape as deserted as the far side of the moon. Now all of China was spread before us. The land was gentler; stretching away below us lay a low sweeping valley carpeted with rice fields. A dozen villages scattered across the valley were joined by a network of roads that buzzed with activity. The Kun Ming railway line ran along the valley floor before disappearing into a great chain of mountains to the northwest. I saw Ta shu tang on the far side of the valley, propped up against the first steep hill.

Suddenly I felt a cold wind against my face. I saw rain clouds approaching from the north. We retreated from the precipice and sought a campsite. We were above eight thousand feet; wind and rain had eroded great chunks of the mountain, exposing huge boulders. We secured ourselves within a circle of rocks surrounded by heavy vegetation.

I set to ensuring that every man was ready for the job. As much as anything else, we needed rest. The bit of hysteria at the river had alarmed me slightly, but I remained confident of the unit's ability to perform. We had proved ourselves pretty well capable of doing what we set our minds to. Once the job was done . . . it was no longer terribly important to me that we got back. But were we fit to carry it off? I took a mental inventory. I had lost a lot of blood, and my hip was causing me great pain. But I could shoot, and I could fight, and probably even run for my life if necessary. My neck and eyelids were swollen from mosquito bites, but that was more a discomfort than a handicap. I had localized infection in my arms where I had dug leeches with the point of my knife; penicillin was keeping that under control. My head was gashed from a fall or fight, and one ear was covered with a scab which bled profusely if I picked it. All the hard points—skull, fingers, elbows, knees—were raw and lacerated. But for the hip, I was in more or less the condition in which I had expected to arrive.

Morrosco and Jackson were in far better shape than the rest of us; they were more or less whole. Prather's hand was holding together, so he was not bad off. We were all dehydrated, and Prather more than the rest of us; no matter how much water we drank, we never quenched our thirst now, and we were all taking salt tablets regularly. Wiley's wound was infected but not gangrenous. He was in constant pain and could maintain the pace now only with Benzedrine. He used it sparingly, afraid of the time when it would let him down. Tan was in reasonable shape considering his wound. He was in constant pain, but he had a way of overcoming pain through sheer will power; he locked it outside his consciousness. It was either that or morphine or letting the pain drive him crazy. Tan wanted the hit too much for the latter two.

The unit was in better shape than it looked. Our uniforms were like stiff cardboard that rubbed the flesh raw at the neck, under the arms, between the legs. We had long since discarded underwear, and the outergarments were in tatters. We had tried to repair them when we stopped for more than an hour, but those times had been precious few.

Prather was the most domesticated of us all; he had even sewn while we waited for Toliver to die. Now he was stitching Morrosco's fatigues; Morrosco was useless at it. I had been watching a deep depression creep over Morrosco. Toliver's death had hit him very hard, and he had not found the strength to refocus his attention on the mission.

"Who's scared besides me?" he said suddenly.

No one spoke.

"Don't any of you guys give a shit about getting killed?" he said.

"Just shut up," Jackson said.

"What do you think the security guard will be? I bet there'll be two hundred of them."

"Knock it off, Morrosco," I said.

"I know you, Rivers," he said, "you don't give a fuck if you live or die."

"Knock it off. That's an order."

"Kiss my ass."

"Go reconnoiter the site," I said, handing him my glasses.

He was right. Dying did not bother me. I did not care. I had come into this war bitter; the more I was involved, the more bitter I grew. I wanted to live, but there was no priority in making a big thing of it.

Dying I could accept. Capture, never. The possibility

had arisen more than once. I was never aware of making a conscious decision against it. The day arrived when I knew I would never hang by the heels in a village square or be paraded before the television cameras in Hanoi.

I was in a large party working just south of the seventeenth parallel. We were creating a diversion to cover a major drive by the Seventh Airborne. We blew two bridges and a railway link, and on the return to our pickup point, we stumbled over a Viet Cong arms cache hidden in a tunnel. We decided to lengthen the mission to ambush the VC when they came for the arms. Six Viet Cong turned up, but most of them survived our ambush and got down the tunnel. They would not surface, so we knew they were retreating through the tunnel, which could stretch for miles underground. Half a mile away, they blew the tunnel out—probably by accident—and tried to escape into the jungle. Two other guys and I went after them. We ran smack into a battalion of North Vietnamese regulars. One of our guys was killed immediately, and the second got his side ripped open by automatic fire. He could walk, so I fought a rearguard action to cover his retreat. I got pinned down against a cliff.

I had only my shotgun, so I could not kill them at a distance. They closed on me and began to rush me in small parties. I was low on ammunitiion and saw myself being sieged out. I was under tremendous pressure, but my mind was problem-solving like a computer. And the final answer was complete contempt for the enemy; I would fight with my knife and my gun butt and take as many as I could with me. I would die fighting.

If these guys had stayed their distance, my ammunition would soon have been gone. But they had no way of knowing that, or how far away my relief was. So they sent in suicide parties of five at a time. I killed three in the first rush, but two guys got through to me. One was five feet from me when he went down, and the second hit me on the shoulder with his rifle just as I blasted him with the shotgun. Now I had two automatic weapons and plenty of ammunition.

A few minutes later, five more guys popped up and tore off in my direction. It is hard to believe, but the only thing in their favor was their numbers. They were firing on the run, with their weapons on automatic, hitting everything but me. They were not coming straight on, but weaving about as they closed; experience had taught me to recognize that the inside men would not swing outside the flankers, so as soon as I saw how wide the flankers were going, I knew the extent of the weave pattern. It became a process of elimination. I shot the first one through the neck, and he somersaulted backward. It was very dramatic and off-putting for the others. They hesitated long enough for me to hit the second one. After that, they were too close for anything but open sighting. The last one was ten feet from me when I gave him a bullet through the upper chest. Before they could regroup, I broke out and fought my way back to the unit.

Morrosco was gone ten minutes, then returned and sat on the ground, saying nothing. I sent each man on his own to look at the target area. It was a way of restoring mission purpose, of reminding them what we were there for, of eliminating any residual doubts about the rationale of what we were going to do. It kept Morrosco's self-indulgence from spreading to the others.

I took the glasses from Wiley and went to look for myself. What I saw this time really took my breath away; I had failed to take it in with that first brief glance. The valley was literally filled with peasants: working the rice paddies, driving ox carts, pedaling bikes along the roads, washing in the streams, repairing the railway line. Getting to Ta shu tang unobserved was preposterous. Like sneaking across Paris or London without being seen. I began to panic. The mission cannot be done, I said to myself. But that was what we had fought a month for, what Toliver had died for. It had to be done.

I needed to collect my thoughts, to be positive I was getting it right. I found myself wishing Toliver were there with me. Then the mission went straight out of my mind; suddenly I was thinking about people a million miles away, times I had spent in another world. But the reflections had a dreamlike quality, as if ours was the only real world, that other world outside was only fantasy. I glanced at my watch. It was 1512 hours. I returned to the campsite. "Lew," I said, "switch on the radio."

Prather fished it out of Tan's pack, switched it on, and set it against a rock. It was just 1515 hours. A very strong sense of purpose began coursing through my veins. I untied the Sahka from its pouch and laid it carefully on the ground, then knelt in front of it. Very slowly I pulled back the waterproof wraps and stripped them from the gun case until it lay exposed on the ground. I flipped the top open. The Sahka lay like a virgin on a velvet couch. I wiped my hands on my fatigues, then lifted the stock from the leather case. I looked at my watch again. The minute hand had passed the half hour. No one could recall us now. I began assembling the Sahka. I would carry it whole into the hit zone.

Wiley sat slumped on the ground next to me, resting against his pack. He had stripped off his shirt and bandages and was prodding his wound tentatively while waiting for Morrosco to dress it. Jackson squatted nearby, assembling his rockets. Prather watched Morrosco as he fussed with Tan's shoulder.

Tan had not broken his silence, nor was he reacting to the pain of having his wound cleaned and bandaged. It was as if his whole life had been directed toward this mission, toward the momentary fury to come. Now I had taken his target away from him. Our wasted condition, the accumulation of wounds—even more, Toliver's death—had robbed Tan of his instinct for survival. I had seen it seeping from him. I had seen it because he and I were much alike, except that Tan was not so good at hiding it as I was. We needed Tan. I had a sudden inspiration. If we could strap his arm tightly enough to put him back on the line, he might care enough to stay alive. Just as I rose to take a look, Prather turned to me.

"You'd best come look at this arm," he said.

I laid the Sahka down and joined them. As Morrosco slowly turned Tan's arm with his hands, I heard the deep sound of bone grating against bone. Tan winced. Sweat was pouring from his face. I squatted beside him. Prather read my thoughts.

"He can't go into the firing line like this," he said. "He can't hold a weapon."

"Can you wrap this arm up where we can tie a weapon to it?" I asked Morrosco.

"I don't think he'll be any good with it, but I'll try."

"Get the heavy tape, and we'll see what we can do."

Morrosco walked over to the medical kit and rummaged through it. I broke open my own medical pack and took out a syringe of morphine. Suddenly Morrosco began to shout wildly. "That's it! That's it!"

"Hurry up," I snapped.

"That's it!" he shouted again, his voice more frantic than before.

"That's what?" I asked, turning on my haunches.

Morrosco held the radio in both hands, his arms extended to their full length in front of him. He was staring at the face of the radio. His eyes were wild.

"Abort! Abort! It's abort!"

Then I heard it too. Soft and steady.

". . . v . . . e . . . v . . . e . . . v . . . e . . . v . . . e . . ."

CHAPTER 13

My first reaction was to glance at my watch. It was 1550 hours.

"It's too late! They're five minutes too late!" I shouted, scrambling to my feet. "They can't send it now! It's too late!"

"It's three days too late," said Prather.

We had all run and gathered around the radio, staring at it as if expecting it to talk. Everyone was babbling at once. I told them to shut up. The message kept coming without a break, "v . . . e" repeated three times, then three "v's" followed by three "e's." I suddenly realized we did not know how long it had been broadcasting; we had forgotten about the radio after 1530 hours, forgotten to turn it off. They could have been broadcasting for twenty minutes now. They knew we had received the message by the built-in automatic response transmitter which indicated our receiver was functioning. But they were going to keep on sending it as long as we would listen.

"Shut it off!" I shouted.

I grabbed the radio and smashed it against a rock. It bounced once and landed at my feet. I jumped on it with my boots. It flew apart; the others joined me, wildly stamping the pieces into the dirt, kicking them into the bush.

Wiley looked at his watch. "It's 1555. If they've been broadcasting at us for twenty-five minutes, every Chinaman in China knows we're here, mates."

The first signal would have been picked up on Chinese radio monitors, and they would immediately have started looking for a receiver. If we had received no more than what we had been promised—eight or ten seconds of transmission—they could not have pinpointed us within five hundred miles; they would have had precious little time to name the province we were in. Given three minutes, they could put us inside a hundred-mile radius. In twenty minutes they would know which rock to look under. Someone flying high in a plane somewhere south of here knew we were receiving, but he held his finger on a button. And signed the death warrant for six men.

"It's a trick. A phony signal."

"We've been set up. Double-crossed."

"Maybe the radio picked up somebody else's signal. Maybe it wasn't for us," Morrosco said, looking around anxiously for encouragement.

"It's a sell-out. We've been fingered for the Chinks."

A feeling of betrayal spilled out in a jumble of confused words, as if it had been on all our minds for days, and we had been afraid to speak.

"Toliver!" I said. " 'A game,' he said. What was he trying to tell us?"

"That motherfucker led us into a trap!" screamed Morrosco.

Everyone began to shout at once, oblivious that we were standing on a hillside a day's march into China. Tan's eyes welled with tears. My stomach was so knotted I had difficulty breathing. I started trying to think the problem through.

"Slow down," I said. "Let's try to think."

"It's simply impossible. Impossible," Prather repeated, shaking his head.

"You know who it was. It's that son-of-a-bitch in the raincoat," said Jackson. "The one with the pictures. 'Photos,' he said. 'Prime targets.' He's conned us. Well, I'm gonna con his ass with a fucking grease gun."

Morrosco turned his head from side to side, then revolved on his feet two or three times, as if he might find the answer somewhere behind him. Finally he slumped to the ground by his pack. Very deliberately, he beat his head against the rocket platform. Tears were pouring from his eyes.

"I got to die," he said, "because somebody's playing games."

Tan began to speak in Korean, then his voice rose to a tirade. "I'm going anyway," he said. "I'm going."

Jackson ran to the edge of the hill.

"Better look out, you motherfuckers! We're coming after you!"

"I'll go with you," Wiley said to Tan. "No, let's get the hell out of here." He paused. "I wanted that signal so badly a week ago; you'll never know how much I wanted it. I've been scared shitless for two weeks. All I wanted was to go home. And now it's come, and it means nothing except that we're sure to get killed. I don't know who I want to kill."

"You don't want the cheese no more, do you?" Jackson said to Wiley. "You just want out of the trap. Well, I tell you what I'm gonna do. I'm gonna kill all them fuckers at that conference table, and then I'm going back to Bien Hoa and kill all them fuckers there. And I might just kill the motherfucking President of the United States. I put eighteen years in this man's army. They ain't selling me cheap."

"It's the U. S. Army," Prather said. "My government would be no party to this."

"What difference does it make? You're dead, pal."

My mind was reeling. It was back to the briefings, and things began to click in place. The chain of command had been so vague. We had been promised no abort after Laos but ordered to listen for it. Who had sent us in? What was their authority? And what were the consequences if we did carry on? I felt like a pilot in Strategic Air Command, racing toward my target and suddenly starting to think that a technical fault might have put me in the air. Maybe we had become more important than the people who had sent us in. Our orders were specific. Abort. Any decision to disobey that order was mine now. If we all died doing it, we could blame no one but ourselves.

"What makes you think there's anybody at the bottom of that hill to hit?" I asked Jackson.

He looked at me, startled. We all grabbed our glasses and ran to a vantage point. Ta shu tang was exactly as it had been reconstructed on our model; the same low houses, the wooden conference hall, the low hill in front that was to be our firing line, the railway and the road leading to the hall. Something was not quite right, but I could not put my finger on it. Then it struck me. Ta shu tang did not look like a place about to receive some of the most powerful figures in Southeast Asia. Or did it? There were two vehicles parked in front of the hall, one black sedan and an army lorry. There were a few people milling about, but from this distance I could not determine if they were in uniform. There were certainly no pickets or military installations along the railway line. Was nothing happening at Ta shu tang? Were the people I saw organizing a conference that would cast the fate of half the world's population? Or were they peasants? Or local officials carrying out a normal day's routine? Maybe administration and security services were to arrive late today or tonight to keep the venue secret until the last minute. Or maybe it was all a brilliant exercise in hypothesis.

"What's happening down there?"

"Beats me."

"Does it look to you like that place is ready for an international conference?"

"Well, does it to you?"

"Man, I don't know."

"The briefings . . ." Jackson started.

"Who briefed you on anything?" I asked.

No one replied.

"What was their authority? On whose orders are we about to hit the top communist commands in Asia? Do you know any names? Who can say we'll stop a war if we go down there tomorrow? And I want to go as much as you do. Maybe we would start one. Maybe somebody in the U.S. hierarchy wants war with China. He sent us to guarantee it. Now he's been found out."

"Maybe that's an empty village down there," said Jackson.

Prather came toward me, but I waved him away and walked back out to the edge of the camp. I scanned the valley below for any positive sign that it was all going to happen. Behind me, I heard the other five raving on, angry, confused. I was being attacked on all sides; by my thoughts, by what I was hearing, by what I wanted to do, by my natural reluctance to draw a conclusion too quickly, by the urgency of our situation, by the need to take positive action to restore order. I was leading men who were used to making decisions for themselves, and all of us were hovering on the brink of hysteria. I was almost out of my depth.

The scene degenerated into chaos; the five of them teetered between despair and rage. Every few minutes one or the other would rush out beside me and shout madly down the hill. I needed desperately to bring the unit back under control.

I just did not give a damn. I did not believe we would ever get out of China. We were less than ten miles from the border, but it might as well have been the middle of Peking. I had marched so many miles, fought so hard to experience the greatest moment of my life, and I was not going to be allowed to enjoy it.

I searched for a reason to justify the abort. Communist intelligence in Saigon had learned about the mission. We had killed too many people on the way up; our kill pattern had been spotted and our route projected. Beyond that my theories got a little crazy. Some dove in the U. S. Government had set the mission up, then exposed it at the last moment to embarrass the Americans. It was a hawk out to force the ultimate confrontation with China. It was some unknown general's scheme for provoking war, and he had been caught out, or gotten cold feet. Westmoreland, how much did he know? We might be nothing more than an experiment to see how far north an insurgency team could penetrate. We might be nothing more than guinea pigs in a jungle laboratory, or we might be the trigger to plunge half the world into war.

My thoughts kept turning back to Toliver's dying moments. There was too much soldier in the man to expose secret orders. But surely he cared more for us— and for himself—than to lead us blindly on a pointless suicide mission. He must have been lied to, promised an abort prior to China. We could have turned back, mission complete, with a reasonable chance of survival. Too late he realized he was among the deceived. The experiment would be played out to its inevitable conclusion.

Fuck it, I decided. We were on our own now. From the moment the abort signal went out, we became free agents. When our people abandoned us, they forfeited responsibility for our future actions. It was my interpretation of the consequences that would determine if the hit was on. Somebody crazy sent us up here. But they never reckoned on our thinking for ourselves. If Giap was at the bottom of that hill, I had the destiny of half the world in my hands. It was almost too much for me to contemplate. I pulled myself up short. I was the decision-maker now, not Saigon, not Washington. I had to take a rational look at the whole thing.

But where to start dealing with this mad predicament? It occurred to me that whoever had sent the signal might expect us to go ahead with the hit anyway, sweep down out of the hills and kill ourselves and everyone at the meeting in one conclusive shoot-out . . . or kill a few peasants and then be hunted down like animals. We would have achieved the desired results, and we could be totally disowned with the same breath. Were we some mad scheme Lyndon Johnson had cooked up as he walked out of the White House to get even for having lost the war? Were we manifestations of Nixon's inferiority complex, a crazy plot to drag the entire world into nuclear war? Was this the only way America's beaten and humiliated generals in Saigon thought they could ever defeat Giap and regain a little self-respect? For the first time, I realized with a start that the Chinese we were to hit were even more important than Giap. What would be the reaction of the American Government if some Chinese assassinated half the Cabinet?

The permutations were too many for me to puzzle out sitting on a hill in China. I had to make my own judgments. I had to deal with the problem within the bounds of our military environment, not get carried away with analysis of why we were there and who had sent us and why in hell the war was going on in the first place.

I tried to sort out the problem rationally, but Giap's picture kept floating into my mind's eye. I had so wanted to kill that man. In the end, it was an easy decision to make. We were the most important people in the arena now. If somebody wanted reaction out of China, they could do it some other way. They could send the B-52s. I walked back to the others. They stopped talking.

"We're going back, fellows," I said. "Let's talk it over."

I made it clear at once that carrying out the hit was beyond discussion. Anything they said to change my mind would be listened to and then dismissed. I said it was the hell with everybody else, we were the ones who mattered. There were a hundred reasons for the mission, and a hundred more for the abort. I told them how I saw it, then just sat back and listened.

Prather was making a hard adjustment. He could not believe what was happening. He did not accept that his government would do this to him. They must have been in the dark from the beginning. With this I concurred; Prather had probably been requisitioned through military channels and stuck in here to embarrass the British. But he did not want to believe it was a setup; the Americans dared not deceive the British to that extent. He was determined to find a valid reason for the abort.

Tan's reaction was just the opposite. He saw it as total betrayal. He had been promised the one thing that every Korean in Vietnam would die for. And he had been deceived. Maybe mission control had been infiltrated by the communists. We had been flashed a false abort. He insisted we go through with the hit. He did not sound as if he believed his own argument. He was looking for an excuse to carry on.

But we were not going to carry on. These men had seen me in action for a month. They knew that if anyone disobeyed my order and struck out on his own, I would shoot him. I was completely detached about this. Our course of action had not been determined with my survival in mind. It was how I saw our best chance of maintaining a sane interpretation of the circumstances. Of getting some of these men back home. We needed everybody and everything we could carry. No one man's self-indulgence was going to jeopardize the group's chances. They all recognized my determination; there was no move to go against me. But these guys deserved a hearing, and I was prepared to give them all they wanted.

It was difficult for any of us to speak coherently. We were so bitter, and we did not know who to blame. First it was the generals, then the politicians; they had been playing war games. The CIA was part of the package. Nixon got his share of the blame. The nameless civilians with their raincoats and photographs. The colonel who had trained us.

Tan pleaded to go on. The others were utterly confused. Morrosco and Wiley did not give a damn about any broad philosophical interpretation; they just had a strong feeling of betrayal. To my surprise, Jackson was the most coherent of all; after his first explosion, he agreed with me that turning back was the best course of action.

"But tell me, Kiwi," Jackson said, "what are we going back to?"

"What do you mean?"

"What makes you think anybody wants us back? Who are we up against? What'll our reception be if we do turn up at Bien Hoa? You think the colonel's gonna slap us on the back? I'd just like to know who the hell is playing what kind of war games with the U.S. Army. And where it stops."

"Are you talking about attitude? Or about somebody shooting us?"

"I'm talking about everything."

I had expected Jackson to agree with me about the hit. He was a soldier from the word go, and sooner or later I knew he would see the abort signal as an order to be obeyed. But the by-product of accepting that order was a shattering disillusionment in the authorities he had so long respected. He knew what was wrong with the Army. He knew the bad side of politicians meddling with the military. But he had always taken the bad with the good. Now he was having doubts about how much good was there.

This was a painful process for Jackson, because he was not an abstract thinker. He had a flexible and imaginative intellect within the confines of the battlefield, but outside it he left the thinking to others. He was a senior NCO in the Green Berets. The Green Berets did a lot more flag-waving than some of the rest of us special forces. Jackson had always been ready to strike at anything that threatened America, but he was content to let his commanding officers tell him what that threat might be. Now he was confronted with the stark realization that everything was not so cut and dried, that all the yeas and nays were not so absolute, that morality was a dilute solution. Someone had been experimenting with Jackson's life. Did it end here, and now we could try to make our way back home? Or did the expected thing—that we would turn around and come back out—lead us into something else?

Jackson and Prather argued over the question of an experiment. Prather had such great faith in his government. The British simply would not do such a thing.

"For Christ's sake, Lew," I said, "they probably don't know you're here. It's the Americans who've sent us in here. And they'll experiment with human beings like nobody's business."

Wiley and Morrosco stayed on the boil, jumping from one side to the other in every argument. They had been under greater strain than the rest of us for the past few days. The strain was showing through now. They wanted to stay. They wanted to go. They wanted to hit their targets, but this gradually turned to the fact that they just wanted to kill somebody. They needed a visible target to vent their wrath for the dilemma we were in. I was sympathetic; I was feeling again my disappointment at not being able to hit Giap. For a moment I wanted to push off alone. Do my job. End it there.

Because, boy, I had come a long way to do that job. I had a vision of that vast chunk of geography that lay between us and safety. We had spent a month getting somewhere, and now someone said come home. It was like going around the world on your feet. Simply impossible. I felt a sudden deflation in my morale, as if all my strength and sense of purpose had been stamped underfoot. Weakening now would be unpardonable. It was time to bring discussion to a close and get us out of there. I ordered Morrosco to bring me the mapping case.

"This has been going on long enough," I said. "Let's talk about priorities. They know we're here."

That killed the discussion instantly. And all of a sudden I was hit by the whole stupid reality of being in China, the idiocy of ever thinking that we could have gotten away with it. We were inside China and no one knew we were there until the abort? It was impossible. That brought the realization that we were up against every conceivable opposition.

"Either we get out of this as a unit," I said, "or we don't get out of anything. We have a lot of enemies now. A lot of people who don't want us to get away with what we've done. Whether they're people who are going to come looking for us here or people that sent us here doesn't make any difference anymore. We've got a common enemy, and we beat it together. Or it beats us."

We became a fighting unit again. We sat down and discussed, in a very strange atmosphere, what we were going to do. None of us expected to get out of China; we expected to find half the Chinese Army waiting for us at the river. We had to plan, but we found it almost impossible to look more than two or three days ahead. Because we all thought we would be dead.

In the short time since abort, the physical and moral decay that had set in to the unit was tremendous. We had been hurt before, but we had a purpose to drive us on, a goal that kept the adrenaline flowing. When thirty past the hour came without a signal, we had been as jumpy and anxious as a band of robbers about to hit a bank. Now we had lost all motivation for fighting fatigue. Suddenly we were exhausted. Deep blue rings seemed to pop out around the men's eyes. I felt my body sagging within me. My spirits were on the ground. Somehow I had found the strength to endure a month of combat; now it was an effort to lift my head. For the first time, I felt wounded. Every part of my body was sore and bruised, crying out for rest. When I started to stand, I knocked over a rifle and did not bother to pick it up. I saw the Sahka on the ground nearby. I kicked it, then picked it up and threw it as far as I could into the undergrowth. For a month, I had lived for that weapon. I had looked after it crossing rivers. I had even thought about it in combat. Now I disowned it completely. It was growing dark, and I was cold. I looked at the men. They were dying. If we did not pull together quickly, we were finished.

I forced them into a briefing on the route back. Since our cover was blown, it was no good wasting time trying to hide. We would take every short cut. Our goal was M Ngoi, the Laotian village where we had rested and rearmed on the journey in. There we would make contact with the Green Berets and rely on them to get us picked up or get us out some other way. By moving straight down the valleys, we could reach M Ngoi in less than a week. We hit the maps before it was too dark to see and worked out our areas of greatest risk and probable opposition. We were running out of food and ammunition. Our medical supplies were almost exhausted. We had no time to avoid obstruction; we would cut our way through them. Gather weapons and ammunition, food and supplies where we could. We had to be totally self-sufficient. All the men were thinking it, so I said it for them.

"If anybody is hit, he has to make the pace. We can't stop. If you can't make the pace . . . well, it's up to you to handle it however you want."

The men were beginning to react. Their movements quickened. In the last hour we had been through rage, then apathy, and now we were beginning to feel rejuvenated. Tan started tearing off his bandages; he wanted to move out feeling a hundred per cent fit. I had to order him to allow Morrosco to bind him up again.

"What about civilians?" Wiley asked.

"No compassion," said Tan. "We don't have time. We can't afford the risk."

"If we need anything from a village, we take it," I said.

The unit was whole, more or less healthy, and ready —almost anxious—to fight its way home. The only man who troubled me was Wiley. I knew him as a very open character, always ready with his opinion even if it was tactless or badly timed. Since Toliver's death, he had grown quiet, morose. He had hardly participated in the discussion over the past hour apart from parroting Morrosco's remarks. Wiley needed guidance. I had grown to expect very human reactions from Wiley. The day after he had strangled the man on the hillside, I had caught him staring at his trembling hands. If Wiley was trembling now, it was inside, where I could not see it. He must have been going through hell. Questioning whether he could pull off his survival. And whether he wanted to. I would watch him closely.

"They're heavy, Alvin," I said to Jackson as he pondered over his rockets. "Don't take them if you don't want."

"I made them, Kiwi. I want to use them."

He broke them down and strapped them back on the rocket packs. We distributed everything across the group: weapons, food, ammunition, medical supplies, canteens, incidentals. We had little ammunition left for the carbines; we had to lay our hands on communist weapons soon. We divided out a few ears of corn and some bean shoots and the last of the K rations. I put on my new uniform. Wiley took my old shirt; his was little more than a rag. The others took the time to sew rents in their garments. We all cleaned our weapons again. This was the first day of a new mission. We would start it as fresh as possible.

I saw Jackson ladling out Benzedrine to Tan and Wiley. Jackson's hand was already shaking. He must have taken some earlier to psyche himself up for the hit.

The gear we left behind was casually shoved under a rock. We no longer gave a damn about discretion. I left the Sahka where it had fallen.

I sharpened my machete, worked the action on my shotgun. The others were communicating with their weapons as well. They were all we could rely on now.

And then we left.

Part 3

THE HUNTED

CHAPTER 14

It was 1800 hours, and the light was fading fast. We had seen the weather changing for a day and a half. A cloud line hit us minutes after we pushed off. Though it was still light in the valley below, we came down the mountain in a smoky mist. By the time we reached the tributary stream, it was dark. We headed straight down the stream bed for the Red River. We had not seen a single patrol. When the riverbank cover grew thin, I stopped the men.

"I'm taking point," I said. "Somewhere down the river in the next couple of miles, the Chinese are going to hit us with everything they've got. Let's give them all we've got."

"I'm ready."

"Let's get it over with."

We followed the river downstream until we reached the ford where the previous day we had thumbed our nose at China. We all stopped and looked around, and a wave of bitterness swept through the unit. Prather started to speak, but Jackson cut him short.

"Get sharp, Lew," he said.

We all got the message. We ran across in the night, our boots clattering on the shingles. We moved very cautiously down to the bridge, then holed up for half an hour while troop transport passed overhead. A short time later, we arrived at the Red River.

We decided not to follow the Red River as we had on the mission in, but to strike directly across and take a valley paralleling the one we had come up. It was a harder route, but quicker. From there we would head due south to the mangroves, then swing well east of Lai Chau. Our route up had passed a few miles to the west of Lai Chau; if they had established our route pattern, they would be looking for us there. From the mangroves, we would strike southwest to the Laotian border about thirty miles south of our departure point and link up there with our route out of M Ngoi.

We crossed the Red River one at a time without incident. We had been in and out of China without identifying a single enemy soldier. We were just coming together on the Vietnamese side of the river, a hundred yards into the trees, when we stumbled onto a dirt track. Parked on it were three motorcycles, one with a side car; a jeep; and a strange-looking vehicle with a rear track and one front wheel, similar to something the Germans used in Africa. All the vehicles were empty. We could not see their occupants anywhere around.

I left the unit in the trees and went forward alone. I could see or hear nothing. I went on across the road alone without bringing the unit up behind me. It was a foolish thing to do; fortunately, Prather saw what I had done and brought the others forward.

I was poised on the far side of the road, peering into the trees, when I heard movement behind me. I whirled around. Standing on the road facing me were eight or nine men in North Vietnamese uniforms and two officers. Where they had come from, I did not know. For some stupid reason, they must have thought

I was alone, because every eye was on me. One of the officers was pointing a pistol.

Before I had completed my turn, I fired the shotgun twice and killed both officers. The roar of the shotgun panicked the others. Before they could recover, Prather led the unit in a charge across the road, and a free-for-all started. The NVA ran in every direction. When two ducked behind the vehicles, Wiley lobbed a grenade in on top of them. The motorcycles burst into flames and fell back into the trees. Bullets were flying everywhere, but we were doing most of the effective shooting. I saw one NVA get back-shot as he tried to run off the road into the trees. The noise was pounding in my ears . . . the racket of their machine guns . . . a jeep exploding . . . grenades going off. I was jumping and running all over the place, trying to reach cover. I saw a face and shot it, and I saw a body and shot it. I was fighting on instinct now. Then there were only two left, firing wildly from the far side of the burning vehicles. We could no longer see one another. They broke off and fled. We ran to scoop up weapons.

"This damn stuff is useless," Jackson said.

He handed me a shoddy gas-operated light machine gun. It looked like a Czech design, very poorly made. I threw it down and ran over to the officers.

"Fuck me!" I said. "These guys are Chinese."

Their Chinese uniforms were unmistakable. I did not recognize their ranks, but guessed them to be lieutenants. A small-caliber automatic was lying beside one of the dead men. He had probably intended to take me prisoner, but our reflexes were so acutely tuned that I had killed two men before he could get the words out of his mouth.

None of us had ever seen a Chinese soldier before, so the others ran over for a quick look. The enlisted men proved all to be NVA. There was no catching the two who got away, so we struck for the hills on the double.

We ran through the bush, expecting to meet people behind every tree; we leap-frogged one another, sounding off in whispers for two hours, moving over undulating terrain, around rocky outcrops, pushing through a low bubble vegetation. Then the going got far less restricted; we could move faster, with less effort. We were an hour past dawn now, beginning our third day without sleep.

When we broke into a river and found a secure spot, we grabbed a couple of hour's rest. We were approaching the mangroves, and we were anxious to regain our old route through; we could move faster on familiar ground.

"Well, they won't be looking for us in China," said Morrosco, referring to the bodies that marked our progress across the Red River.

"Pity, that," said Prather. "Otherwise the Chinese might have maintained control of the operation. The communications and logistics delays would have given us a break."

"I'm not sure we were meant to be found in China. We may have been allowed out," I said.

"What do you mean?" asked Jackson.

"Don't you find it odd that we never saw a soldier inside China and ran into Chinese officers the first five minutes we were back in Vietnam? They must have had pretty accurate co-ordinates on us in China. Who knows, maybe they were watching us the whole time. So they let us leave. Once outside China, then China is no longer the subject of the mission. The Chinese don't have to admit the infiltration, and the allies don't have to deny it. We're back inside the confines of the Indo-Chinese war theater now. They can kill us with impunity. And the war has not been extended across the borders of China."

We moved out over rough hill country, traveling fast to intercept Highway 138 before dark. We were pouring with sweat by the time we reached it, dropping down into the roadway from the mountain above. I expected opposition, but we dashed across without seeing anyone; possibly I was overestimating the enemy's communications. Below the highway, we were boxed into a narrow valley with a hamlet just above it on the hill to the west. Beyond lay a wide plain where we hoped for easier going.

We had been on the highway, which was little more than a track, for five minutes when Morrosco, at point, rushed into the trees without waving us down. We faded into the undergrowth and waited. Nothing happened. It was growing dark, so I decided to go forward before we lost one another. I crawled on my belly to where I had last seen Morrosco, but he was gone. I lay perfectly still for five minutes, then I heard him give a hiss. He was hidden under some brush no more than fifty feet away. I signaled the others to hold their positions, took out my knife, and crawled to his side.

The body of a peasant man lay beside him. The man's head hung in a curious way; the neck seemed to be cut all the way around. I looked at Morrosco. He opened his left hand. It held a garrote—three strands of piano wire, each about a foot long, twisted together and attached to two small wooden toggles. I had seen these before in Vietnam, but I did not know Morrosco was carrying one. It had sliced through the man's neck like a cheese cutter, clean to the spine. I smelled the stench of the man's bowels.

I started to raise up, but Morrosco pushed me down sharply. Then I saw three more men beating through the bush in our direction. They were peasants as well, and I thought they might walk past us. But they were looking for the man Morrosco had killed. They felt no sense of danger; they were just chatting, wondering what had happened to their friend.

When they were within a few feet of us, one of them spotted a basket on the side of the road that I had not seen before. They got a bit excited, as if they might go back to the hamlet for help; they had started to think something was wrong, but they showed none of the fear to suggest they suspected something like us. A snake perhaps. They walked past us, and I decided we could not risk their turning back.

"In the open," I whispered to Morrosco.

We jumped up and ran out on the track, making sure they heard us so that all three would stand and fight. If we had stalked them, we might have killed two and lost the third. We charged them, Morrosco with his machete, me with my knife.

They ran back a few yards and grabbed up something from the roadside. Then they turned on us. They were wielding wooden spades the peasants use to build up mud in rice fields, something like an ax handle with a flat wooden blade for turning the mud. Morrosco and I stayed close together to give them the encouragement of three on two.

"Fun and games, you bastards," I heard Morrosco say.

His voice was almost light-hearted. He had a lot of anger to release, and he was looking forward to this fight. For me, this was just another job, and I was conscious of having to spread myself across two men. I could not rely on Morrosco's help, nor he on mine.

We squared off for two seconds, then one guy swung at Morrosco. He ducked, but slipped. He jumped up, and he and the bloke started circling. Another rushed me with a wild chopping blow. I stepped inside it and brought him into me. I went down on my back and took him over my head, sticking him with the knife as he flew upward.

I rolled off him to take on the second man. But I could not see him. A crushing blow caught me in the small of my back, like being hit with a cricket bat. I fell to my knees and toppled over to one side. The spade came crashing down on the ground beside me. I tried to stand, but my legs would not work. My back was throbbing, and pain was shooting up and down my legs like an electric shock. The guy saw that he had me. He started to finish me off, then saw that Morrosco had just killed his companion. He hesitated a second, then broke into an indecisive run into the bush. I grabbed my knife and heaved it at him, and it clattered harmlessly against the ground. The guy looked back, and I saw from his expression that he knew he had made it. The guy turned, Jackson stepped from behind a tree, and the guy just ran into his mouth. He was dead in a fraction of a second. Jackson strolled to where I was lying on my side.

"Well, you two screwed that one up, didn't you," he said.

He had seen what was happening and anticipated the result, so he slipped through the trees and cut off the man's retreat. I was on my feet almost instantly, but my back and legs were swelling quickly. I recovered my knife, and we moved out. We had to leave the trail, because these people would be missed. I forced myself to run. We had a compelling sense of urgency to flee these scenes. We were lucky, because five minutes later a mobile unit came down the track, moving very quickly. We struck out across country, avoiding all the trails. Every rogue wind seemed to be blowing us off course now. We stopped talking about specific routes, about making landfalls, about time and distance projections. From now on, we would make our way however we could to M Ngoi, move as far and as fast as we could, rest when we had an opportunity.

We marched nonstop through the night. It was still dark when we broke out of the thick undergrowth into the flaxen grass that preceded the mangrove swamp. We reached the mangroves by the time morning was well established, and we were deep inside by midmorning. At the beginning, we were in a less inhospitable swamp than before; the streams were better defined, the ground between them firmer. But the trees overhead were filled with bats. Our voices panicked them; they fell out of the trees almost to ground level and then screamed their way back to their roosts, their wings flapping and beating with a roar in our faces on their erratic flight skyward. We could see vultures through the cracks in the canopy of foliage, but they were not following us. When the trees closed overhead, it was pitch black around us though the sun shone brilliantly above. The heat grew stifling. The leeches found us again. A tree limb moved. Unseen things slipped through the watery floor beneath us.

"I heard there's a baboon in here that will pull a man's ear off," said Wiley.

"Bullshit," Jackson replied to that.

Dragonflies three inches long rose off the stagnant water and swarmed around our heads, seeking the salt in our sweat. They clogged our noses, filled our ears with buzzing. I thrashed wildly at a snake, severing its head as it swam between my legs.

"Hey, Wiley," Jackson said, "there's a beetle in here that gets in your ear and eats its way right through your brain. There's no way to get them out. I've seen guys go crazy, run down a hillside screaming. Shoot themselves."

"Now that's bullshit."

"Maybe. But I'm puttin' cotton in my ears."

When we saw Jackson stop, we all did the same, plugging our ears with wadding. We were struggling now, sweating out more water than we had brought with us. Fighting off sleep. Every step was agony for my legs and lower back from the blow I had received. We had to hack a path with our machetes.

Tension was an added drain on our reserves: we had to be on constant alert. We could not get caught out because of preoccupation with the environment. It was hell. It was jungle warfare we could not be trained for, we could not prepare for, because there was nothing like it, and we were in it until we got out.

The jungle grew too thick to penetrate with our machetes. We moved into the stagnant streams. They were filled with rotting vegetation and foul water life, but they were shallow, and we could push along them. It was terrifying. Everything that moved or brushed against us was a snake. The mosquitoes swarmed on our upper bodies as we walked waist-deep in water. It was difficult to find our way; the vegetation closed over us, and the rivers seemed to disappear in the undergrowth. We would hack our way for a hundred yards, and we would be back in an open stream. Snakes and water animals dropped into the water all around us, then disappeared.

I had never been afraid in combat. When I knew my enemy, I was ready to take on almost any odds. But the nerve-racking fear of the mangrove swamp was almost unbearable. The ground moved under me, and I thought I was being swallowed up by quicksand. I struggled to free my boots from the slimy, sucking bottom. Something brushed against my legs, and suddenly a thousand jaws were tearing at the flesh.

"Piranhas!" I screamed.

"Then we're really lost," said Prather, "because piranhas live in South America."

We pushed on into the night making pitifully little progress. We fell over in the streams and tore our faces on the overhanging branches. When a tree blocked our path, one of us had to haul himself over and drop down on the far side, praying that the water was only waist deep.

Wiley was getting knocked about constantly. When I dropped back to talk with him, I realized that his night vision was not as keen as the rest of ours. He was running into branches that we could see. His morale was crumbling. Crossing the swamp by night must have been the most frightening experience of his life. I said nothing about his eyesight. It was no good making people aware of weaknesses in a unit. Then they began to be allowed for, and the unit could take a certain action to which there were better alternatives. We had to deal from our strengths, not weaknesses.

We left the mangroves in the early hours of the morning via a river, then joined a trail. We were shattered. We desperately needed rest, but I did not want to stop until we were across Highway 6, which we could see in the distance. We were within a day's march of the Laotian border now. If we could get past the highway and into the Nam Meuk, our chances improved considerably. Our only obstacle was a small hamlet blocking our exit from the valley ahead. We intended to skirt it by climbing the hills at the end of the valley.

When we got there, we found the hamlet cutting our only acceptable route. The hills to either side were steep and bare; we would have to go rock climbing, and we were in no shape for that. We stopped outside the hamlet. I was indecisive. The sun was rising now. We could not stay where we were, and we could not spend a lot of time planning a maneuver.

The hamlet held some twenty houses laid out neatly against the base of the hill. We waited outside for an hour, growing anxious all the time because we were not well hidden. Our maps had proved inaccurate for the past couple of days. Earlier they had been so good we could almost count the fence posts in a village this size, but they had not been interpreted correctly for this area. We could not afford to rely on them. Jackson and I crawled forward for a closer look.

We lay almost totally exposed in the dawn light at the edge of the hamlet, peeking from behind a pile of rubble. I dared not even raise up to get a full view. People were moving about, and we observed no signs of a military unit in the hamlet. We were gaining nothing by sitting there. I brought the others forward. The village men were gathering to leave for the fields.

"We have to take this place," I said, "and we have to do it before the men leave."

We dispersed around the hamlet and crawled up under the houses. I could see clearly now. The houses in these tiny villages were usually tidily placed in a circle or a square; here they lay in two parallel lines with a clearing between and a steep hill behind. The track we wanted left the hamlet at the far end. There were fewer men gathering than I had expected, all old or very young. The rest must have been off somewhere playing soldier. As I waited for Prather and Morrosco to take up positions on the far side, I puzzled over the best way to handle this place.

The peasant men began gathering their tools, so it was time for us to move. I waved. Wiley and Jackson ran straight across the clearing toward the second row of buildings. The men saw them and began shouting and shuffling about in panic. I ran out and let go with two rounds of the shotgun into the hill behind them. It had its usual effect. Prather and Morrosco stayed hidden. Tan came with me, and the four of us started shouting and kicking people about to instill fear and confusion. We knocked two of the men down with rifle butts to show them we meant business. The women started screaming and ran into the huts. We kept the panic going for a while. The only way a small force can take and hold a large group of people is to terrify them. We were doing it pretty damned seriously. We split a few heads with our rifle barrels. We did not give a damn about these people. We were in bad shape, and we must have looked like the hand of death to them.

One woman kept screaming hysterically, running about without knowing what to do. Wiley grabbed her and flung her toward the group we had herded together. The woman stumbled and fell. He booted her in the stomach and dragged her with one hand into the group. We had the fear running in. It was no good walking in and asking people to put their hands up and be very quiet; it never worked. If we let the momentum drop, we would start doubting the odds ourselves.

I told Tan to make them shut up and to get everyone out in the middle of the clearing. A man came forward who must have been the village head. They did not want trouble, he said. They would do whatever we wanted. But the men started to mumble among themselves, and I asked Tan what they were saying.

"I don't like the look of it," he said.

Then Prather came piling out from hiding and ran straight at one of the buildings. I saw three guys at the veranda window trying to draw beads on us. Tan and I went back to back and fell to our knees. He covered the peasants, while I furiously scanned the rest of the houses for more snipers.

The three guys never saw Prather. He came across the front of the building and killed all three with one sustained burst. Jackson and Wiley ran through the houses and dragged out two unarmed men.

As I turned back to the peasants, I saw a flicker of movement on my right. I pivoted and fired in one motion. Too late I saw it was a woman running to where the three men lay dead. One must have been her son or husband. I had fired instinctively, and I had made a mistake. Two men ran to the woman, though she was already dead. I saw what they were doing. But I fired anyway. I killed one of them. Jackson killed the other.

All this time, Morrosco had been working his way beneath the buildings. Now he surfaced, shouted, and pointed at one building, and disappeared again. Two men started sniping at us from the last house in the hamlet. The villagers began to scream and wail and wave their hands in begging gestures.

"They've got children down there," Tan said.

I saw Morrosco leap on the veranda and burst inside with his Armalite blazing. There were ten seconds of sustained firing, at first a few single rounds, then all automatic fire. Morrosco came outside and fell up against the building. I thought he had been hit, but he waved that he was all right. No one else seemed to be shooting at us, so I went to join Morrosco and see what had happened. Prather came with me.

We climbed the porch and went into the small building. Six children were cowering together in one corner, staring at me without making a sound. I waved them out the door, and they dashed out, ducking as they went past as if they expected me to hit them. Two men and three children lay dead on the floor. Prather put his hand over his mouth, then over his eyes. He turned and ran out of the building. I watched from the window as he ran to where the peasants squatted. He grabbed up the head man off the ground.

"You bastard!" he shouted. "You killed those children!"

He brought the blade of his hand down across the man's face, crushing his nose. The man sagged, but Prather held him up by his shirt. He drove his fist straight into the man's mouth, splitting his lips and knocking out his front teeth. I turned back into the room.

I pulled the three children together and laid them out. They were so bloody small. They had all been hit by Morrosco's Armalite, which must have been spraying bullets everywhere. I had little time for sentiment, but this sight affected me. A man's body can absorb a lot of punishment. But a child that has been shot is a grotesque thing. These kids' bodies had disintegrated. When a 5.56 round hits a four-year-old child, it just takes arms and legs straight off.

The children were the only ones I regretted to see suffer in this war. I did not give a fuck about the rest of them. When we had started to subdue this crowd, I had no plans to come down on them hard. But when they allowed their own children to get killed, I had nothing but contempt for them. The action had been forced on Morrosco. There was nothing else for him to do. Morrosco liked kids. He felt as bad about it as anybody. But there was no blaming him.

I covered the small bodies with the rush matting from the floor, then walked out and put them out of my mind. The peasants could bury them in their own way after we had gone.

I learned now that Morrosco had been slightly wounded in the upper arm, and a bullet had torn the flesh to the bone on one finger of his left hand. But he was too angry about the children to talk about it. Prather and Morrosco needed to let off some heat, so I ordered them to herd all the people into one of the houses. It was a rough business; they broke heads and smashed down anyone who did not move fast enough. They made everyone squat on the floor and put their hands on their heads, not for security but discomfort. We took turns guarding them while Wiley and Tan organized some of the women to wait on us.

The women knew that the quickest way to be rid of us was to give us what we wanted. Several set to work at a furious pace. They got water on to boil, and we took turns washing while they stitched our shirts and gave them a quick scrub. We grabbed stew meat from a pot with our fingers before they could heat it. They gathered us chickens and cornmeal and bags of doughy preserved meat that hung in the houses. One woman brought several eggs wrapped in rough sacking. They would be broken in our packs five minutes after we moved out, but we would throw the mess, shells and all, on a fire somewhere and gulp it down.

Jackson and Tan searched the hamlet and found several weapons, but they were too old to be of use to us. The peasants stayed very quiet. The women whimpered a bit, but the men remained silent; their eyes were filled with such hatred, they could have attacked us with their bare hands. But peasants want to live as much as anybody else. A man of forty had had about forty years of this existence, and killing me had a very low priority in his life. Sooner or later I would go away, and the whole thing would be forgotten for a while. Next week, he might be a refugee. In a month's time he would return home. Nothing much would have changed. The buildings would be gone, but he could build another house. The rice would still be in the fields. In a year, it would happen all over again.

We gave ourselves a good scrubbing down. I even took my knife and had a go at my beard. Then it was time to leave. We told the peasants that if anyone moved within the next hour, we would return and fire the hamlet. We regrouped and moved out.

We crossed Highway 6 by midday without incident, though we saw a lot of military traffic. We decided against going back into the river because of what had happened at the hamlet, so we worked our way down smaller rivers that would carry us toward the Laotian border. For half a day, we walked in virtual silence; no one felt like talking. The streams grew smaller and more frequent as we approached the border. East and south of Lai Chau, we spotted observer aircraft which we presumed were looking for us. We saw distant patrols as well, but they were always a day's march behind us. The enemy seemed to have underestimated our speed. We reached the Laotian border and rejoined the Nam Meuk after two days' unmolested walking. We would join up with our outgoing route half a day's march to the south, where the Meuk intercepted the Nam Pa. We reached the Meuk in late afternoon and found a safe encampment before nightfall. I was happy with our progress and decided to indulge in a good night's rest. We ate and relaxed, then set about repairing bodies and washing uniforms. Our spirits were lifting.

"I'm glad to leave North Vietnam behind," said Morrosco.

"Yeah," said Jackson, "there's combat and combat. But that was some ugly stuff up there."

"Maybe it will get a little easier now, mates," said Wiley. It was the first positive sign from him in days. "How far now to M Ngoi and some of that good chow?" he asked me.

"Sixty-odd miles. I calculate three days and a bit."

"That's where it ends," said Prather.

"Don't kid yourself, Lew, about what lies between us," said Jackson.

"I don't," he replied, "but it can't be worse than what we've seen to date. We'll survive it."

"I believe you're right," said Jackson, preparing to turn in.

I was delighted with the restored mood of optimism. The weather was warm, so we slept out under the stars with our groundsheets beneath us. I gave the men the first full night's rest we had had since leaving Thailand a month earlier; everyone got five hours' sleep. I took a good share of guard duty, because I was feeling responsible for the unit. But even then I body-slept. I consciously relaxed each part of my body until I was approaching a state of total physical rest while remaining mentally alert. I was almost as fresh as the others when we pushed out the next day.

We broke camp slowly. Everyone was chatting cheerfully. We thought we might be picked up even before M Ngoi because by now somebody must have been wondering where we were, perhaps even looking for us. We pushed off down the Meuk, and even the terrain was favoring us now. We reached the Nam Pa and marched for another day and a half without seeing anyone. By midafternoon on the second day, we were at the river and road junction where Jackson had been pinned down by the NVA patrol. We encountered no obstruction, not even much road activity though this was a busy track. Either we were moving faster than our pursuers anticipated—assuming we had pursuers—or they thought we had gone somewhere else. But it was unproductive to analyze our opposition to that degree. When I was on the run, I dealt with what I found and just tried to anticipate the obvious. I could not predict everything the enemy might do, because I did not know how far the enemy extended.

We were feeling good; knocked about a bit, but whole. We were on our way to intercept the Nam Rue, which would carry us to M Ngoi. There, at worst, we could rest, rejuvenate ourselves, and rearm; at best, we might get carried straight out of this war. We made camp about midnight at the junction of the rivers Pa and Rue. We preferred moving by day; though it was slightly more dangerous, it made easier going. Then before we settled down to sleep, for some instinctive reason I decided we would push on. This was accepted without complaint. We left the Nam Rue to slip between the villages of Pak Luong and Phou Gi. We were moving into an area where the Luang met the Rue, and the countryside was thick with roads and tracks. I wanted to be beyond these two villages before sunup because it was a bad area to hold up in and a worse place to move.

It was just coming dawn when we reached an elevated spot north of Phou Gi. We saw a large unit of NVA troops moving out to the north behind us— six jeeps, a dozen canvas-topped troop carriers and pick-up trucks; in all perhaps a hundred men. We went to ground and watched them pass below us and disappear in the distance. We jumped up and hurried like hell to get back into the river, passing very near Phou Gi without being seen. We came off some high land toward a trail three miles below us which would carry us to the river. For a day now, I had had a bad feeling about the way things were developing, and I was very suspicious of the trail we were approaching. I stopped the unit when we reached a point where we could observe the trail from above through heavy woods. It was just wide enough for two vehicles to pass; we could clear it in nine or ten good strides. Prather and I went forward alone. We crawled the last hundred yards in total silence. We reached the edge of the road and lay perfectly still for a minute. Slowly I raised my head and looked about. And froze.

CHAPTER 15

Sitting on our side of the road no more than ten feet away was a small canvas shoulder bag. Immediately I looked up into the trees. There they were. NVA snipers. They had seen the unit approaching. They were looking out over Prather and me, glasses trained where the others were holed up. It was the purest form of instinct that had told me we were walking into a trap. We had seen nothing to forewarn us; the only enemy we had spotted had been moving away from us.

The snipers expected us to come down the trail, because they had the tree trunks between them and the road, leaving themselves exposed to Prather and me. I counted three, settled in about thirty feet above the ground in three different trees. All three had sniping rifles; two of the weapons carried scopes. Prather had not seen them from where he lay ten feet behind me, but he had frozen when I did. Had we not been looking out for booby traps, we would have been moving faster and making a lot more noise. When I was hunting mines or trip wires, I did it with such care that a spider's web stood out like bloody ship's rigging. But for this caution, we surely would have been observed. I thought to myself how lucky we were to be alive, but perhaps not lucky enough to live much longer. I had left the Armalite behind; I was carrying only my shotgun, which could be ineffective at thirty feet through the branches. Fortunately Prather had his M-3.

The snipers were sitting very quietly, like sharks waiting to pounce on bathers. Prather had seen them now. We looked at each other in distress. I could figure no way out of this. I put my face in my hands, searching for a solution that did not come. I looked back at Prather for encouragement, and he poked his tongue out. I could not imagine what the hell he was going on about. He started cutting his eyes from side to side while thrusting with his tongue at the same time. Finally I realized he was trying to point. I looked across the road, and the bushes were full of these guys waiting to hit us at ground level. The hair stood straight up on the back of my neck. My body flushed with heat.

I looked up again. The guys in the trees must have been observing the unit, because they were staring even more intently now. They would not shoot from this distance, because they wanted maximum coverage. They might hit one man, and the rest could disappear.

I could not count the men across the road, nor did I know if there were others in hiding elsewhere. Prather and I were finished, but we might save the others. I debated for a couple of minutes and finally decided to draw fire first from the men across the road and hope that it took the people above us some time to zero in. I was only asking for seconds.

I unclipped a grenade from my shirt, sure that the snipers would spot even that much movement. I showed it to Prather and pointed across the road. He took a grenade as well, and I shook my head and pointed my thumb up in the trees. I unhooked another grenade, but I honestly thought I would be dead before I could throw the second one.

The noise of the pin being withdrawn from the grenade seemed to echo through the forest. My mind was racing, my heart pounding. I jumped up and heaved the grenade across the road, then threw myself to the ground, grabbing up my shotgun as I rolled. Prather hit the trees with his AK-47 and brought down the man directly above us. My grenade exploded harmlessly in the middle of the road. A bullet slammed into my back. I saw Prather get hit at the same instant.

"In the trees!" I shouted as I went over backward.

I had not had seconds; I got half a second. One of the snipers must have seen me coming off the ground and fired on reflex, hitting both of us. Now there was firing everywhere. Somebody blew a second sniper out of the trees, and the third one lost his balance and fell out without being shot. I saw him come floating down as if in slow motion. He hit the ground on his feet about five yards from me. He must have broken his back. He was still going down when I biffed the second grenade just beyond him in a sidearm throw. Stones and dirt and shrapnel went everywhere and ripped the man's body apart, and a lot more of it slammed into my side like a sledge hammer.

I must have blacked out for a few seconds because the next thing I saw was Tan staring into my face, and I somehow knew it was only moments later. I rolled over and took a firing line facing the road. Our guys had just time enough to form up in the trees when the guys on the other side heaved a lot of grenades in our direction, and nine of them charged over the road with fixed bayonets. We brought three down in the open, then the rest were upon us. I missed one with the shotgun; after that they were too close to know who was doing what. We were in prone positions, firing almost straight up at men trying to shoot us and drive their bayonets through us at the same time. I hit the first one to me, but as I pumped the shotgun another was coming down on top of me. I blew his arm and half of his side away, and he went flying. A third reached me before I could react, and someone shot him off my back. I blew one guy off Tan with the shotgun, somehow without killing Tan as well. Just when it seemed the noise and killing would never cease, it stopped as suddenly as it had begun. We looked around, but there were no more targets to hit. Then I saw that Jackson was locked in a silent death struggle. Before anyone could reach him, he turned a bayonet away from his stomach and impaled his opponent through the chest. The man slumped over, his rifle hanging to him, six inches of blade thrusting out the back of his neck.

"Stay where you are!" I yelled out. "Watch the road!"

We were waiting for another rush. I shot the only man who was still flopping in the road. We lay without moving for two minutes, then slowly began to surface. I sounded off. Everyone responded. A quick look around told me that everyone was exhausted from the last charge. We needed time to put ourselves together, even if there were more of these guys about. Without a word, Morrosco and Wiley raced across the road, prepared to take on the world to give the rest of us a few minutes respite. I heard them sounding off every three or four seconds. In a minute, we knew we had killed them all. We started to crawl around and check each other out.

Prather was the worst hit. The bullet had entered in a downward angle by the left side of his neck and exited through the back of his left shoulder; the wound was remarkably similar to Tan's, but on the othr arm, and Prather had no broken bone. I was surprised to find Prather conscious. A wound like his usually brought on shock, but I was getting a continuing education in what a body could take. Tan went to work on Prather while Jackson looked me over.

The bullet had not hit me until it had gone through everything in my pack. It had ripped out the canvas bottom and scattered my belongings all over the jungle before tearing more or less harmlessly along my back. The grenade had done far more damage. I had caught a lot of shrapnel and was bleeding heavily from my torso. Jackson saw the condition of the pack and immediately thought I had been back-shot. He started cutting frantically at my pack straps.

"Piss off, Jackson," I said. "I'm all right!"

I tried to sit up, and keeled over. He tore my shirt up to the collar.

"Shut up, Kiwi," he said, "I'm in charge here."

There were a score of tiny metal shards in my side, plus one flat piece about the size of a penny match box which fortunately had hit me on the flat. I had a couple of cracked ribs, and my side felt as if glass splinters had been driven into it, but I was far more concerned about directing our defense than what had happened to me. I was waiting for another wave of these guys.

"These pieces have to come out," Jackson said, probing my side.

"For Christ's sake, no morphine!"

He accepted my plea. I could only survive another charge if I was not doped. He rolled me onto my back, and I tried to sit up again and could not. He took four pieces out of me with the point of his knife. I did not scream. I wanted to, but there was a sense of urgency here that did not allow me the luxury of succumbing to my pain.

Pain was not new to me. The first time I got hit had been bad. But after a year in combat, I had almost grown to disbelieve that my body could be immobilized. I remembered Toliver. Half his stomach had been hanging out, and he had marched into the mountains. If we had been under normal combat conditions with a helicopter eight minutes away, Toliver would have lived. A new boy would have died five times over. It was a matter of what you knew and what you wanted.

A GI—he was just a young kid—had taken a

grenade very near his body. His flak jacket had been ripped off his back, and his eyes were bleeding because of burst blood vessels.

The boy was crying, and we were gathered around him; a medic held him in his arms. We were trying to convince him that he was all right, just hang on, the choppers are on their way. The kid started going through this ritual of dying as the Church had taught him to do. He took a cross from around his neck and held it trembling in his hands, and he fumbled blindly in his shirt until he found a picture of his mother. He kissed the photo and asked for the last rites. And he died.

The medic started crying and he looked up and said, "When they die as easy as that, what can you do?" This kid became another statistic because he thought it was his time. He had come to Vietnam, and he knew he would not see home again. He should never have been sent off in the first place. Kids like that have lived such a sheltered existence—community, Church, family—they know nothing about survival. When a man is praying, he is dying.

This kid had the Church around his neck. He ripped it off, and it took him three minutes to die.

Tan came to assure me Prather was all right. The arm was useless, so Tan had stuffed the wound with wadding, strapped the arm to Prather's side to stop the bleeding, and shot it full of morphine. Morrosco bandaged my chest tightly, and I found my feet. We policed the area on the run.

The NVA were all dead. The battlefield looked like hell. People being shot at point-blank made a terrible sight. The bodies on the road were grotesque . . . limbs blown off . . . stomachs ripped open. . . .

We got another AK-47 off an officer and twenty magazines from his two carriers. The rest had been carrying a sort of Lee Enfield we did not bother with. Morrosco scanned the bag on the road; when he was satisfied it was not booby-trapped, he ripped it open. Nothing but personal effects. Jackson kicked one man out of his shirt and slipped it over his own torn one. In ration pouches we found rice, and hard sausage, and a soft doughy bread, a few large gritty sugar cubes like coconut fudge.

We counted twelve bodies. These men had belonged to a larger unit that could not be too far away. The others took Prather's gear and mine, and we ran. Prather was not used to carrying wounds. He was sweating from shock, but he refused to be carried; this was his way of overcoming the wound psychologically. But he was obviously in agony. I was in terrible pain myself now. This had been a hell of a fight. All fights were messy. But in ten minutes, there had been half a dozen occasions when we should have all been wiped out. It did not happen. All I could think was Jesus, why hadn't it happened?

It was almost night. We hit the trail for half an hour, left it for the river, then set out on a direct bearing for M Ngoi, ten miles away.

Though we had rested and rearmed there with impunity on mission-in, M Ngoi lay inside a Pathet Lao region only forty-five miles from North Vietnam. The village could have gone over to the Green Berets because the peasants favored the national government, or because they liked the money. Now there was little they could do about it. If they tried to turn over, the Green Berets would punish them. So would the Pathet Lao, for past transgressions. The villagers would do what they had to and keep very quiet. If a Pathet Lao unit walked in, they would get the same courteous treatment we had. The Green Berets would surface again when they left.

The Green Beret unit might be three men, or one. He would not sit there and operate a regional headquarters. He would live with the peasants. Take to the bushes when he had to. The Pathet Lao could ambush us ten miles away, and he might not know about it, nor they about him.

How safe was a safe village anyway? We might

arrange a pickup from M Ngoi; the pickup point could still be thirty miles away and fighting all the way. In another village, safety could mean being hidden or simply handed a sack of rice as we passed through. Or not being shot at. Or just ignored. Small mercies, that was all we were asking. We would not walk into any village, throw our gear down, and assume we had made it.

The ambush had put to rest any thoughts that we were being ignored by the enemy. At M Ngoi, word could go out to a few friends that we were alive. We were anxious to get there. We were sharp, but our bodies were slowing us down; it was near dawn before we closed on the village. We stopped to rest, and I sent Jackson and Wiley forward to observe. They were back in half an hour.

"The village looks safe enough," said Wiley.

"It looks safe, that's all I can say," said Jackson.

"What do you mean?"

"I don't like the feel of it."

"Be specific," I said.

"I can't. It's just too quiet . . . too perfect . . ."

"Everybody would be asleep now."

"I'm telling you, I don't like it."

"Well, like it or not, we've got to go in there. We need what that village can give us. We're in a fuck of a shape, Alvin. If nothing else, there's a radio in there somewhere."

We moved off slowly, with Jackson and Morrosco at point. We were no more than two hundred yards short of the village when all hell cut loose. Bullets whistled around us. I could not see where they were coming from. We scattered and went to ground.

"Where the hell are they?"

"Can anybody see them?"

The people doing the shooting were between us and the village. We had set off an ambush prematurely. There was a terrific amount of fire, but it was passing over us. I identified at least one, possibly two, Armalites. There were AK-47s, and other weapons. The firing died down, then stopped. We stayed under cover but moved close enough together to talk.

"Did anybody see anything?"

"How many?"

"At least six weapons," Tan said.

"Then you can bet your ass there's twenty of them."

Someone had fired too soon, and others had followed suit. But in any ambush, enough men would obey orders to hold their fire that I always counted two or three times as many guns as fired in the first salvo. We heard moving in the trees to our right quarter. They were trying to outflank us. Someone began shouting furiously in Laotian. Tan told me it was an officer dressing down the men who had fired. Then just shouting back and forth, covering one another as they moved, wondering where we were.

"Tribal mercenaries," Tan said.

"Tribal mercenaries!" I said angrily. "It's the villagers."

"The bastards have double-crossed us," said Jackson.

I was sure the villagers had set us up because the price on our heads had made it worth the risk. It was important to verify this, because if the villagers were being held by mercenaries, and we could free them, they would take our side. But if the village had turned over, we had no help from any quarter. I told everybody to stay together, that we were going to take the village, though I knew we were in no condition to be so bold. We were in such terrible shape that it seemed the only alternative, twenty men or no. M Ngoi was the one village in the region we could be sure had a radio. If we could not get a radio there, we had another two weeks' walk ahead of us, back to our starting point.

I suddenly realized that no properly co-ordinated drive was being made for us, because the enemy patrols we had been meeting were not carrying radios. We had been set up at M Ngoi not because of a radio message out of a military command post, but because news of our ambush on the road had traveled ahead of us. If a big price had been put on our heads, the mercenaries of M Ngoi would not have told anyone else we were on our way. They would have set out quietly to get us on their own. Ten thousand dollars a head could tempt any village to turn.

I remembered we had not found the village head we had expected at M Ngoi, nor any sign of Green Beret presence. There could be a hundred and one reasons for this, but they all led me to the conclusion that the villagers were directly involved in our ambush. My determination to get into M Ngoi was redoubled, if for nothing more than to clarify the situation. We had had a door slammed in our face, and I wanted to know who had done it. The villagers? A Pathet Lao unit? Mercenaries from elsewhere who held M Ngoi? The ambush party was still moving about noisily.

"They're confused about where we are," Tan said.

"Let's keep it that way," I said. "Move on out to left."

We lagged toward higher ground, overlapping one another, while they tried to flank us on our right. We moved across a firebreak and had just faded into the trees when their lead party exposed itself behind us. They had not seen us and came carelessly into the open, where we could see their bodies silhouetted against the sky.

"Get them," I shouted.

We wheeled and hit them as hard as we could. We brought down several within seconds, but we received heavy answering fire from the village. The din was deafening. With fire coming in from two directions, there was nothing to do but withdraw. We struck up the hill behind us, firing every step of the way. An hour passed, and we had covered only a few hundred yards. The gray light of dawn crept over the battle-field. We could never hold our position in daylight, so we leapfrogged into higher ground. Jackson and Morrosco helped Prather along. He had been firing his M-3 quite effectively with one hand by resting the barrel on a rock or a fallen tree. The pursuing party got slightly stretched, and when the trees thinned, we pinned some of them down. We pulled out of effective range. Our pursuers broke off the chase and turned into M Ngoi to join up with the people there, whom we had never seen. We were high above the village now and had good cover, but we were grossly outnumbered.

"We can't go into M Ngoi," I said. "Do you want to use your rockets on the place, Alvin?"

"Wouldn't do any good in the open. Don't worry, Kiwi. I'll find a use for them."

We kept moving higher, seeking cover, distance, time to figure our next move. Our route-in had been southwest of M Ngoi. Now we were moving almost due east. We would have to keep climbing until we were clear of our pursuit, then work our way back to our original route. We climbed for three hours, the last hour over open ground which would expose any party chasing us. Then we dug in. No one appeared behind us. I spotted a Pathet Lao unit route-marching up the river toward M Ngoi. M Ngoi was being strengthened. Someone had certainly expected us there.

"What weapons did you hear from the village?"

"Armalites and communist."

"Whoever is holding the village has access to American weapons. Which would have come from the Green Berets. The village has been exposed, or it has turned over. Either way, we're not going in there."

"What do we do?"

"We take our original route back toward the Mekong. A lot of people know about us. We expose ourselves to any friendlies, or go back to Thailand."

"You know," said Jackson, "we got a lot of briefing on the trip up. A whole bunch of intelligence about Ta shu tang. But they didn't tell us much about the trip back, did they? Just kind of 'Get to M Ngoi, boys, and everything'll be all right.' "

This was heard in silence. We knew that we had little to look forward to for a couple of weeks. We moved to the top of the hill and along the ridge, striking due south to follow a valley that paralleled our route-in. The ridge rose to four thousand feet; we had a clear view back to our route-in. We knew the lay of the land, so we knew what we were observing. As we continued south along the ridge, we saw several Pathet Lao units going north up the valley floor to intercept us. They had underestimated our speed and the height to which we climbed, but their presence prevented us crossing the valley and rejoining our old route. They obviously knew our route-in. The villagers at M Ngoi could have told them, or we might have been seen by enough peasants whom we had not seen to chart our route-in pretty accurately. The ridge we were following swung eastward, turning us away from familiar ground. We had no choice but to head for the Nam Suong and use it to get back to the south-west.

The unit was in an ugly mood. Our progress was slow. Prather was in great pain, and my wounds had opened in the scramble out of M Ngoi. Morrosco was clearly worried about Prather, but he was fighting an instinct to get emotionally involved as he had with Toliver. As a consequence, he was almost brusque with the older man. With every passing day, Morrosco was becoming more the youngest brother in the family. We all recognized it; he recognized it, and he resented it. Wiley was growing up in a hurry. Things were no longer so unpredictable to him. His bravery went without question, but now he was more self-reliant, perhaps a little less concerned about his own safety.

Even with the fresh wounds, we were by no means as washed out emotionally as we had been coming out of the swamps. We had pulled off two drastic pieces of action, and we were almost matter-of-fact about what had to be done. We were a long way from safety, but we no longer felt that anvil about our necks of being in China or North Vietnam. We knew how to look out for ourselves. And we might run into help at any time.

Physically we were weak. Particularly Prather, from delayed shock and loss of blood. We all depended on Benzedrine to keep us going, and we all knew it was a luxury we would have to pay for. We had to get back to our route-in at any expense, because if our high command knew we had survived, that was where they would look for us, assuming they wanted to. We were far north for helicopters, but they could send Green Berets or even mercenaries to pick us up.

We spent a day walking the ridge before starting down to join the Nam Suong. It was not hard going, and we talked nonstop. We were all confused, not knowing what to believe, too excited to analyze with any logic the events of the past few days. The feelings of betrayal we had shared in China were resurfacing; movement against us that had once appeared unpredictable we could see going on all around us now in a very organized, methodical manner. Events began to seem more sharply defined and cut to a preordained pattern. But how had the situation come to exist? We refused to blame ourselves. We felt we had done pretty well so far. Who was to blame? The people who had put us there? What was their motive? Would they give us any help?

At the end of the day, we dropped down into the valley, onto a rich grassy plain that spread out from both banks of the river. We reached the Suong at midnight and struck camp. We would intercept our outbound route at dawn.

I was feeling pretty sorry for myself. The wounds in my side and back were painful and growing infected. Prather was willing to keep going, but we both desperately needed rest. Everyone was tired from the pace we had been making. Tan had begun to use his shattered arm under pressure of combat, and this had allowed him to break through the pain barrier; he now started to move the arm about a bit, though it was a terrible mess. I told Jackson to organize a four-hour break; because of our condition, Prather and I would stand no guard duty. Jackson and Wiley took first detail. When I fell asleep, Tan and Morrosco were having an idle chat.

I seemed to have been asleep about five minutes when the sound of firing jolted me awake. Incoming and outgoing. Jackson and Wiley were firing at targets I had not yet spotted. We hurried into our gear, strapping on packs and kits while trying to fire. By the time we had scrambled into a defensive position, I was beginning to sort things out.

"Sound off!" I shouted.

Everyone responded.

"How many?"

"Twenty. Twenty-five NVA." It was Jackson. "They're trying to sweep us on the flank. Pin us against the river."

They must have seen us strike camp and waited until we were quiet. But Jackson had spotted them. They were quickly closing our flank; we had to move or get pinned in. We could never survive hand-to-hand combat with these numbers. They had to move across open ground to sweep us. I waited until their flank was slightly stretched, then we hit them hard. We brought down several.

"Tan, Prather," I shouted. "Make for the high ground."

They took off, and the rest of us spread our flanks to fight a withdrawal. I gave them four minutes, then we moved out behind them. We went into low shrub where we could not be outflanked because it was bordered on both sides by open ground.

When I grabbed at my shirt for a fresh clip for the Armalite, I discovered I had only two left. The others must have been as short of ammunition as I was. We kept our pursuers off with sparing fire and fought an orderly withdrawal. It became a race for high ground. If they got above us, we were finished. They were moving in three parties in a semicircle behind us now. We were bringing people down, and we had not been hit, and suddenly I saw that we had stretched their right flank.

"Hit the guys on the left," I hollered.

We pivoted left. This drew their stretched flank even closer to us and put them on the double. They were convinced they were overtaking us. They broke into a run, strung out along the hill behind us. We led them onto a patch of low vegetation. We dropped off Jackson and Wiley and they went to ground. We kept going until our pursuers were clear of the tree line, then we turned into them. They thought we were making a last stand and charged right at us. We caught them in a crossfire and wiped out all nine of them in ten minutes. Then we pivoted right and drove the other two parties back into the trees.

They would regroup and try to sweep us, but we had four minutes to breathe. We stripped the bodies of everything we could carry, then turned back east again and ran up the nearest slope. When we crested the first hill, I looked behind us. The NVA were in hot pursuit in a chase to which I saw no end. They had stopped firing now to climb more swiftly. It was hopeless trying to outrun them.

"We've got to take cover," I said.

We scrambled uphill until we found some rocks that were the only cover for several hundred yards. The NVA moved in below and began to harass us. They tried a frontal rush, hurling grenades, but they were throwing uphill, and we drove them back.

There was sporadic firing for an hour, then they let off a sustained burst for a couple of minutes. The firing stopped. For five minutes we waited anxiously. Then three men jumped up off the ground less than a hundred feet below us. They nearly overran us; we killed the last man as he breached our defensive circle. They tried the same trick twice more, but we drove them off.

Their officer was using his men quite effectively. I could not see us holding out after daylight. At first light we broke for the east and kept climbing. If we ever came back down, we would have to strike for another river that paralleled the Suong.

The NVA followed us over the crest of a hill and down into the next valley. They tried to flank us; Wiley and Jackson moved into them off our flank, firing from the hip and throwing grenades. They managed to kill several of them. I was surprised to see how deadly effective we still were. Not one of us was playing the numbers game with automatic fire. We were taking out individual targets. We were rapidly diminishing their numbers and had not been hit ourselves except for a stone splinter or two.

We played cat and mouse all morning, until we ran up against a river. The river was shallow, its bed flat, with a wide expanse of open ground between banks. The NVA were three minutes behind us, in the trees just out of firing range. Tan, Prather, and Wiley sprinted across first; the rest of us followed in a body. We had just reached the trees when I heard the NVA burst out on the far bank. They were gaining on us rapidly. We had to fade out in the forest. I turned to look behind me and immediately changed my mind. These guys were being led by a major who was really determined to get us. He was shouting and waving his arms and counting us dead. But they were growing careless; they were spread out all through the trees, appearing singly by the river. There were still about fifteen in all.

"Hit the ground," I called out. "Keep it quiet."

Tan and Jackson crawled over close enough to converse with me.

"They think we're still running," Tan said.

"Jackson," I said, "take out the major as soon as he goes into the river."

The major was getting excited as the kill approached. He lined his men up on the riverbank, then could not make up his mind how to send them across. Finally he ordered them to charge over in a bunch. They broke out across the shingles, practically running over each other. To my dismay, the major and two aides stayed on the far bank. Jackson held his fire. I kept watching for the major to fall. The guys were practically on top of us before I realized that Jackson was not going to shoot him.

"Grenades," I shouted.

Grenades landed everywhere among them. The explosions knocked them all down, but half jumped up and kept coming. The major started screaming, driving the men on. His aides charged into the river behind the others. I jumped to my feet and fired at the major with an open sight, and I saw what Toliver's adapted weapon could do. The bullet hit the major in the chest and just ripped him open, tore his body apart, and killed him instantly.

I pivoted and took out an aide. There was firing everywhere. The grenades that had gone off on the shingles had stripped flesh right off the bones. But half of them had landed in the water and been muffled. The men who had survived were on top of us now. I stood up, and they ran right past me into hand-to-hand combat with the others. One man broke for Prather, who was sitting up with his M-3 propped between his knees. Prather drilled him full of holes.

I kept my weapon trained on the opposite shore while trying to watch the fighting around me. I feared the major had been waiting for more men to arrive, so my eyes were darting all over the place while I covered our rear. I saw Jackson lose his weapon, then take one away from another man and shoot him with it. People were screaming everywhere. Wiley and Morrosco were fighting with their knives. I tried to draw a bead on the NVA setting into them, but these guys killed them with their knives before I had time to fire. One bloke hit Jackson under the eye with the point of his rifle barrel, then Morrosco killed him with a knife thrust into the kidney.

They were all dead. We were near collapse. We had been in a running fire fight for a night and a day which ended in hand-to-hand combat; it had almost been too much for us.

Jackson's face swelled immediately. When Morrosco tried to probe it for fractures, Jackson screamed so loudly we had to leave it. We were all torn and bleeding from the running, and the men who had been fighting with their hands looked like they had been dragged across a road on their faces. We had to finish off several guys in the river, and we were too tired to run down there. One had ducked under water when the grenades started flying. His brains had been scrambled. He was bleeding from every possible direction. I put a bullet into him and strolled over to the major. I had hit him just above the belt buckle, a much better shot than I could have hoped for. He and his aides wore a blue shoulder flash which I assumed meant they were some sort of special troops. These guys were carrying field rations, so we got little food but lots of ammunition for the AK-47s and some stick grenades.

We could not use the river now. We had to go back to high ground. We threw caution to the winds and took off up a trail. We had not gone a mile before we spotted another NVA unit of fifteen men moving right at us. We ambushed them and killed nine, but six fled back up the path. We stopped to gather ammunition. There was a soft crump, and I was nearly blown off my feet by an explosion a hundred feet behind us.

"They've got a mortar!"

"Up the hill!"

We could not go after these guys because we did not know how many we would find. We struck out through the undergrowth. Again we were being forced in a southeasterly direction, away from our old route. I was confused about our exact location; we were some-where near Ban Houay Ket, but we saw no sign of the village. We climbed higher to look about.

"There they are," Prather shouted, pointing behind us.

This was not the sort of party we had encountered;

this was one hell of a bunch of NVA moving up the track where we had the mortars thrown at us. Forty or fifty men. I panicked. Jesus, I thought, there is just no way out of this. We had to keep moving because in ten minutes they should find our last action. A few might stop there, but the rest would keep after us. These guys looked very sharp. The officer in charge was debriefing his NCOs on the move; they were practically jogging, but very cautiously, and covering a tremendous amount of ground. Our only chance was to get over the hill, down the far side, across the road and river before they spotted us. They were only a couple of miles behind us.

We sprinted up the hill and tumbled down the far side, gasping and spewing with exhaustion. We reached the river and cut it quickly, but there was no decent cover on the far side, so we had to keep going. We swept southwest of the village of Ban Hap Khouang and headed up a steep slope. We climbed a firebreak to the top of a mountain. We jogged up this thing until our lungs were bursting.

Prather, Tan, and Wiley were moving like zombies. Wiley stopped to rest, then slumped to his knees. I kicked him and jerked him by his shirt to his feet.

"You son-of-a-bitch," Prather said. "I'll get you for that."

"Shut up, Prather, and keep running," I said.

I had never seen such hatred in men's faces, but if we stopped, we would not move again. I drove them on. We had been running and fighting for three days; only the mechanical functioning of our bodies kept us moving. At the top of the mountain, we pulled off the firebreak into the trees. The main body of NVA was moving off from our last action toward the north. They were still looking for us toward our original route. They had lost us again.

We crested the mountain and looked down into a gentle valley, with a trail leading downhill from where we stood. It was tempting to take the trail, but it led toward rugged lowland in the distance. I wanted to get as fast as possible into even higher ground, where we could stop and consider our next course of action. We pushed off through heavy brush for two miles, then crossed a stream. We climbed fifteen hundred feet straight up the side of a hill; when we reached the summit, we had a view of the entire countryside. It was well past midnight when we lay down beneath the undergrowth. And faded out.

CHAPTER 16

I was the first to come around. It was midday, though whether the next day or the following I did not know. I had lost all track of time. How far were we out of China? Twelve days? Fifteen? Only night and day counted for us now.

I looked around, and despair hit my innards like a knife. The others were scattered like dead bodies through the grass. Half had fallen asleep before they could strip their packs off. I was trembling. It took me a moment to realize I was soaked through. We had slept without waking through a heavy rain. I was desperately cold for the first time on the mission, and I was too tired to do anything about it. I sat and stared at the others for a long time. They had nothing more to give.

I walked out a few yards to a spot where I could observe the countryside. I saw the river we had chosen not to use. I followed its course as it bent south into a wide, inviting valley that led where we wanted to go.

Ahead I saw a trail that would carry us to the Nam Khan, and I saw the rugged chain of hills that lay between us and the river. We were not far east of the Plain of Jarres. That was violent country that I knew well. I was trying to contemplate our situation, my mind still cloudy with sleep, when Jackson joined me.

He sat silently beside me while I studied our maps. They were not greatly detailed here, because we were far adrift of our original route, but they showed the lay of the land. Enough for a good soldier to spot the danger points. I was still hoping to get south of Luang Prabang. Somewhere between there and Vientiane we must run into an American unit. I told Jackosn of my intentions.

"Forget that, Gayle. Looky here."

The valley behind us, where ten minutes before I had seen nothing, was swarming with Pathet Lao troops. A couple of hundred men were spread out on our side of the river, sweeping toward the base of the mountain we were sitting on. They were within four hours of closing.

As much as I wanted to think otherwise, they had to be looking for us. The Pathet Lao worked in small guerrilla groups; here they were being used quite openly like regular soldiers, sweeping the valley in a carefully co-ordinated way. Somebody was putting a lot of importance on us. I thought about the units we had wiped out. They may have thought we were a much larger party.

There was only one way for us to go. East. If we could not get down to the Nam Khan—and I expected it to be obstructed—we would have to cross the mountains. This would take us so far east of our original route that for the first time I thought about finding another entrance into Thailand. I studied the map for twenty minutes. We would go south by southeast to Borikhan, a major communications center just north of the Mekong, then pick up a highway a few miles from there and follow it to Muong Poxan on the Mekong. We would steal a boat and paddle to safety in Thailand.

This meant pushing off into unknown territory, abandoning all our plans, forgetting everything we had been fighting for in recent days. But when I made the suggestion, Jackson accepted it with equanimity.

"We got no choice anyhow," he said. "We're the target of a search and destroy mission now. That means our high command can pin us on a map. A movement that large," he said, pointing back down the valley, "don't go unnoticed."

Jackson woke the others. We had a quick council of war and adopted alternatives. We would head for the Nam Khan. If we reached it, we would strike southwest again and try to find an American unit. If the river was obstructed, we would turn east, cross the mountains, then take the Nam Ngiap on to the plains and head for Borikhan.

We broke camp slowly. We had the privilege of knowing how far our pursuers were behind us and where we were going. We were making for the south side of a forty-eight-hundred-foot peak which would carry us safely past the village of Houay Ket. We had to avoid being seen. Any village in the region would be sympathetic to the Pathet Lao; we knew that by the open way they were using the trails. We were moving into high ground by early evening. Farther east, mountains rolled ever grander into the distance. We felt a certain sense of protection because of the elevation and the open landscape. American units had been operating east and south of here, around Men Kuong. As a last resort, we could head there.

We reached the Nam Hang and its junction with the Nam Khan before midnight. The Khan was a clean, swift-running river. We found a campsite a short distance from the river and broke for the night.

There was no urgency now. No deadline. We had no reason to push hard, because we had left our pursuers behind. We just had to make it back. We decided to break our pace a little.

We drank our first good water for days, fresh and clean. It had a fantastic effect on the mind and body. Water suddenly became a very thick and nourishing substance. I drank what seemed like gallons.

I took off my boots and soaked my feet in the rushing stream. It was like no other luxury. The rest joined me. We stripped off our shirts and waded into the water. We beat our shirts against the boulders and rubbed them with sand, washing out two weeks of accumulated dirt and blood and sweat and scabs. We took turns washing one another's wounds. Our bodies were torn and swollen, and we were gentle.

Tan and Morrosco speared some river crustacea with their knives, while Jackson built a small fire in a sheltered area. They returned with their catch, and Wiley cooked us our first hot meal in days. We knocked together some simple shelters, then sat down to dress our wounds.

Prather was in far better shape than I had expected. His wound opened constantly as the bandages moved around, and it had been infected. The infection was subsiding now, the swelling going down. Morrosco dressed the wounds carefully with liniment.

Tan was healing well. The bleeding had stopped days before, though the pain lingered. But Tan bore his pain in silence.

I was in better shape than I deserved. I had been pretty messed over, because I had been bleeding and sweating and fighting the jungle and a blazing sun and going without medicine or enough to eat. But I was doing all right. We all were.

"Things are not so bad, Kiwi," Wiley said.

That was the first positive statement from him for days. We were all feeling good about the way things were going. A break like this—we had had extensive rest for two days now—sharpened everyone. We were showing more patience with ourselves and with each other. We could think a bit more clearly. We chatted around the campfire, looked after our weapons, re-distributed the load.

"Hey," Morrosco remarked, "we're talking in normal voices."

It was true. I could count on my fingers the times we had been able to speak openly. For a month we had almost never exchanged words at an audible level. We had been in hiding, or too exhausted.

By now we had grown used to the idea that we were forever blown off course. We had two goals: survive and reach friends. This was what we were trained for. We would go about it very methodically, with far more experience than the people we might run up against. I could see the entire unit regaining its equilibrium simply because we were not being chewed up by fatigue and mental exhaustion. Now was the time for us to call on our endurance. We had that in abundance. Endurance alone had kept me alive before.

It was late in the day. I was walking an old VC supply trail, abandoned months earlier because of heavy bombing. Cramps hit my bowels like a pitchfork; I had been plagued with dysentery for days. I stepped into the bush and squatted. As I stood to button my fatigues, twenty VC came around a corner in the trail, pushing bikes loaded with mortars and ammunition. I ducked back down before they saw me, balancing on the balls of my feet. I slid my shotgun up between my legs and primed myself for combat. I kept very quiet. This is it, I thought. But I was not going out in a blaze of glory if I could help it.

They spread out and decided to make camp right there all around me. One guy was no more than four feet away. I could not change the position of my feet. I could not exhale loudly. Within half an hour my legs were cramping. So I began the mental therapy that is what endurance is all about, the wiping out of the concept of time.

I started to withdraw. It was the only hope I had

of staying alive. I cut my body off from the waist down. I forgot it was there. I had to stay alert without allowing the bottom half of my body to function in my thinking. I followed the hands of my watch. I played counting games. I composed math problems that were difficult on paper and tried to work them in my head. I thought of everything I could that was detached from human emotion. No memories. No dreams. No reflections. Nor could I let patience or boredom impose themselves upon my will. They might have impaired my judgment, taken the razor's edge off my readiness.

It was the next day before they left. I waited half an hour, then fell over on my side. I had been squatting for twenty-three hours and thirty-two minutes. My body was blue from lack of blood. I unpeeled muscles for the next five hours, screaming the entire time. I could not throw morphine into myself, because I would have been too fucked to fight if more of these guys came along. Straightening the knees was the worst: absolute agony. And the calf muscles. It was worth all the pain. I did not die.

"You took us through a bad stretch, Kiwi," said Jackson.

"I hope next week is better than last."

"You're a hard man to climb a mountain with, mate," Wiley said.

That was their way of apologizing. We had all had to reject the state our minds and bodies had been in, otherwise we could not have stood it. Rejection needs a target, and I had been the handiest. It was as simple as that. But I needed no apologies. Their hatred had been nothing more than a mental notation for me. It was anger and temperament driving men on. I did not care how they felt about me. I had enough personal problems to make what they thought immaterial. Our predicament was my real concern. We were all preoccupied with it. There was a long conversation around the campfire, a lot of speculation about China, about the past few days, about what lay ahead.

"What I still can't make out," I said, "is what exactly happened at M Ngoi. Who set us up? Who was in the village? Damn it, if we knew that, we'd know what's happening now."

"I can't honestly say we were up against more than Pathet Lao and NVA regulars," said Morrosco.

"Those were tribal mercenaries at M Ngoi," said Tan. "Believe me."

"Even so," said Jackson, "they must have been working for the NVA. They could have obstructed our people from reaching us."

We were all hanging on to the hope that friends somewhere were trying to reach us.

"The village may not have turned," I said. "If there is enough head money on us, those mercenaries could have come halfway across the country after us. But that doesn't change the craziness of what we were sent to China for. It's that that makes me worry."

"It was the best move of the war," said Tan. "We should have done it. I know we should."

"You didn't think it crazy when we set out," said Prather. "It was a damned fine strategic stroke, if we'd carried it off. We're the ones who've messed it about and made it look crazy. Made it so ugly."

Prather was thinking about the children. It had remained a constant torment for him; he had been having nightmares about it, tossing and calling out in his sleep.

"We didn't make it ugly, Lew. Don't blame yourself. And as far as I'm concerned, it was absolute madness from the start, whether we recognized it or not. You can't prevent a war by killing the enemy high command. You can only start one. The question is, who are the crazies who sent us in? And what was their mandate? If we knew that, we might know what kind of support to expect."

"I don't see support coming our way from any quarter," Morrosco said. "If it was an unauthorized mission that got found out about, then they'd be happy not to see us again. And if it was authorized, I figure we're damned if they did, and damned if they didn't."

"I can't believe a word of that," Jackson said, "but one thing's for sure. If we're being set up, they can't let the troops in the field find out. That they're hitting Americans. So we can just walk into any unit in the field, and they'll take us in."

Because of my wounds my rest was still a priority. Jackson adopted a secondary command role and detailed Morrosco, Wiley, and himself to stand guard. We doused the fire and went to sleep.

I woke up with a hand across my mouth. I grabbed for my knife, and another hand pinned my arm against my body. I saw Morrosco's face in mine. He did not need to signal me to stay silent. I heard moving in the trees all around us. Morrosco left me and crawled toward Wiley. I woke Jackson beside me, and he woke Tan. We lay where we had awakened.

A Pathet Lao party was walking right through us. They were looking for us; I heard no more than the swish of fatigue trousers. The occasional clink of metal, bushes pushed aside, whispered commands. We abandoned half our gear, grabbing only what was in reach, and crawled out to the river. Jackson killed one man, trapping his body with his legs while he flopped and thrashed in the agonies of death. We fought the icy currents of the swift river for fifteen minutes, with Jackson pulling Prather behind him, before collapsing on the far bank. We crawled until dawn dodging people at every turn, covering a hundred yards an hour. When the sun rose, we saw that we were clear. We kept climbing as morning pursued us.

We reached a major river and moved a mile along the bank, then cut overland when the river meandered to the east. We rejoined the river on lower terrain and made good time walking the shingles. When a hill jutted sharply up beside us, the others lay low, and Morrosco and I climbed it for half an hour to get a look around. A mile to our northeast the river we had been walking was joined by a second major river. I got out the maps. Morrosco studied them over my shoulder.

"I make that to be the junction of the Nam Hang and the Nam Khan," I said.

"You're wrong. It's the Nam Hang and the Nam Khao. The Nam Khan should be just west of here, over there." I looked where Morrosco was pointing. My breath caught in my throat. The Nam Khan Valley was swarming with troops spread out for miles along the riverbank, beating through the underbrush. Traveling fast. And north. Where we had come from.

Twice they had stretched a net to catch us. Twice we had been a day ahead of them. The country was being swept by an army steadily moving away from its prey. Morrosco laughed. He put his hand in his fatigues, drew out an imaginary object, kissed it, and returned it to his pocket.

"My rabbit's foot," he said. "Christ, we're lucky."

"So they're behind us. Who knows who's ahead of us?" Morrosco's superstition annoyed me. "We can't use the river. Go fetch the others. I'll wait for you here."

I was alone for the first time since we had departed. I did not waste the opportunity for uninterrupted thinking; I started analyzing, problem-solving, reflecting, projecting. I wished we had brought a silencer for the Armalite. With the night sight, we could have sniped our way out a lot faster the previous night. Then I realized I had not even used the night sight. Tan had it in his pack. I did not usually overlook such opportunities. I stored it in my mind to take the sight off Tan.

Our alternatives were rapidly being reduced. The Khan was cut off to us now. We had to strike south, stay east of a great mountain called Pau Sa along the eastern edge of Plain of Jarres, cross Highway 7, and keep moving in a southeasterly direction toward Borikhan.

An hour passed. I watched the unit struggle up the

hill toward me. I was appalled. They looked not so much physically whipped as damaged. Like animals crawling off to die. The wounds were only a part of it. Swollen glands in Wiley's neck and throat had twisted his features grotesquely. Morrosco and Jackson had been racked by dysentery for several days; their eyes were blood-red, and they clutched their abdomens when the cramps struck. The tension had given Prather a violent migraine headache. I saw him stop and squeeze his temples with both hands until it seemed he would crush his skull. Wiley's hands were trembling, and the left side of Morrosco's face drew up continually. I noticed for the first time a tic in my own neck; I drew my head sharply, then shook it every few seconds.

Body decay preceded decay in morale. I resolved to restore some self-respect, some vestige of interest in our bodies. The men were too beaten to force anything more upon them, but I could maintain my own body as an example to the others. I rummaged through the remainder of my rations for a packet of salt. When they arrived, I was rubbing it on my teeth with the end of a split twig.

"That will stop some decay," I said.

I cleaned my fingernails with the point of my knife, then shook my canteen. Corroded bits of metal rattled about in the water.

"I'm cleaning that in the next sandy river," I said, "and this uniform."

We moved into the highlands just west of Highway 6, which we could see in the distance carrying a lot of military traffic. We stayed well clear, for fear of running into NVA units. We were not many miles off the North Vietnamese border.

We were also watching for mercenaries. The Plain of Jarres had known horrific struggles through the years; we saw the tracks of great tank battles and earth seared by napalm. The civilians had no loyalties here. While they had survived, and the ground was still fertile, they cultivated rice in great paddies that fanned out over the undulating landscape. And they fought for anyone who paid and provided arms. If we ran into a unit working for the Green Berets, we were home free. They would have the backup to get us out. I just prayed we would not be hit by mercenaries carrying American arms. That would be soul-destroying for men who were already having doubts about the cause of their present predicament.

We moved along the edge of the plain, sometimes in dense undergrowth, sometimes in open country. We moved down a river, then picked up a track that passed between Bouan Long and Highway 6. We passed another hamlet that appeared deserted. We took the path out of it to make some quick time. The path, along the side of a mountain, was a genuine luxury: cover above, cover from below, a flat surface, a good view of the valley. Jackson fell back a quarter of a mile and followed us walking backward. Tan, at point, made a good pace, and we quickly covered four miles. The path took us to the base of Pau Sa. In the waning light, we saw activity toward Highway 6, so we pushed out across Pau Sa as night closed in. We were east of the mountain by midnight. We rested briefly. I decided to push on through the night, to be down to Highway 7 by the following night.

The moon came out of the clouds as we pushed out south across a vast slope. It was a fantastic sight; this great mountain washed in moonlight, an empty landscape that seemed to stretch forever about us. The whole world was hundreds of thousands of miles below us. The night wind blew. The peak of Pau Sa shot up out of nowhere and hung four thousand feet above us. I lost track of where we were. My mind drifted to other places, other times. I thought of hunting with my older brother in the mountains of New Zealand. I was a boy again, not a soldier with two months of self-destructive combat behind me.

"If we ever get out of this, Kiwi," Prather said, dropping back to walk with me, "I want you to come to stay with me on the farm in Devon. We'll hunt pheasant and fish for trout. I've a mile of chalk stream that's some of the best fishing in the west country."

"I'd like that, Lew."

"I want a second bite at life."

The trio talked about women they had known. Wiley had fallen in love too many times to count, and Morrosco and Jackson had both experienced an early turnover in their lives. They had become involved with a woman when very young. They had married, and it had fallen apart. I felt similar in a way. I had met a girl I cared for, but I had a pretty wild youth, and it had not worked. For weeks now there had been nothing more than the moment to live for. Then suddenly, walking along together, we were thinking idiotic things, like Prather's second bite at life.

We came down into a heavily scarred valley pocked with bomb craters, the earth scorched from napalm. We reached Highway 7 by midafternoon. This was the biggest road we had seen on the mission: tar-sealed, wide as a dual carriageway. We paralleled the road until dark, skirting well clear of the outposts. We crossed without incident and struck out on a southerly course across the highlands.

We were feeling pretty good. Our wounds were holding steady, and morale was high. As we moved unhindered, I asked myself if we were being observed, if someone was reserving the right to pluck at us farther down the line. We crested a ridge. Morrosco was the first to spot them. Laotian nationalist troops moving in the valley ahead of us. He let out a whoop.

"We've made it!"

CHAPTER 17

I was still cautious.

"Let's make sure who they are. Are we all agreed they're nationalists? Friendlies?"

Everyone nodded.

"Tan?"

"They can't be anything else. Their vehicles are American. Look at the way the troops are dispersing."

"Could they be mercenaries in nationalist uniforms?"

"Never. Not moving that confidently."

"Let's get down to them."

"They're moving away from us!"

"We can cut down to the low ground and intercept them on Highway Forty-two."

We had to negotiate several steep hills and a small river; it took two hours to cover the five miles to the highway. The highway was quiet when we arrived. The others stayed in the trees while Jackson and I went forward. We went out on the side of the road about a hundred yards apart and started walking in the direction of the troops we had seen. Suddenly five open lorries with troops in the rear appeared around a curve behind us. Jackson turned, then waved and shouted frantically at them. To my astonishment, the lorries roared into low gear and sped past Jackson. He ran into the middle of the road and waved both arms over his head.

"Government troops!" he shouted. "Stop them!"

I stepped to the middle of the road and tried to wave the lorries to a halt, but they swerved past me and disappeared around the next bend. As soon as they were out of sight, I heard the lorries grind to a halt. Jackson ran to me.

"What on earth are they playing at?"

"I don't know. But I don't like it. Stay where you are," I shouted to the others.

Jackson and I ran down the road and ducked into the trees at the bend, then moved forward cautiously to take a look. Two lorries were pulling off in the direction they had been going. The other three were reversing on the road. Belts were being passed up to load machine guns on two of them, and all the troops were piling into the third vehicle. We stared amazed at what we were seeing.

"What the hell is going on?"

"I really don't have a clue, Alvin. I don't know. But we're not approaching those people."

"Maybe they just want to identify us positively as American troops."

"What do you think we look like, Eskimos?"

"I want to risk it."

"We're not exposing ourselves to these people. That's an order."

"Order's ass. This is a chance to get out of here."

"These people are out to shoot us. Go back to the others. I'll follow."

"What are you going to do?"

"I don't know."

I had to play safe. There was no exposing ourselves to these people, then running if they proved hostile. They were too many. And they had not jumped for joy when they saw us. Usually these guys hero-worshiped special forces.

"Get across the road," I shouted to the unit. "Quick!" I ran to join them.

We had just taken cover when two more vehicles came past and went around the bend. I positively identified them as government vehicles. We heard them stop.

"What's happening?" Morrosco asked.

I explained quickly.

"What are you going to do, Gayle?" Prather asked. "This may be our big break."

"I guess it's now or never. I'll expose myself."

I walked back toward the edge of the road. Just as I started to step out of the trees, two lorries came very slowly back around the bend. Troops stood shoulder to shoulder in the rear, rifles at the ready, searching the bush for us. Roof-mounted machine guns were sniffing for targets. My mind was whirling. I could not think of any sensible action, so I went to ground. They went past me, reversed, and cruised back again. And stopped opposite me. I lay without breathing while the drivers talked between the cabs. To my horror, Jackson and then Morrosco crawled up alongside me.

"What the fuck is all this about?" Jackson asked.

"Just look for yourself."

At that moment, another vehicle with a mounted machine gun came in sight. It cruised very close to the edge of the road, barely creeping along. The machine gunner and loader were darting their eyes all over the place. There was no way they could have held off on the gun if they had seen movement.

"I'll chance it anyway," Jackson said.

"You're not getting us all killed," I said.

He and I were arguing bitterly beneath our breaths when Tan joined us.

"These guys are after us," he said. "They're going to blow us away if we surface."

"If they're after us, then why aren't they combing the trees?"

"Maybe they want us to come out on the road. They'll kill us and leave us there. Then anybody can be blamed for it."

"Bullshit," said Jackson.

I exploded with rage.

"That's it. We're leaving. No more argument."

We faded back into the trees and gained high ground where we could see the road. The lorries cruised up and down for an hour. They were joined by a jeep. After some discussion, two of the lorries continued to cruise, and the rest drove off to the south. To cut us off, I presumed. I said nothing to the others, because it was an interpretation I feared would lead to a violent and unpredictable reaction in the unit. I was questioning everything now, even my own sanity. If I could not recognize these people as friends . . .

We moved out on the high ground, from which we could watch the road below. We reached a river that we knew had to pass under the road somewhere. We moved into the river. By midafternoon we spotted a bridge that carried the road across. My heart sank.

Sitting in the middle of the bridge were two canvas-topped lorries similar to the ones we had seen. Machine guns crowned the two cabs, one facing in each direction to sweep both riverbanks and the bridge approaches. There were a loader and a gunner on each gun, and one rifleman stood down on the bridge. I was sure these people were waiting for us; by now we felt the focus of every movement in the entire region, even as we approached safer terrain. We were only a few days from the Mekong, a couple of days from areas of intense American activity. We were very close to slipping through our pursuers' fingers. There was a good argument to be made that they were communist troops, Pathet Lao in government uniforms.

The unit was badly split over the question. Tan supported my instinctive fear of these people, regardless of who they were. Jackson was convinced communist troops would never move up and down the road so boldly. He thought Tan and I were being paranoid. He kept an open mind about a doublecross, but he was all for finding out one way or the other. Morrosco rallied to Jackson's side. Prather was in the worst shape of all, mentally and physically. He had reached the point where he just wanted the whole thing to end. His attitude was what the hell, old boy, we're not going anywhere anyway. We might as well get it here as the next spot. Wiley disturbed me even more than Prather. He simply would not talk. He was cutting himself off from the environment, even from us. I tried but failed to draw him into the conversation. I made a note to watch him.

Fully expecting it to create loss among us, I decided we would expose ourselves. If these people were friendly, we would never match this opportunity to cross back over. We would wait until almost dark, then impose ourselves upon them. The men on the bridge were growing careless; they looked to have been on duty a long time and were getting bored. There was a general milling around, smoking of cigarettes.

Two hours later, they were joined by two jeeps carrying six men and an officer. They conversed for a while, confidently, very casually; I began to doubt that they could be communists. The guard changed over; six stayed behind; the others departed in the jeep. My combat instinct told me there was no military presence either side of the bridge; the officer made no attempt to contact any party farther along, and when they left, we heard their vehicles drive without stopping until they were out of earshot.

When the sun at last fell behind a distant hill, I took Tan and Jackson forward to reconnoiter before we made our move.

"It's wrong," Tan said flatly. "Those guys are looking for us. I don't care if they are communists or nationalists or what. I can just tell you they are waiting for somebody. And as far as I'm concerned, we're the only people in the area worth waiting for."

"Let's see what they have to say," I told him.

"Look," Jackson spoke up, "they've got government uniforms. American trucks. Those are our boys. I know damn well they are." His voice rang with the irritation he was beginning to feel toward Tan.

We slipped into the water a hundred yards upstream and climbed out on the bank directly beneath the bridge. Every footfall from above was amplified on the heavy wooden planking that surfaced the stone structure. We listened for five minutes, but the guards were standing forty feet away in the middle of the bridge, and Tan could not make out what they were saying. I thought I heard the word "American" more than once.

"Climb up under the bridge and see if you can hear what they are saying," I whispered to Tan.

Tan swung a leg over the wooden beam and began inching his way out with great difficulty, pulling himself along with his one good arm. He sat on a beam directly below the vehicles for fifteen minutes before dragging himself back. He swung off the beam and sat down. He stared at me for a long time before speaking.

"They're after us."

"Shit," Jackson said. He and Tan glared at one another.

"Keep your voices down. What did they say?" I asked.

"They're just talking. They didn't say anything."

"You see! They're not after us. It's his imagination."

"They were confused about their orders. They can't believe them."

"What does that mean?"

"They've got orders to get an American insurgency unit."

"If they're surprised, they can't be communists. But 'get a unit' . . . what does that mean? Find them or kill or what? How do you know they are going to hit us?"

"I just know."

"He's crazy," Jackson whispered, trembling with anger. "If we're ever going to get out of here, these are the people to get us out. Tan's making it up about us getting hit. He's over the top."

I saw the hair rise on Tan's neck. He turned and looked deeply into Jackson's eyes without saying anything. I thought he might kill Jackson on the spot. We're breaking up, I told myself. The unit is falling apart. It gave me a feeling of great sadness. I laid my knife lightly along Tan's forearm and grabbed Jackson by the shoulder.

"No more! Now shut up, you two. Jackson, you're going to expose yourself to the people on the bridge."

Tan crawled back and brought the others forward. I tapped my Armalite and pointed up at the lorries. I kept Jackson and Tan with me and waved the others under the bridge. I gave them five minutes to take a firing position.

"Give me ninety seconds, then go out on the road as close to the bridge as possible," I told Jackson.

Jackson moved off with Tan behind him. I climbed up and away from the bridge until I was level with the lorries. Through my night sight, I watched Jackson slip off his rocket pack and belts and climb toward the road carrying only his Armalite. I saw total contempt in Jackson's face for what he was doing. Either he knew he was going to die and no longer cared, or he was that convinced that these were friendly troops. I swung the Armalite back to the machine guns. There was only one man on each gun. The loaders were standing down on the bridge. But the gunner facing our side of the river could take us all out if it started too soon. The other man would have to swing his gun in a 180-degree arc before he could fire; I had time to take him out. I settled the cross hairs on the first gunner. From the corner of my eye, I saw Jackson step out on the road and start walking toward the bridge.

"American special forces unit!" he shouted.

He had his Armalite at the ready without pointing it toward the lorries. The startled Laotians scrambled for their weapons. The near machine gunner swung his barrel sharply and took aim on Jackson. One of the loaders began climbing up the side of the lorry. I tightened my finger on the trigger, but I did not pull off a round. I had to allow them reaction time. The second gun swung around. One of the riflemen who had been smoking in the cab of the first lorry threw on the headlights, pinning Jackson against a white sheet of light. It was too late now. For Jackson's sake, they had better be friends.

Fewer than a dozen seconds had passed since Jackson had surfaced. The belt operators were still scrambling up on the cabs. But it was enough time for the initial confusion to subside. The gunner had positively identified Jackson as an American. He seemed to relax. They have recognized us, I thought. I exhaled heavily.

"American special forces unit. What is your unit designation?" Jackson yelled as he advanced.

I never moved my sight off the first gunner. I heard a cab door open and a man jump to the bridge. Instantly he let off a burst of automatic fire. I saw the gunner glance down, then he raised his eyes back to Jackson. And squeezed off on the machine gun. I heard Jackson scream. Events began to whirl, and time tumbled and pitched forward at an astonishing speed. I fired at the first gunner, swung and fired at the second. They both went down. I swung back to the first gun to hit the loader, but before I could fire, the man was blown off the lorry by a burst from below the bridge. Tan ran out on the road and dragged Jackson to a ditch at the side. There were several seconds of sustained firing, then a grenade was lobbed onto the bridge, deadening the action immediately. One lorry burst into flames. I could see no more targets, so I broke for the spot where I had seen Tan drag Jackson. As I mounted the embankment, I saw Morrosco and Wiley run in among the vehicles, firing from the hip. Wiley jerked open a cab door and dragged out a wounded man, then crushed his skull with his rifle butt. Prather came loping up the other side. He had only one clip left for his M-3 and had not fired a round. He and I reached Jackson at the same time. Jackson lay unconscious on the ground, his life running out of him. He had been stitched from the waist down; half the muscle and flesh had disappeared from the inside of his right leg. Tan fought desperately to stop the bleeding, but the surging wounds swallowed up the gauze pads. Prather and I dropped down on either side of the unconscious man and hacked at his trousers with our knives. Wiley began to shout, but I could not understand what he was saying. As I pulled at Jackson's webbing belt, Wiley lurched up behind me and threw a weapon over my head. It landed with crushing force across Jackson's chest.

"Fuck you, Jackson!" Wiley screamed from the edge of madness, unaware that Jackson was unconscious.

I jumped to my feet in amazement. Instinctively Prather and I threw Wiley and pinned him to the ground. He did not fight back. I jerked him upright by the collar.

"Have you gone crazy?" I shouted at his face.

"Somebody's crazy!" Wiley roared, grabbing up the weapon he had thrown down. It was an Armalite.

"Fucking American weapons! We're being shot at with fucking American weapons!"

CHAPTER 18

There was no time for argument. I was frantically trying to fill Jackson with morphine before he regained consciousness; his body could never withstand the shock of these wounds.

"Strip the lorries," I ordered Wiley.

"Over here, Barry," Morrosco called him.

Wiley jumped up and sprinted back to the bridge, Prather at his side. The three raced in and out of the flames, stripping the vehicles of everything of value. Morrosco found boxes of ammunition. Wiley grabbed an armload of weapons from a burning tailgate. Prather found a stretcher and a wicker creel of medical supplies which he brought back to us. I had planned to cut the canvas tops to make a sling for Jackson. I was suddenly struck with an idea.

"Get the good lorry off the bridge," I shouted at Tan. "We'll drive it to Thailand."

Before Tan could take a step, the second lorry burst into flames. The scene was absolute chaos. We had to get out of there before the lorries exploded.

While the others continued to scrounge, Tan and I sorted out some Armalites that were in good working order and quickly piled them with Jackson's gear. Jackson looked like a dead man to me. I did not want to lose the guy. We put him on the stretcher and bound him down with leather straps.

"Let's get out of here," I shouted. "Grab weapons, ammo, and Jackson's gear."

I saw Wiley hesitating over the pile of gear.

"Leave the rockets," I said.

"We'll need them," he answered, grabbing them up. We were all looking for excuses to kill. But Wiley wanted to destroy.

Wiley humped the rockets up on his shoulder, then he and Morrosco grabbed up the stretcher. There was no thought of leaving Jackson. Our fates had become inextricably intertwined. I was no more concerned for my own life than the lives of the rest of the unit. We were all thinking as one on this score.

Taking Jackson increased the odds against the rest of us. There was support in numbers; Jesus, there were only six of us. But I could not see Jackson ever being more than baggage. He would not walk again. He was a dying man. If he had been hit this hard in China or North Vietnam, I would have given him an overdose of morphine. Or put a bullet in him. We needed morphine. But now we would carry him until he died, or we died, or we made it. He was part of us. While we lived, he went where we went.

We dashed across the bridge and hightailed it into the hills. We followed a jungle trail to higher ground where we could look back down on the bridge burning furiously below us. We saw headlights racing toward the bridge and heard sporadic gunfire. People apparently thought they saw us in the trees. A short time later, we heard the lorries explode.

We crashed on through the night, moving higher. We had to stop often because Jackson was bleeding profusely. He was saturated in his blood. There was virtually nothing we could do to stem the bleeding, because we were in almost total darkness. We could not even see the extent of the damage. We would give him a few minutes' rest, tighten the bandages, and push off again. I took point and led the unit south for the rest of the night. I used the night sight to scout our trail, and I set a murderous pace; I felt a great sense of urgency to get clear of the last battle. All through the night I was blaming and vindicating myself for Jackson's wounding. Why had I held my fire? What else could I have done? We had to give them a chance to recognize us. Instead, Jackson had been torn in two.

We reached morning in a shattered state. We crested a ridge just as the sun came up, and we stopped to survey the damage. Jackson regained consciousness. At first, he did not know who or where we were. Then briefly he was lucid.

"You boys go on without me," he said. "I'm dying. I don't care. I'm not interested anymore. Too much ... I can't walk. You can't ..."

He lost consciousness. We stripped him down. He had been stitched up the inside of the leg from knee to the groin as if someone had hacked at the flesh with a machete. His scrotum was ripped, but his testicles were intact. Incredibly, neither bone nor the main artery had been touched. What flesh remained was torn and shredded. Tan and Morrosco worked like mad trying to keep him alive.

To my surprise they managed to stop the bleeding. Then Morrosco took off his shirt and began to strip threads out of the seams. He found a needle in the Laotian medical pack and stitched the open wounds together with the heavy waterproofed canvas thread. He was threading infection into the wounds, but that was better than leaving them open to bleed.

I assumed we would sit there until Jackson died, so I went out to scout the route ahead. And to think.

All night I had been weighing my decision to bring Jackson with us. It was what we all wanted. But what was it doing to our chances of survival? Jackson would die sooner or later. Was it going to cost all our lives to carry him for another day or two?

I had never felt so desperate or alone, I was in command of these guys' lives, and I was so worn out I could no longer think. I was out of my depth. How much longer could any of us carry on? Our problems were just too many, too big for us. The whole thing appeared almost ridiculous. I found myself thinking about friends I had left behind in New Zealand. They were getting married or starting law school. And I thought, this cannot be real.

I snapped out of it. I could not accept that way of thinking because it was not logical enough for me. Quite logically I made up my mind. To save five men, we must abandon one. It must be what they all wanted, deep in their hearts. It was our only chance of surviving.

I walked back to where the four were gathered closely about Jackson's outstretched body. They all looked up as I approached, and Morrosco stopped wrapping a bandage.

"We're not deserting him," Prather said.

All four were watching me. They had read my mind, and I had misinterpreted their feelings. They were not offering an argument; they were telling me how it was to be. I had gotten over the psychological barrier of making the decision, but it was an easy one to retract. I made no reply.

We spent the morning resting and tending to Jackson. No one wanted to talk much. In little more than twelve hours, we had had a flare-up between Jackson and Tan, Wiley had thrown a weapon at Jackson, Prather and I had thrown Wiley, and I had made a decision to abandon Jackson. The incident between Tan and Jackson was not serious. Their blowup had been like a release valve on a steam engine; they were letting off feelings that had been building for days. Two minutes later, Tan had dashed out in the road under fire to pull Jackson to safety. Nevertheless, it remained the first sign of personality conflict in the unit, and no one could ignore it.

Nor could we ignore Wiley's explosion, which had had very little to do with the event of the moment. He could no longer contain his sense of desperation. These things manifested themselves in momentary illusion-stripping scenes, then went back into cold storage.

Physically, Wiley was with us and willing to do any chore set for him, but his thoughts were a million miles away.

Tan and I went forward to survey the route ahead. A vast plain stretched before us. We decided to cut straight across it, aim directly for Borikhan. The others agreed. We were within twenty miles of Borikhan and about a day and a half from the Thai border on the Mekong. At Borikhan, we could join a relatively safe road to Muang Pakxan on the river. At Muang Pakxan, there was a Bailey bridge protected by Laotian government troops at one end and Thai forces at the other. If we could not reach the bridge, we would push west and south along the Mekong—it curved away from us like the outer rim of a half-moon—until we found another way to cross. We abandoned forever any thought of returning to our old route.

None of us felt safe even this close to the border. If we came across an American unit, we agreed to take every precaution before approaching it. The feelings of betrayal that had arisen in China and returned with a jolt at M Ngoi were resurfacing again.

"How do you see it, Lew?" asked Morrosco.

"The sad fact is that we're no more than the victims of a snarl-up somewhere."

"No way. Setup, not snarl-up. What about you, Kiwi? You have any sensible explanations?"

"I've only managed to come up with one sensible explanation, and it's a bloody complicated one."

"Let's hear it," said Prather.

"The Pentagon has got its dominant thinkers. And

there are certain political dominant thinkers who serve as a buffer zone between the Pentagon and the White House. Some of the close-to-the-heat guys like the CIA, got wind of the conference through somebody. Maybe from the communists, from a little country that doesn't want to be swallowed up by China. This might have been a year before we were thought of. The intelligence was fed through the military analysts until someone decided to take an article of action to counteract what was envisioned as taking place. This was taken to the political arena for acceptance, and the buffer-zone people agreed to the implementation of our mission. But even after we moved out, we were being discussed. Argued. Compared to the alternatives. So you had the hard-liners and the soft-liners and the pure military all working together. All the time we were marching to China. They couldn't reach a decision, so the only thing to do was to spend us."

"Do you really believe all that?" asked Morrosco.

"It's the most likely possibility I can come up with. But, no, I don't believe it. Sometimes I believe we are an experiment. Sometimes I think it was an American general pushing all the chips up on the table. If certain political decisions were not taken—by the Chinese, or the Americans, I don't know—prior to mission date, he was going to let us do it. That man wanted war with China. He was hoping the mission would take place before it was aborted. I agree with him. If we had carried out our job, the war might have been over in a year. He was found out. And we're being sacrificed. Either that, or some people knew they would be getting mandates or briefs of what would take place at the meeting while we were on the march. If it was unfavorable to the west, we carry through. If it was favorable, we get spent."

"All you've said is there's a contract out on us," said Morrosco, "and we don't know friend from foe."

"Oh, we know. Everybody's our enemy. We have no friends," said Wiley. It was the first time he had spoken all day.

"A contract?" I said. "That sounds like a gangster film."

"So what? A contract's a contract."

I said no more, though I concurred with Morrosco. I started to see Stacey, my commanding officer, and these other people, and I decided that I was going to kill Stacey. I had a fantasy about the two guys who had briefed us for the hit. We had gone back to barracks, all charged up to save the world, and they very calmly discussed the finality of our existence. Our lives were of no consequence to the importance they put on their jobs or whatever it was they had us doing. My resolve to survive was redoubled. I would settle that score.

We spent most of the day talking, waiting for Jackson to improve. He did not get better. He needed more than we could give him. Tan and I went back out to survey the valley. Several miles away, we spotted a small hamlet on a river. We had to get help for Jackson.

We struck out at once and reached the hamlet before nightfall. Tan and I jumped two peasants; Tan stopped me from killing mine. The men were babbling that theirs was a safe village. They took us into the village. When the women saw Jackson, they rushed to him before we could get the stretcher on the ground. Tan pushed them away. While the others held the place under arms, Tan and I went to work on Jackson. The entire village crowded around us. The women were frantic to help. Tan relented, and they went to work on the wounded man. This was a very poor, backward village that wanted to stay isolated from the rest of the world. I started to relax. Before we had our packs off, they were pushing fish soup at us. I grabbed up the fish and ate it whole, like an animal. We ate and rested in rotation throughout the night.

When the women cleaned Jackson's wounds with salve and herbs, he regained consciousness within an hour. He remembered nothing since being hit and was amazed at how far we had carried him. The peasants were delighted to see the improvement. They did not want a dead American on their hands.

With Jackson on the mend, the peasants turned to us. They washed our uniforms and produced great wooden tubs of hot water for bathing. I climbed in first and nearly fell asleep. My energy seemed to melt away with the weeks of accumulated dirt.

I called Tan back from guard by the river. He felt comfortable with these people, which increased my growing sense of security. One guy reminded me of a newsreel I had seen as a child of the Second World War, where the troops were passing by, and a guy was picking rice in a paddy. The war and the world ran over the top of these people. It did not matter to them if we were American or Laotian or communist or whatever. The quicker we were made welcome and given what we wanted, the sooner we would depart. When the next party came in, they would keep quiet that we had been there.

We spent the night repairing ourselves and sleeping. Only I did not sleep. I had not relaxed sufficiently to sleep for days. I did not want to sleep. My mind was racing . . . Jackson . . . where we were going . . . how long it would take. I was one hundred per cent insomniac by now.

As dawn neared, I told the others to prepare to move out. Jackson was still conscious and aware of the extent of his injuries.

"I'll stay here, Kiwi," he said. "My leg's as dead as Kelsey's nuts. These people will take good care of me. You send somebody to get me."

A peasant spoke to Tan.

"He says Alvin can stay here."

"You're safer in the jungle."

We pushed off just before dawn, carrying Jackson by shoulder straps Wiley had fashioned during the night. We seemed to me to be in fairly good condition. As soon as we got on the trail, Prather dropped back to walk with me.

"You've got to sleep, Gayle."

"How can I sleep? I have to keep my guard up, so the rest of you can relax."

"If you don't rest, you'll collapse. Give us one more man to carry."

"Rubbish."

"You're not restocking your reserves. You're not functioning as a man now, Gayle. You're a bloody machine. And you're running low on fuel."

"You can't get along without me."

"We can take care of ourselves. We don't want to have to take care of you."

For the first time, I realized I had detached myself from the others; I was an outsider, trying to manipulate us as from a great distance. My job . . . I was obsessed with the job of keeping these men alive. I had to go to the limit. I had to watch the others, be somehow a step removed from them. Keep them from making a mistake. How could I afford to sleep? Was I going mad?

We pushed out toward Borikhan along the river, then over a track that took us near the road. The going was easy, over open ground. We took turns on the stretcher and walking point. Jackson was conscious and not complaining much. He lay in the stretcher fully armed, with his weapon at the ready. We hoped to reach Borikhan early in the night by a track from the east.

With two hours to go until nightfall, we moved quickly down an unobstructed trail. We may have been lulled a bit by the easy going, because we came around a bend and walked straight into a party of mercenaries. We had no time to run; they had already seen us. There were eleven in all, a shabby lot, but very heavily armed. Morrosco, at point, froze in his tracks. He had his Armalite at the ready. The leader held up his hand in greeting.

"Allow them to come forward," I told Tan.

Tan told them to advance, then he walked to where Prather and I were holding the stretcher. The mercenaries came past Morrosco and stopped in front of

Tan and me. Everyone had weapons trained on every-one else.

Their leader was quite friendly. He was an ugly son-of-a-bitch. Most of his front teeth were missing; the remainder were brown and rotten. His crew were filthy, practically walking around in rags. They could see by the way our eyes were darting around that we were ready to go. Prather and I eased the stretcher down. I laid my Armalite on the stretcher with Jack-son and casually unslung the shotgun.

The boss of this ragged outfit kept smiling as if he did not see any of this. He asked Tan what unit we were from. Tan translated for me but made no reply. The guy said they were from a village just down the trail. He asked us if we wanted to fall into their village to rest.

Tan asked him something about Borikhan, how far away it was; I heard "Borikhan" a couple of times. The guy replied, gesturing with his arm.

"It's a trap. He says Borikhan is about a kilometer down the road."

Borikhan was at least ten miles away. Without ex-changing a word, we all made ready for action. Prather was the first to spot the others.

"They're more in the trees to the left," he said in a casual voice loud enough for all of us to hear.

"For Christ's sake," Jackson said. "Get me off the road."

My mind was racing like a merry-go-round. Instinctively I told Tan to tell those in front of us to move, so we could put the stretcher down on the narrow trail. They saw that we were about to jump out of our skins, so they lowered their weapons as they moved away.

We hauled Jackson to the side of the trail, and Wiley and Prather nonchalantly slipped off their packs and piled them in front of Jackson so that his chest and head were hidden. The gear would not stop a bul-let, but it was psychological cover.

The eleven guys were all standing on the road, five

in front with the leader, then four a few feet farther back with his second-in-command. Tan walked up very close to the leader, and I followed him. Gradually we pushed the front group back down the road, away from Jackson, simply by violating their psychological space.

"Come back a few feet," I said to Morrosco. "Make it look casual."

He was fifty feet past the second group. He sauntered toward us. I could see three guys in the trees closing behind him. When he was almost even with the second party, I stopped him.

"Stay there," I said. "Be ready to go to ground. I'll take the ones in front. Wiley and Prather, go into the tree line on the left."

Tan, his rifle resting on his shoulder, was conversing with their leader, but he was hearing every word I spoke. The two units were close enough to touch each other. And these guys were cool. I could see the dollar signs, the head money, rolling around in their eyeballs. The leader had slung his rifle, an American M-1 carbine, and was chatting and offering Tan tobacco. He was waiting for his men to position themselves in the trees, then they would come out with a bead on us and take us alive. But it was taking them longer than he had expected. Tan refused to lead the guy along. We stayed like this for a couple of minutes, with just this strained chatter coming from this guy. Everyone was nervous. His henchmen were getting jumpy, because they had been briefed on what would happen, and it had not happened. And suddenly the conversation came to this strange end. The guy had run out of stall time.

I had been easing myself toward the side of the road, out of Morrosco's firing ilne and away from Tan. Their two groups were being forced together, by people trying to remain at a psychological distance from one another.

Suddenly we were all functioning again like highly tuned machines, like a Ferrari instead of a delivery van. It became a matter of watching the movement through the trees . . . the shuffling of the people on the road . . . measuring the arc of my weapon . . . checking the disposition of the unit . . . setting the thing up so that we had maximum fire power before they could retaliate. I could take two out immediately. Tan two. Morrosco was in position to hit a lot of them from the rear. We were ready. I was waiting for the right moment . . . that instinctive feeling that would tell me the scene was balanced in relation to how we were disposed, how we were thinking. The time came right.

CHAPTER 19

I fired the shotgun twice in quick succession. I bowled two guys over with the steel balls and felled two more with the pellets before they knew the fight had started. Then I danced away.

With one smooth stroke, Tan brought his rifle off his shoulder and smashed the barrel across the leader's skull. The rifle fell into Tan's hand. He dropped to one knee and started firing, bringing down two more men. Morrosco opened up with automatic fire and killed five of them in seconds. One of the guys I had hit with the pellets climbed to his feet and stumbled backward into the trees. He was terrified, firing everywhere. It was funny to see. I fired at him. And missed. Three guys came tearing out of the trees toward me and Tan, but their line of fire was blocked by the man I had missed. Prather and Wiley shot them down from the trees.

I began to lose the pattern of things. There were only three or four still alive, and we were all firing furiously. As Morrosco came charging forward, a man rose up off the ground with a pistol in his hand and shot him in the back. Morrosco pitched forward on his face, and I blew the guy's head off at point-blank range. There were two left 'and five of us firing at them. We fired and fired. We shot dead bodies. We wasted more ammunition than we had on the entire mission. We were still wound up and there was nothing left to fire at. Tan ran to Morrosco, glanced at his wound, and shouted that he was all right. I dashed to Jackson and found him with a smirk on his face.

"What's so funny?" I said.

"Look around."

The trees were torn to shreds, the road dug up by flying bullets. Somehow not one round had touched Jackson. I ran back to Morrosco. He was lying on his stomach, his back soaked in blood. Tan had stripped off his shirt.

"They got me, Gayle," he said. "The bastards have finally done it."

"You're all right," Tan told him. "The bullet hit the pack and deflected into your arm. No bone broken. Just some torn flesh. You're all right," he assured the disbelieving Morrosco.

I saw that Tan was right. If the guy had been using anything more than a small-caliber pistol Morrosco would have been dead. The wound was not severe. I was more concerned about our performance, about the obvious sign that we were cracking when I thought we had come to life again. I had missed an easy standing target. And the aftermath . . . the way we kept firing. The place was a hellish sight. We had to get out of there while the adrenaline was still pounding at our hearts. We bound Morrosco's arm, gathered ammunition for the Armalites, grabbed the stretcher, and took off.

We left the track and went into a river to avoid two hamlets. We could still reach Borikhan by midnight or the early hours of the morning and strike from there to the Mekong. Once past the hamlets, we stopped for two hours on the riverbank. Carrying the stretcher was exhausting us. Morrosco was in great pain. As Tan was dressing the wound, he suddenly pulled free, then probed his arm carefully with his fingertips.

"The bullet's still in me," he said.

The bullet had entered the upper arm, and the flesh had closed around it, like a ball pushed into Plasticine. It was resting against the inside of his bicep. We had to get it out to avoid infection. We had no morphine.

Prather bound his dog rag very tightly around the upper arm, cutting off the flow of blood. We waited a few minutes for the arm to go numb. Morrosco put his shirt collar in his mouth to keep from screaming. Tan and I sat on his chest, and Prather knelt across his forearm while Wiley dug out the bullet. It was only a small thing, and we had it out quickly, but we made a mess of the job in the dark. We wrapped the wound quickly and strapped his arm, then loosened the tourniquet. He lay in a cold sweat, fighting off his desire to scream, as the blood flowed back into his arm.

We washed and cleaned ourselves up. Once again we were covered in the shit of other men. When we were fighting hand-to-hand, the one thing we could not stop was the other guy's bowels opening. When a man died, his body reacted against his death. If he had been done with a knife, or Morrosco's garrote, it became quite grotesque; his guts and the contents of his bowels came spilling out. I could stop a man from screaming with my hand, but he was shitting, and I was floundering around in it. If he was wearing a loincloth like these mercenaries, it was very ugly.

When Morrosco could stand, we moved on. We left the river to join a road that led into Borikhan. We fled into the trees to duck a line of mercenaries heading for the river. We reached the road, only to find it occupied by forty or fifty men. Half were government troops, the rest mercenaries; they were chatting and sharing a meal served out of the back of several military transports.

I was desperate to find out what they were doing together, but Tan could not get close enough to eavesdrop. It was enough for me to see the two groups together. The government was paying mercenaries to do a job in the region.

Two vehicles went off toward Borikhan carrying mercenaries and government troops. Other parties went into the bush. We were about to get caught between these guys and the first party we had seen. We had to forget about Borikhan. We would head straight for the Mekong. We raced away southward. As the vehicle had returned to Borikhan, the city was in government hands. The feeling that we were being paranoid was fast fading. It looked as if everyone was up against us.

We had a nightmarish struggle with the stretcher through thick jungles. We broke out on a rushland to find it crawling with government troops. They were in battalion strength, sweeping through tall bamboo reeds, moving and stopping at the bark of a whistle. Through the night sight, I saw them probing the reeds with their bayonets. We sat and watched these guys for a while. They were sweeping toward the Nou River, which we had hoped to take to the Mekong. We had to go back to high ground.

"Wouldn't it be ironical," Morrosco said, "if they were looking for us to bring us in."

"With bayonets?"

Again my choice of route had been made for me. We could never cut through a force that size; we had to keep moving east. We would go east and south until we found a river that would take us to the Mekong.

Physically we were not in bad shape. I was the worst of all, fatigued beyond the measure of fatigue. But Jackson was growing stronger by the minute. Morrosco was simply impatient with his wounds, tired of the pain and restriction. Prather and Tan had learned to accept theirs. My hip had become infected, which was annoying; otherwise, I was healing. Exhaustion was depleting our energies far more than wounds.

When we reached high ground, I sent the other four down a narrow valley with Jackson and the stretcher, and I climbed to survey with the sight. Any movement southwest toward the Mekong was blocked by pockets of military activity; I could not identify the troops. We went high again and kept moving southeast. So it went for days. Every time we tried to turn toward the Mekong, we found our path obstructed.

We kept climbing until the thought of dragging the stretcher up one more hill became unbearable. When we reached a junction of four rivers like noughts-and-crosses southwest of Ban Hatpakmut, we moved into the bed of one stream that seemed to aim for the Mekong. Just as the stream broke into open terrain, I heard a sound which I did not recognize at once.

"Look!" said Prather, pointing toward the southwest.

Just above the horizon I saw three helicopters moving slowly east to west; these were the first we had seen since leaving Thailand. From time to time, they hovered or dropped low to the ground. They were too far to identify as U.S. or Thai, but they were American-made machines, and they were looking for something. They appeared to be on our side of the Mekong.

"If they come overhead, do we try to contact them?"

"I'm going to ground."

We were an uneasy lot; strange things were running through our minds. From a high vantage point, we saw a highway several miles to our southwest. It carried so much military traffic that I began to doubt it was connected with us. We rested on the river the remainder of the day and had a long debate about our next course of action. We thought we were on the Nam Kading, west of Ban Phangiaung. The nearest safe Mekong crossing I knew was at Nakhon Phanom, more than seventy miles to our southeast; I had worked out of Phanom West, a Thai airstrip near there. Muang Pakxan appeared impossible. There was no division in the unit over this; none of us was willing to risk confrontation with Laotian government troops.

We agreed to turn ourselves over only to Americans, or to Thais if we got across the river. Until then, we would keep moving southeast.

"If we can find a radio," I said, "I'm calling out for choppers."

"What if they shoot us down?" asked Wiley.

"That's a risk I'm prepared to take," Prather said, and the others concurred.

We pushed off after dark and made fifteen miles that night, not bad going considering our condition. Or had we been two days doing it? Things were beginning to blur in my mind. We intercepted a dirt highway west of Ban Phonkho and moved along high ground that carried us above mangrove swamps to either side of our route. We took a trail, then had to lie low for hours while people moved up and down it. I began to forget where we were and what we were doing.

We were in a terrible state by now, moving on instinct alone. Prather had contracted malaria and carried a constant fever. Dysentery struck Morrosco as we were ascending a steep grade. He fouled his fatigues with watery excrement; he cursed and moved on. I had a fantasy of walking away from the unit, sloping off into the woods all by myself. I was sick of the sight of them. Tan was the only one functioning well. He was moving like a lizard, he was so sharp. I could not understand it until I saw him choke down three Benzedrine tablets at one go. I began to watch him. He was taking speed every three or four hours. We had all been using it, though not in quantity. I stopped when I found myself dependent on it to keep moving. I spent a hellish twelve hours until my adrenals started to work again.

We debated cutting southwest to the Mekong, then decided to keep moving southeast, paralleling the curve of the river. We knew somebody was deploying Laotian troops against us. But it just was not rational to think that the entire government army was after us.

Prather suggested that one area commander was directing operations against us because of what we had done in his region. If we could get clear of him, we would be far safer. This was little more than a way of reassuring ourselves that we had alternatives. We were working hard to make this thing appear better than it was. It was hard to accept that we were public enemy number one.

It took us another day and a night to get down to where Highway 137 began near Ban Nonglao. We arrived at a hamlet near there just after nightfall. We were in a bad state; we needed what a hamlet could give us—food, rest, tending to our wounds, a psychological rejuvenation, a brief respite from the relentless chase. A quick look told us that the place was occupied by mercenaries strolling about casually with weapons in their hands. Most of the armed men were concentrating around one central dwelling.

"Who are they?" I asked Tan.

"Obviously mercenaries. But friends or foe? There's no way of knowing."

"Do we go in?"

We wanted that hamlet desperately. They all waited for my decision. I could not make up my mind.

"What about the mercenaries?"

"I say we take a chance with them. Change our luck," Prather said.

"Might as well shoot yourself out here in the bush. It's quicker."

"I'm tired, Gayle. I'm just about ready to do that."

"I'm still in charge here. Nobody's committing suicide—individually or the entire unit. I'm taking you all back to Bien Hoa."

I decided to let the people settle for the night, then take the place quickly. We never saw more than five or six men with weapons, but they were constantly coming and going from the one building. Women and children were wandering about unmolested, so they had the confidence of the mercenaries. When things grew quiet, we parked Jackson in the undergrowth, and the five of us moved in for a close look. We were slipping up a trail fifty yards from the first hut when we came face to face with two peasant men. We must have been a frightening sight, but I gave them time to recover from the shock. I prayed they would smile and make a welcome sign. They just stared. Then one of them tried to shout out a warning. Before three words were out of his mouth, we had killed the two with our knives. We waited, but there was no alarm.

These two were ordinary peasants, not mercenaries, so the hamlet was definitely unfriendly. It was either held by mercenaries, or the village men were themselves mercenaries. Since M Ngoi, I had harbored a deep hatred for these kinds of people. We went forward very quickly, up under the buildings. The hamlet was quiet but for one large building, where people were having a party of some kind. We could hear singing and general carrying on. We crawled back to Jackson.

"What do we do?"

"We can hardly go round the bloody place without going miles out of our way," I said.

"I'm sick of being hunted, of running and hiding," said Wiley. "These are the people that are making life miserable for us. Let's go on the offensive for once."

"We'll hit them hard, take what we need, then get out."

"This is what we've been carrying the rockets for," said Wiley. "Those guys have got the village women in there with them, and I bet they're raping the shit out of them. Let me go on the far side and hit that building with the rockets."

Wiley hurriedly stripped the rockets from the packs and began assembling them. The rest of us primed our weapons. For weeks we had been rats in a drum with no way to get up the walls. Wiley's remark was an excuse we all grabbed at to hit this place. We could avoid combat here, move around it, and take a safer village. But straight through was the quickest, simplest way. Killing was the only positive thing we had left in our lives now. What the hell, why not? For once, we could enjoy the luxury of initiating an action.

"Let me go with him," Jackson pleaded.

"Sorry, Alvin," I said. "You stay here. If we have to leave in a hurry, this is our best way out."

I allowed Wiley time to circle to the far side of the hamlet. There were a few people milling about, but I managed to move under all the dwellings one at a time. I checked to see who was in them, listening for boots rather than bare feet, or the sound of brass buttons or weapons being tended. Everything seemed in order. Most of the villagers, the children and the adults not working as mercenaries, were sleeping. The four of us took position facing the entrance to the longhouse. It was a bamboo and thatch building with one long, low window. I saw several half-naked women pass the window and heard sounds from inside which convinced me they were sky-larking around and having a gang bang.

I had the night sight trained on the window and was waiting for a target when Wiley hit the building with a rocket. Somehow he had fired it almost in a direct line so that the rocket entered at an angle through the base of the wall. The rocket went off inside the building, and it was total devastation . . . a tremendous explosion . . . the whirring chains biting through the air . . . shrapnel whistling . . . the structure engulfed in flames. He blew a neighboring building apart with a second rocket.

People came jumping out of buildings with their clothes on fire, and we shot down everything that moved. A few peasants had grabbed up weapons and were firing wildly at us. We heaved grenades and hurled bodies everywhere. I saw Morrosco run up to the longhouse and shoot everybody that was still alive. As people spilled out of the other houses, we shot them down at the door and heaved grenades in behind them.

Gone was all thought of hitting the hamlet and moving out. We fired and fired. I wanted to kill everyone. I felt that everything that moved, everything left alive, had contributed to the hell we had been through for the past three weeks.

"Stop it, Gayle," Tan shouted. "We're the only ones firing."

For the first time, I saw what had happened. In our overindulgence, we had wreaked havoc on this place. Bodies were strewn everywhere . . . children . . . soldiers . . . old people. If there was no price on our heads before, there was now. We hurriedly searched the surviving buildings and found a terrific amount of arms, communist and American. The hamlet was burning profusely. We must have seemed like a hundred men to these people. Tan herded the survivors in front of one building, screaming at them in Laotian. While he and Prather were bringing the peasants under control, I sent Morrosco and Wiley to fetch Jackson. The hamlet was larger than I had imagined; we herded together about thirty people. We must have killed the same number. I went into the longhouse, which the flames had consumed to ash. There was a lot of weapons, a lot of naked, dead bodies. Brass buttons and belt buckles. The men had been in some kind of uniform, though there was no identifying it now.

There was plenty of wailing among the people left alive. Two women broke away and ran into a hut. We did nothing to stop them. They brought out some children. Several more children and two women came forward from where they had been hiding. When Jackson came in, he made it clear there were more of us hiding outside the hamlet. Tan sent four men to bring us all the arms we had not found. They returned with some dated weapons and some communist automatic rifles, as well as M-1s and Armalites.

Morrosco found a pile of American uniforms, and he went a bit haywire. He dragged two men out of the crowd and threw them to the ground. They rolled in balls, holding their heads in their hands.

"Where do these come from?" he screamed. "You bastards. You've wiped out an American unit."

He raved on and began kicking these guys. They did not know what the hell he was saying, and they let themselves be kicked. Finally I stopped him, because by this time it had all calmed down, and everything was getting a bit sick.

I had a gutful. I did not want to absorb any more of this scene. I was beginning to differentiate between the needed and the needless, and it seemed needless for Morrosco to be kicking around two peasants after we had wiped out half the village.

I had a hard time calming him down; Prather came to help. Morrosco was like a man crazed with drugs; his weapon was dancing in his hands; his eyes were pleading for someone, anyone, to move so he could shoot them down.

We grabbed up some food, medical supplies, ammunition. Tan found a huge old American radio, but he could not make it work, and it was too heavy to take with us. It looked like a base radio; the Americans must have run these people once, then had their own arms turned on them.

We made the villagers clean Jackson's wounds. They were healing quite well, though there was terrific scarring and bruising all along the leg. I was ignoring my own wounds, though they were gravely infected. Prather pleaded with me to get attention, but the more he argued, the more I rejected help. His wounds were by no means healing, but they were closed and manageable; he had considerable use of his bad arm. Tan's arm had deteriorated; he had practically no lateral movement. Morrosco's wound was healing fast.

We left and headed downriver, hoping somehow to reach Nakhon Phanom. We pushed up some low hills for several hours before stopping to rest. I was too whipped to post guard, and no one took the responsibility upon himself, so we just splayed out on the ground without a word. We were very grim, almost silent. No one made any real effort to go to sleep, because none of us trusted sleep now. But we could fight it only so much. As I sat there thinking, I watched the others drift into sleep and drift out, and I drifted into sleep a couple of times, but the fatigue and my nerves jogged me awake. As dawn approached, we moved.

We cut down toward a flat valley of rice paddies interrupted by marshland and vast sandy areas like dried lake bowls that were scarred with vehicle tracks from some recent battle. We skirted several mangrove swamps in a very hot sun. Dehydration was telling on us all. East of Ban Nakok we headed toward a trail that would take us in sight of the Mekong. We pushed across an open landscape with low, gentle vegetation. It was easy going, but we were pushing through a sticky hot sun. We saw constant air activity, which meant we were approaching a battlefield. We walked in almost total silence. We were all thinking more than we were saying, and none of us felt like sniping at one another. The tension was unbearable. I no longer knew where the limit was.

As we approached the track, fifteen Pathet Lao came cycling down it, then stopped and dragged their bikes off into the woods. We slipped across the trail. Morrosco and I went forward a quarter of a mile, dodging from cover to cover in sparse vegetation. We were just out of the trees, down on our bellies, when Morrosco tapped my shoulder and pointed. We were within three hundred yards of a Pathet Lao encampment. This entire area was unsafe. We would have to go farther south, then east.

Just before we got back to the unit, some instinct told me there were people about. I waved Morrosco down. Three men passed without seeing us. We were in sight of our guys when we saw two more of these blokes walking to where the unit was hidden. Neither party had seen the other. They were on a collision course.

Morrosco and I moved quickly through the trees to intercept them. One was between us and the other, so I signaled to Morrosco to take him first. I moved away. Morrosco underestimated the time it would take me to get set. I was several feet off my man when Morrosco knifed his. The guy made a noise. My man turned and saw what was happening. He whipped his rifle up to shoot Morrosco.

I flew out of the bush and drove my knife straight into his stomach. We fell down together, and the guy grabbed my throat with both hands. I tried to stab him again, but my knife was stuck in bone. The guy was jumping around on the end of the blade like a speared fish, but he was choking the life out of me. He was a strong son-of-a-bitch; I felt myself growing weaker. I struggled with my knife and beat him on the face with my free hand, but I could not break his grip. He was bleeding from the mouth; he was going to die. But he wanted to kill me first. All the time, I was conscious of attracting attention and trying to do him silently. And he had me; his grip was getting tighter and tighter. As I began to lose consciousness, Morrosco slipped his garrote over the man's head and ripped his throat to the bone. I grabbed both his hands but did not have the strength to break the grip. Morrosco pulled the fingers from my throat. I collapsed, and Morrosco rolled me on my back. He checked me over while I caught my breath, then pulled me to my feet and pushed my gun into my hands. He pulled the knife free and slammed it into the sheath at my side. I looked at him. I bashed him on the arm, and we took off.

We all dashed across open ground, then over the road completely exposed. We had just reached cover when we heard four shots. The bodies had been found. Within minutes the area was crawling with these people. They saw or heard us, because they got on our trail. We managed to stay just ahead of them in the heavy undergrowth. Farther east, we overran a party of five and wiped them out. We ran for half a day with these people not many minutes behind us. We dodged another party of seven. The countryside was crawling with armed men. We reached a highway that led into Muang Kham Mouan and moved along it to cross it at a safer point. I was out front, walking fast. We broke out of the trees fifty yards off the road.

A gun fired, and a bullet slammed into my thigh. I spun and went down on my back. Once again I had triggered an ambush prematurely. Guns went off everywhere, but the others had dropped the stretcher and run back into the trees. There was a lot of yelling on our side, trying to figure out where they were. I finally spotted them at ground level, firing from a depression on the far side of the road. When they did not rush me, I crawled for cover in the undergrowth. The firing stopped. They were going to wait and pick us off. I lay there for several minutes, trying to make out their firing position. I counted eight, but could have counted some of them twice. They were mercenaries, but no ordinary bandit rabble; they were pretty well organized.

We began moving against each other, crawling through the bush to draw flank. Firing was sporadic, so I took time off to shove a wad into my trousers. I was bleeding like a pig. I dragged myself out on the flank and drew a lot of fire, then I got a bead and took a couple of them out. I could not see my people, so I was out there on my own, stalking and being stalked. I was charged by two men and shot one, and he fell dead beside me. I fired at the second guy, but the Armalite was empty. I raised up as far as I could and swung the Armalite at him. It slipped out of my hands and went flying off into the bush. The guy stood right over me. He fired, and the bullet must have passed between my arm and my chest. He stopped to draw a more careful bead. A bullet smashed into the side of his chest. He pirouetted and landed right beside my head. I rolled over and killed him with my knife. Half a dozen bullets tore into his body that were intended for me. I was down to my shotgun and thirty rounds now. It was useless unless I was charged, so I kept working my way to our flank. We gradually regrouped and pushed them back on one side as they tried to flank us; I was hoping to stretch their flank, but it was not working. They were a tight team. We fell down toward the road. I managed to reach my feet and walk with a stiff leg, but it felt as if the leg was not there. No one could help me, because we needed everyone firing. We got to the edge of the road and started to dash across.

"Jackson!" Prather shouted.

We had forgotten him where the others had dropped him in their scramble for cover. At that moment, we heard firing. Wiley and Morrosco ran into the trees and down the line to where Jackson had been. They came tearing back.

"The stretcher's empty," Morrosco shouted.

"Bodies all over the place," Wiley said. "He's gone."

"Here!" Jackson shouted.

I saw him waving from where he lay by the road a hundred yards away. These guys were grouping in the tree line to rush us. We rushed them first, hurling grenades, then dashed back to the road. I yelled to Jackson to go across while we covered him. The poor bastard was a pathetic sight, dragging himself across on his hands and knees. They spotted him and started yelling and firing. Bullets bounced all around him in the dirt, but he escaped unhit.

"Can you make it?" Prather shouted at me.

I said yes, not at all sure I was telling the truth. I hobbled across, feeling as if I had only one leg to support me. Tan and Prather followed me without being hit. Before Wiley and Morrosco could get clear, they were jumped by four guys. We laid down covering fire while they dealt with these four. Two of them were shot immediately, but the other two went into hand-to-hand combat.

One guy came at Wiley waving his rifle like a club. Wiley disarmed him, then brought him in close to stab him. They fell and rolled on the ground. The second one swung his weapon like a cricket bat. Morrosco ducked, but the stock caught his forehead. He went down like a rock, and Prather shot the guy off him. I saw Wiley grab up his knife from where it had fallen in the struggle. He was looking at his man and did not realize he had grabbed it with the blade pointing backward. He tried to plunge the knife into the man. The man pulled Wiley into him and onto his own knife. The knife went into Wiley's stomach. I thought he was dead, but he got it out and killed the man. He stumbled to his feet and pulled Morrosco upright, and they both staggered to our side of the road. As they fell down beside us, we started cutting down a party that was grouping for a charge.

Toliver's Armalite was gone forever, and my shotgun was ineffectual at this range, so I lay there feeling sorry for myself until I saw the amount of blood surging out of Wiley's shirt. I tried to roll him over, and he pushed me away.

"I'm all right," he said. "Don't worry about me.

"Get back in the trees," I said, "and get that wound tended."

When he started to argue, I jerked his weapon out of his hand and kicked him away. I started firing across the road. He crawled back to the trees. Prather and Tan ran to help Jackson, who was now on his feet. He was in terrific pain, he was limping, but he was upright for the first time since he had been machine-gunned at the bridge. They helped him to the trees and then joined me on the firing line. The mercenaries failed to reach the road by frontal assault several times, so they moved out in two groups to cross the road on either side of us. I saw there were far more than I had counted. They wore American fatigues and carried American arms, and they were bloody well organized.

We had all we wanted of these guys, so we moved away as fast as we could. They dogged our trail for hours. They forced us into open ground between Highway 12 and Muang Kham Mouan. We were in no shape to fight a rearguard action on the run. I had lost a lot of blood. Wiley was in agony; when he ran, his heart pumped his blood out his stomach. Jackson was being dragged by Prather and Tan, but he was hopping along and even using his bad leg from time to time. Morrosco was seeing stars, but we could not bother about that sort of injury. When we dared go to ground, we scrambled frantically to patch one another up. Half of us needed morphine, but we could not have taken it if we had any. I gobbled Benzedrine, but the effects would not last long enough to support the condition I was in. Prather was trembling with chill and fever, but he was surviving because he at least had legs. Legs were the weapons we needed most now. The fighting slacked off when night fell, and we kept moving as fast as we could. We covered several miles by midnight, then collapsed in the bush to take a desperate rest.

For a few moments, we lay on our stomachs without a sound, watching the trees like crazy. Even in our condition, we had carried out an automatic function of falling into a defensive arrowhead. This was partly psychological; if shooting started, none of us wanted his line of fire blocked by another's body. We dropped down in a semicircle facing where we expected them to come from. Then it was like a crowd watching the races—one man put his head out, and the next man up the line went out a bit farther, and someone went out even farther until we had quite naturally assumed an effective posture, though we were no more than ten feet apart.

We lay for a long time gasping for breath. When we had filled our lungs, our most pressing need was for nourishment. There was no thought of food. I sucked at a clove pack, and one or two others broke off a piece of glucose and tried to get it down dry throats. The rest took pills. We were so dehydrated that the saliva would not run in our mouths; anything we swallowed lodged immediately in the throat until it melted. I had water, because I used it like a watch to measure my endurance, but it was stretched to the limit. We shared it around, nipping just enough to wet our mouths and swallow stiffly.

We needed water. What did we not need? I knew

everyone was low on ammunition, because they had been firing on single shot in the heat of action. I gave Wiley back his Armalite. I had a few rounds remaining for the shotgun.

"Ssh!"

We froze. From the point of the arrow I saw four men silhouetted against the night sky, two on either side of me. They were walking very cautiously, taking three or four steps, then turning in a full circle with their arms at the ready. They had not seen us down on the ground. They were going to walk right onto us.

We had to take those four silently in case there were more. I showed my knife to Prather. He withdrew his. I ran my knife blade down my sleeve, which meant it was to be done silently. I touched my nose and held up two fingers; I would take the two to the right. He touched his nose and held up two fingers. The rest would cover us.

I came off the ground and put my knife in the first man before he saw me. I leapt at the other man and tripped over the fallen body. I fell right at this guy's feet; I could see his boots. As I glanced up, his rifle came down on the back of my neck.

I came around with Tan slapping my face. It took a few seconds for my head to clear, then it was racked by pain. Everyone was lying prone in complete silence. The four mercenaries lay dead, one from a bullet wound. When no more appeared, we very quietly stripped the bodies. They were carrying Armalites and a lot of clips and wearing U.S. fatigues. I had lost the night sight, so we moved slowly until we broke out on open ground. We were dragging along. Fortunately, my leg was numb. But I had bled inside my fatigues, and the blood had caked on the insides of my legs and broken into sharp pieces which were cutting into my scrotum with every step. The skin went raw, then began to tear, and my testicles swelled from the bruising. I bit my lip to keep from screaming. I began to get disoriented.

Running . . . we never stopped running. . . . We

were somewhere in the open . . . it was night . . . we went into cover . . . on high ground . . . in the heat of another day . . . we dragged along like zombies . . . stumbling . . . struggling over fallen trees . . . trying to vomit when we stopped to rest . . . running again. We broke into a river and ran wildly down its bed until the sun was on our faces. Our condition was worsening. I fell into the water to soften the blood on my legs, then tied my testicles to one leg with my shirt. How Jackson stayed on his feet, I did not know. Prather was supporting him, so Tan dropped back to help me. I refused his help, and he took Wiley's weight on his good shoulder. We moved like this for hours, with no idea where the river was taking us.

CHAPTER 20

We were lost. I still had the maps; along with a few weapons, they were all we had left from the beginning. But it had been days since we had looked at them. We knew only that we were moving vaguely east. We left the river and raced across open ground for cover in some distant trees. We ran until we were in high ground, then we collapsed. We were too tired to talk, so we crawled about helping one another, redistributing load and ammunition.

Half an hour later, we started taking stock of the situation. We reckoned unanimously that we were a prime target, because we had been in running action for weeks with people who showed absolute determination to kill us. We were so few in numbers, they could simply have observed us, then written us off when we moved out of their areas. But they had underestimated what we were capable of. They had been losing men at a desperate rate, and on the rebound they had resolved we could not live.

"We've got to be somewhere near the dead end of Highway 135," I said. "We'll strike for the highway."

"What for?"

"I don't know . . . follow it . . . make for the Mekong."

"Right," said Prather, "make for the Mekong. Is that a joke, Gayle?"

"How many goddamn times have we tried that already?" said Jackson.

"And if we got there, what would be waiting for us anyway?" said Morrosco.

The conversation started building on itself, people expanding other people's observations. The unspoken thoughts we had been nursing for days began to spill out.

"We're not only being hunted," said Tan, "we're being maneuvered. How many of you have worked around here before?"

We all had, but for Prather.

"I bet you never had this much trouble. Faced this kind of opposition. Have you ever seen so many freshly formed units over such a wide area?"

"You know what we've got here, don't you?" said Jackson, picking up a weapon by his side. "These Armalites are brand-new. Look at them. They'd never been fired before today. And the fatigues those guys were wearing. They still had the crease in them. You think these guys turned over before they fought their first battle? You think they walked out of a U.S. armory and joined the other side?"

"We're puppets on a string," said Morrosco.

"What do you mean?"

"You know what I mean," he said, then retreated into his shell.

Morrosco and Wiley were growing more silent by the day. They were almost environmentalized now, like an animal doing what had to be done to stay alive, and no more. They both had a positive sense of betrayal and almost total disinterest in conjecturing where it might come from. It was easier to count everyone as an enemy.

The rest of us had more command experience; we knew how a higher command might work, and we wanted to make some military sense out of it. Tan noted that there was a marked absence of low air activity along the Mekong. There should have been constant movement of American troops. He said they were being kept away so they would not see an American unit being hunted down by allies.

There was argument in the degree of the sellout. I thought we were being sold out by people who knew who we were.

"This is a bastard sellout. No way can we win. We're finished," I said. I was feeling pretty lousy. Prather refused to let loose from his myths.

"It may be our fault. For not exposing ourselves to the units that have been looking for us. Perhaps they were friendly. Possibly those last blokes were looking for us."

"Yeah. They were planning a surprise party."

"What I mean," Prather insisted, "is that an area commander may have been told to look for us. And was not told what we have been up to. Fair enough. He's friendly. He's going to pick us up. And we burn his villages down and slaughter people and wipe his men out up and down the countryside. Then he doesn't care who we are. He's going to kill us."

"It won't wash, Lew. You're trying to explain away the obvious. That we're being used."

"It's all a farce anyway," said Wiley. "It was nothing but war games from the start. Right mates, if it's games we're playing, I retire. I just want to be let out of here."

"You retire and you die," said Jackson. "It may be a game to you, but it's fucking serious to me."

"You fight your war and I'll fight mine, Jackson," Wiley answered.

"You're a piss-poor soldier, Wiley, when you talk like that," Jackson said.

"You're talking shit, Jackson. You know how good I am."

"You're gonna be good and dead if you don't stick with us."

"Wiley is right," said Tan. "War games. We're an experiment. Somebody built the best unit they could put together. To see what we could take. Submit us to the extremes of trauma. And they're watching us all the time. We're laboratory rats. They've put us in a huge trap, and they're waiting to see if we'll start eating each other."

"Killing each other. That's what they want us to do," said Morrosco. "I'm not killing you people. I'm getting back. I've got some other people to kill."

Revenge. It had been keeping me alive for days. If they wanted us to kill each other, they had picked the wrong unit. We would kill the people who had done this to us. I saw determination grow in every face. And stubbornness is the basis of endurance; endurance, of survival.

Hatred began to work on us like a powerful intoxicant. Tan started looking for targets in the American Army, then suddenly he hated his own government. Tan, the most loyal Korean I had ever known, hated his people, his country, and everything it stood for. The conversaton got very strange. Jackson started cursing his wife, calling her every filthy name he could think of. If she had made a better marriage, stood behind him, he would have quit the Army years before. The others encouraged him, joining into rage against their homes, their backgrounds, their families. It was preposterous, but a very human reaction to our condition.

I was swept by despair that rolled over me like waves in a heavy sea. For the first time, I was afraid of death. Morrosco and Wiley were souped up on the Benzedrine that was fast running out. We were all mentally disoriented. I could hear the conversation getting senseless, but I could not quite understand why or how. We must have been approaching a collective insanity. I could not imagine myself insane. But where does insanity begin?

I looked at our state. We were sitting in enemy territory, no guard posted, arguing with one another, shouting at people a lifetime away. Anyone could have come up upon us and just sat and watched us rambling among ourselves. If we had been hit, I was not sure the unit would have bothered to move. We would have fought it out on the spot, made the engagement come to a definitive conclusion. Which is a way of saying suicide. I think we might have shot it out with an American unit.

The only thing I trusted in the whole wide world was my gun. I was sick of the others. We were all sick of each other and began to say so. It was superficial; deep inside we could not forget how many times we had saved each other's lives. It was the decay that had set into us all. It was the absolute despair of being completely on our own, our lives of no consequence to anyone but ourselves. Everything we had been through was no more than a fly on a piece of paper. I started to get angry again. Some people had grossly underestimated us. Like a mean drunk in a bar who only knows how tough he is. No one stopped to think how tough we were.

I had seen it so many times. A guy is showing off in front of his girl or his mates, and you can see right behind his eyes into his ignorance. He cannot know what he is getting into. The only mercy that he is going to share is how lightly you choose to handle it.

When you have killed people with your hands, and a year later you are in a bar in Saigon or Tokyo facing a guy who is trying to pick a fight, his mind can no way reach out to the extremes of violence that you have known. His fantasy of how the fight might go would carry him to where he put you on the ground and put a boot in your head. Your mind has gone right past that, past seeing the man altogether. Get in a fight, and you know how easy it is to take his life away. His detuning from the fact that he could hurt you and kick you in the head can no way be compared with your detuning from the knowledge that you can kill him.

You are going to take the fight to a more effective level than he ever dreamed of. But you do not let that happen, because you have got this feeling in your guts that it does not have to come to that. He is full of himself and thinks he is the better man. And you see beyond his ignorance that he has no idea how lucky he has been. He has no idea of the man you are.

For a couple of weeks, we had been entirely self-motivated. We had done our regrouping, rearming, fighting. No one had made any effort to help us. Now we were arguing among ourselves, and we were all we had. Even my cool, collected exterior broke down. I had argued as much as the others, and I was just as scared as anybody. Of my inability to think and act. Of dying. Or worse, coming out of it unwhole. Missing an arm or a leg. We must have raved this way for an hour before it died down. Now we looked closely at one another. This was not our way of working. None of us was ready to surrender to failure; without comment, we went back to the job of surviving. We were past the wrangling and the indecision. We started talking rationally.

"We'll forget about the Mekong and keep going southeast," I said.

"That makes sense," said Jackson. "The population down there is a lot less committed than around here. We'll have a better chance with the peasants at least."

"Green Beret units are operating there," said Tan. "What do we do if we meet one?"

"I'm not giving myself up to any party that's not so large they couldn't possibly have been sent out to hit us," said Morrosco.

"How far east?" asked Prather.

"Forty, fifty miles and we should be in relative safety."

"This job does prolong itself," he said.

"Are we north of a village called Ban Thahat?" asked Tan.

"As best I recollect from the maps."

"Then I've worked here before. We should be able to strike east to the Nam Xe Noy and into a range of hills I know well. We can move relatively safely in them as far east as we want to go."

"I don't want to see any more of those people back to the west," said Morrosco. "Let's take the easy way out. I don't care how much farther it is."

"None of it is easy," said Wiley. "If the Yanks find us, they're going to gun us down."

Morrosco looked pained.

"Don't you believe your people would hit you?" Tan asked.

"They're not my people. I'm a spic, remember? What do they care about one more spic?"

"It's all the same," said Tan. "The Koreans will hit us if they get a chance. And I'm not a spic. Not in Korea."

We let the subject die there. Running into an American unit was the only straw we had to hang on to.

We moved out and crossed the Nam Hoay without difficulty. We kept off the trails until we were convinced we had high ground between us and any pursuit. We pushed south for a couple of days, hurting and repairing all the way. We were so shattered and overtired that none of us felt the need for sleep; we had passed the limits of our endurance now. We marched around the clock without rest. We met the Nam Xe Noy east of Ban Bangbet by night. We found a safe encampment on the river, between a range of hills and a wide plain. We had been almost two and a half days without combat. It was time for that extra something we could not give ourselves on the move.

Prather and Morrosco lashed together some rough shelters at river's edge. We dipped our groundsheets in the water and hung them over the lashed shelters to cool the steamy night air. Jackson and I were in the worst shape; the others cleaned us up, and we crawled under cover to rest. Wiley was in pain but functioning well enough; the knife had pierced no vitals. He caught crustacea and eels in the river and cooked them with wild vegetables over a small fire.

The stop two days earlier had pulled everyone up short when we saw what shape we were in. Not a man among us had failed to recognize our irrationality. Wiley must have given thought to Jackson's criticism; he was a better soldier than he had been for weeks. We had all subsided from a fever of antagonism to a better level of communication.

We were able to relax a bit, though we were maintaining a state of readiness again. We ate, cleaned ourselves and our weapons, and became a little more approachable.

"Where do we go from here?" Prather asked me.

"Keep moving southeast. The farther we go, the safer it gets."

"How far?"

"The seventeenth parallel . . ."

"The demarcation line? That's in Vietnam."

"Yes, but it also more or less divides loyalties in Laos because of border incursions. We may have to go as far as South Vietnam anyway."

"How far is that?"

"A week. A week and a bit. But we may be a day from running into friendly hands."

"But we know there are friendly units operating within a day of here, back to the southwest."

"We're not strong enough to go that way, Lew."

Prather grew silent. I knew what he was thinking. As unit leader, it was my responsibility to suggest it.

"We move too slowly. We're too badly hurt to run over anybody that obstructs us. Do you want to try it on your own? You and Morrosco? You can move fast. If you find anyone, you send them to fetch us."

We all tried to imagine what it would be like to split up. Little by little we began to talk about it in a very practical way. We all knew it was a good gamble. We never voted on it. I never put it forward in the form of an order. We simply worked out the logistics, treating the decision as an accomplished fact.

The slower ones would keep moving south and east toward a high range I was familiar with. I wanted to keep Wiley with me because I distrusted his state of mind, and also his physical condition would allow him to help the rest of us. Prather and Morrosco would turn on their heels and strike due west. If they made safe contact, they would institute a search for us. I estimated we would reach the seventeenth parallel on the range ahead in two days' time. If they could not sight us by air, we would be on the seventeenth parallel on the morning of the third day. I could give no exact co-ordinates. We would go as high as possible on the range; a thorough helicopter search could hardly fail to find us. The men pushing west would have to be fit; the Mekong had turned due south at Muang Kham Mouan and was now several days' hard march from us. They would be facing swamp as well as heavy enemy troop concentrations. They would have to travel on rough compass bearings without maps to tell them what the countryside looked like. If they met no friendly forces in the first two days, it was their choice to push on alone to the Mekong or turn back and meet us on the seventeenth parallel. We would wait two days for them.

Prather and Morrosco left the following morning. We stayed in camp another hour, then broke out to the south. Seeing those guys disappear down the river had made me realize what a small party we were. No one felt like talking for a long time.

After a day and a half of undisturbed climbing, we stopped to rest by a mountain stream. We had half a day's hard climb to where the parallel crossed the highest point on the range. We could hear extensive aerial activity to the west, big noisy things like Sky raiders and TR-6s bombing and diving, operating as ground support for a major movement. Prather and

Morrosco would have to run into somebody. We moved on, then pitched camp after nightfall.

We were being very cautious now; doubling up on guard, no fire, all the usual precautions. We were lying on our bellies, talking quietly when Tan grabbed my arm. Wiley crawled to my side. He too had heard a noise. Then I heard it . . . the slightest ruffle of the bushes to either side of us. We woke Jackson and waited. The noise stopped; they knew we had heard them. They must have been few in number from the amount of movement I had heard. We had to take these guys silently.

These people were really good. We stalked each other for half an hour; we spotted the area of movement by sound and tried to flank them. They cut through us without making contact. One crossed my path twice, then disappeared into the bush. They were going to get through us, so I slipped to Tan's side and showed him the shotgun. We put our knives away. I picked up one on my left, then lost him in the dark. I saw Tan bringing up his weapon to fire. His target silhouetted in the night fifty feet from us.

"Freeze!"

CHAPTER 21

It was Prather. He had turned just as Tan drew a bead on him. We called Morrosco in and returned to camp. I was enraged.

"You stupid bastards got lost," I said.

"We never got lost. When we got to the villages around Ban Bangbet, they were crawling with Pathet Lao. Two or three battalions. We couldn't go any farther, and it was not easy getting back. We were on our way to meet you."

Prather was cut across the bridge of his nose, and Morrosco was nursing a swollen hand. They did not enlarge on it.

"In that case, I'm glad to see you back."

"How are you, Pete?" Wiley asked. "Are you all right?"

"Welcome, my brother," Tan said to Prather. He embraced the taller man and kissed him on each cheek.

Their return had made us appreciate anew the depth of our commitments to each other. After my initial outburst, I found myself very pleased to see them

Morrosco and Wiley fussed over one another like two monkeys picking fleas. Our love and respect for one another was growing beyond all bounds.

We talked through the night, rethinking the situation. The area to the west we had thought was contested was in communist hands. That explained the air activity. To our immediate south was a low-lying plain with almost no cover. We had to stay within the range that would carry us to the southeast toward Ban Maloua and Highway 9. We would try to signal a helicopter or find a Green Beret unit.

We were as physically bashed as we were mentally improved. We were low on everything. I had few rounds remaining for the shotgun. Long before, we had abandoned all other weapons but Armalites. We spread the Armalite ammunition around, and it amounted to a few clips per man. The morphine was all gone. Benzedrine was fast running out. We had to go into a village, friendly or otherwise, at the first opportunity.

We came off the slopes in the early hours to find one. We saw several in the valley and chose the one nearest a river, so that we could leave in a hurry if necessary. We arrived there at sunup, then watched the place for an hour. I was uneasy because I heard no sounds of children; the village appeared almost deserted, though it was obviously lived in at the time.

Almost gently, we rounded up the few women who were about; we were in no condition to treat anyone rough. And they were people who just needed a bit of pushing and pulling around. We heard more female voices, and Tan and Morrosco found the rest of the women working in a vegetable field nearby. When they brought the women back, the racket attracted the men, who came storming down a trail. It was quite funny; they arrived with hoes and Christ knows what in their hands, and they were confronted by us. They mellowed in one second and became completely docile. Tan told them we were going to stay there three days. This scared the wits out of them. It paid off, because they told us in a panic that the communists had just been through. To my surprise, they said the troops were Vietnamese, not Pathet Lao.

We spent the morning being patched up. The women sewed cloth into our uniforms, making us look like very grim clowns. While we were eating, two men came running in. They were very excited, raving on to the head man. When they saw us, they really panicked. Tan shouted and jumped to his feet. We grabbed our weapons and made everybody freeze. The two guys told Tan a communist unit was coming in. We were right in the middle of being cleaned up. Jackson's wounds were undressed, food was cooking. I thought this was the end.

The head man, who was about ninety, grabbed Tan by the arm, talking all the while, and pulled him along.

"He's going to hide us," Tan said.

He led us quickly to a small dwelling at the far end of the village. I ran inside to take a look. One end of the building was stilted, the other was built up against a mud foundation. The old man lifted some floor plankings and indicated that we were to hide inside. If things got bad, we could go through the wall and out the back.

"What are the chances?" I asked Tan.

"Terrible. Worse if we stay out there. If we take kids with us, we're a little safer."

We grabbed several children and three young men and went inside. Two women came running up and threw our uniforms in behind us. We watched through the cracks in the timber.

These guys arrived. They were not North Vietnamese regulars, as we had assumed. They were Viet Cong, a typical wandering band, but a big unit. Twenty or twenty-five men.

The village tried to make these guys welcome, but they were a sinister breed. They circled around the hamlet and took up positions without saying a word. They were dressed entirely in black: some in baggy trousers, others with a loincloth tucked between their legs. They all wore coolie hats and sandals. They had ammunition belts hanging everywhere and were heavily armed with automatic weapons.

They closed the circle, then stood silently for a quarter of an hour with their weapons pointing into the village. Twice the head man approached them, but he was ignored.

A second unit of five arrived. The leader was apparently a regional adviser or political commissar of some kind; he was dressed in a primitive uniform. He called the village head forward and had him gather the villagers in a bunch and sit them in the open. Then he proceeded to make a speech. The first lot were still standing at the perimeter of the village.

We lay there listening, scarcely daring to breathe. We would not have made a dent in this crew, not in our condition. We had gradually been reduced to carrying out soldiering as it was presented to us. We had left behind days before the cunning and sharpness and initiative that had served us so well for two months. Numbers mattered now as never before. And there were too many numbers out there.

This guy raved on nonstop for an hour. It was unbelievable; he just went on and on and on. The guy was taking himself very seriously, but he looked like an idiot to me, acting exactly like I supposed political commissars indoctrinated people. Finally he let his men come in. He ordered the village women to fetch vegetables from the fields. His men stuffed them into the typical Viet Cong wicker baskets. They had a hot meal of fish and rice. They relaxed a bit and moved about the village, though they never said very much to the peasants.

It seemed these guys would never leave. We were sitting there, our guns pointing at the hostages. We were staring at them, and they were staring at us. And we were all waiting for the big moment to come, for the villagers to drop us in it. But it did not happen. These guys suddenly picked up and took off in the direction we were heading. They had arrived in a shifty way. They marched out like a band of storm troopers.

We lay there for half an hour to make sure they did not come back. Two peasant men ran out of the village, and I assumed it was to tell on us. But they returned to say that the Viet Cong had kept moving on.

We ate what the Viet Cong had left behind. The head man thanked us for taking the hostages. The VC unit had been a press gang, and we were holding the only men of the age to go with them. We departed. The peasants were as indifferent as they had been to the departure of the VC unit. But we were well fed, and Jackson's wounds and mine had been cleaned and dressed with fresh garments cut into strips.

We crossed the river and moved back into the highlands over a trail that would eventually join Highway 23. We were below the demarcation line in Vietnam, though still several days west of the border. There were all sorts of Green Beret and airborne units working around here, and for the first time, we heard artillery to the east, big guns fifty or sixty miles away. We saw choppers in the distance. Surely, we must run into friends soon. We were floundering in a way, because we did not know where to look for these units. We came out of the highlands to hunt for activity on Highway 23.

As we descended by a riverbed, we ran smack into four peasants. They spotted us at the same time, and before we had time to react, they gave us a very warm greeting.

"American! American!" they all cried with wide smiles.

Tan asked if they had seen any American units in the area. They very excitedly told us that there was a village six miles to the south with an American unit in it. We had them take us to the village.

We arrived at dusk, and Prather and Wiley went

cautiously in, marching the four peasants ahead of them at gunpoint. Tan followed slightly behind. It was a neat hamlet, built of low-roofed dwellings. It was larger than the last village we had stopped in, and it had an orderliness about it.

As soon as Prather and Wiley were spotted, the villagers came flocking forward. The head man came out of a distant dwelling and walked to the center of the village. I saw the peasants looking at one another. He welcomed the two in a very friendly way. Tan went forward to translate. The rest of us came in. The head man took Tan and me to his house.

This guy had some gear! He had American arms, he had ammunition, he had medicine. Tan and I saw it simultaneously. A radio. We have made it, I told myself. I waited for a wave of jubilation to sweep over me. Instead, I do not know why, I suddenly was extremely cautious.

"Get on the radio," I said to Tan.

When Tan moved toward it, the head man started jabbering; I did not know what he was saying, but he was excited. He was going on like a Frenchman, waving his arms, shrugging his shoulders, moving his hands around in the air.

"He says the radio is broken."

"It doesn't look very old to me."

Tan went to work on it and immediately got a carrier wave. But there were no earphones to tune out the static on the receiver. Nor was there a microphone, though it had the fitting and socket. The head man swore he did not know where they were. Tan kept fiddling with the thing and the static got louder and louder and began to pound at my nerves. I was just getting ready to go outside when Wiley called me.

"Rivers. Get out here."

I went out on the veranda to find Wiley crouching with his rifle at the ready. Instinctively I went down on one knee.

"What's the matter?"

"Look at that."

He pointed to one of the women standing in the clearing. She was wearing an American fatigue shirt.

"So, what's the problem?"

"I haven't seen any Yanks around here yet."

It was a valid point. We had been in the village long enough for them to surface. There seemed to be an organized American presence here. But no soldiers. I went back inside.

"There's a woman outside wearing an American uniform. Get that guy to tell us exactly what the position is here."

Tan questioned him sharply.

"He just keeps saying the Americans are here. Everything is all right. We're safe. He's just about as vague as he could be."

"Americans here," the head man said to me smiling.

The atmosphere was becoming quite strained. I heard the villagers set up a racket outside, then Prather called me to come out again. The head man came out as well and shouted something which quieted the people milling around in front.

"I was looking around," said Morrosco. "That hut over there is full of American weapons and ammunition. It's not stacked. It's just thrown all over the joint, like somebody wanted to hide it quick when we showed up."

I went to take a look. They were all American weapons—M-1s and M-3s and Armalites. I began to get very nervous. Tan questioned the head man about how the weapons came to be there, and the man avoided answering by breaking into broken English, saying Americans here, Americans here. Tan was getting this look in his eye; he could recognize deceit in an Oriental far better than the rest of us. I called Prather and Morrosco back to me, and Jackson joined us from where he had gone to try his luck with the radio. It was whistling and carrying on, but it would not lock onto a frequency. It was a normal backpack radio with a phone clip on the back. And the phone clip was missing. I began to think that it had been stored in parts; we had the body; the rest was hidden. We kept questioning the head man, but we could not get a straight answer. We had to look for the rest of it. This radio was our biggest break on the entire mission.

We tore the hut apart, but we could find nothing. The head man kept shrugging his shoulders, as if he did not know what we were looking for. We had been in the village half an hour now, and I was growing more anxious by the minute. I sent Wiley and Morrosco to the river to keep watch.

I interrogated the head man through Tan, and I got the impression he was trying to string it out, to keep us there as long as possible. I had him order some village men to bring up the weapons we had found. Then I changed my mind. I took the radio and the head man down to where the weapons were lying. The man started betraying a strange apprehension.

There were twenty or thirty weapons scattered everywhere with ammunition mixed among them. We sorted out what we needed. Jackson took an M-3, so that he could carry more clips without having to strap them to his bad leg. The rest of us took new Armalites. Wiley and Prather came running up, shouting that they had seen activity in the river. I told Wiley to arm himself and keep the villagers under close observation. The people had brought food out by now, but we ignored every friendly overture. I went to the river.

We saw a large force moving in our direction, too far away to be identified positively, but they were moving in a military column. I heard a commotion from the village. I took a mental picture of how far away these people were, then ran back.

Wiley was standing over a man he had killed. Prather and Tan were up on the veranda, their weapons trained on the villagers.

"What happened?"

"That woman over there is wearing a fatigue shirt with a Green Beret flash on the shoulder. I went over to take a look at the shirt. Something funny was happening, so I ducked in this building. This guy was inside, wounded. He was trying to rest a rifle on the window ledge."

"For God's sake, did you have to kill him?"

"He needed killing."

I was sick. The guy could have told us what was going on. But that was the frame of mind Wiley was in. If we were going to learn anything now, it had to come from the head man.

Tan dragged him down to where I was standing. I hit him in the mouth with my fist, then Tan questioned him about the man Wiley had killed. Tan was in midsentence when he broke off and walked over to the dead man.

"This is a fucking Cambo," he said.

"What do you mean?"

"This is a fucking Cambo," he repeated. "A goddamn Cambodian mercenary."

"How do you know?"

"Because he looks like a Cambodian, that's how I know."

He was dressed as a peasant, but he must have been a mercenary, because no other Cambodian would be that far north. He was armed with an American carbine. It all started to fit into place. This village had been used by Americans who were now probably buried in the bush.

We took the head man and the four villagers who had brought us in and lined them up against a dwelling. We gathered food and some clean clothing to make bandages. I gave the head man one last chance to explain. He kept saying Americans here. Then Wiley found more American uniforms in another hut.

I lost my patience. I knocked the head man down. I pulled him to his feet by the shirt. His shirt tail flew up, and I saw the mouthpiece from the radio tied around his waist. I yanked it off and stared at it in my hand. The head man realized the game was up. And he started to smile.

Wiley and Prather ran through the village but found nothing more. We herded the villagers together in the clearing. Jackson stood on the veranda covering them with his M-3. He was very nervous. He looked ready to shoot them down.

I knocked down the head man. I wrapped the mouthpiece cord around his neck and jerked him upright. Without taking my eyes off the head man, I yelled to Tan to tell him he had his one last chance to explain what was going on. I knew by the courage and substance of his resistance so far that I was dealing with a dedicated communist. He had an ideal to back him up. He was leading a village that had turned over, or had never been what the Americans thought it was. Now they had wiped out an American unit. I was filled with loathing.

Holding him by the cord around his neck, I pressed the head man back against the veranda steps. Tan shouted at him to tell us what we wanted to know. The man's smiling demeanor broke and he began to scream. And he did not scream exactly what I wanted to hear. Tan translated for us.

"Communist troops are on their way here now. We'll be dead in an hour. If we kill him, we only make our own deaths that much worse."

I heard the word "Cambodian" more than once; there were Cambodians in the area. But the man kept breaking into English with this strange "Americans here" business. It made no sense. He had this cunning way of looking at us, as if we were bandits in the final hour of our existence.

I kicked him in the groin. As he went down, I held up his head by the cord and pulled it as hard as I could between my hands. I killed him.

Weapons were breeched all around me. I told Tan to forget about the headphone. We had to get out of there. I sent Jackson and Prather toward the river where the party was advancing on us.

"Shoot those four guys," I said to Tan, pointing to the peasants who had brought us in. "Lob a couple of grenades into the hut where the weapons are."

Then I changed my mind. I made the four peasants carry the head man's body into the hut with the weapons. We lobbed grenades in behind them. The building erupted. One man was thrown through the wall. Both his legs were missing, but he was alive. Tan shot him.

Jackson stitched the ground very near the villagers. His eyes were darting wildly. He wanted them to break out, so he could shoot them down. I wanted it as well. He let off a second burst closer than the first. Several people went down, hit on the ricochet. They were screaming everywhere. I told him to knock it off. He and I backed out of the village.

The men below had heard the explosions and were coming on the double. We stayed above the river so we could see anyone tracking us in it. We raced southeast all day toward Highway 23, which we intended to cross where the river passed beneath it. Getting on the far side of the highway and clear of this last village was both a psychological and geographical goal to aim for.

Late in the afternoon, we were moving quickly through heavy bush. I was at point, Prather at my elbow, the others almost within reach behind us. I ducked a thick vine, then Prather chopped it aside with his machete. The vine flew skyward with a whooshing sound. I thought someone was coming down on top of me. Instinctively I fell to the ground and flattened myself. Behind me I heard a crunch, then bodies being flung about. A flock of wooden darts went whistling over me at waist level. The rushing of wood through wind and leaves ended as quickly as it had begun. Cautiously I raised my head.

The others were tangled like a pile of dominoes. They began to unwind, until everyone but Morrosco was sitting up.

"What happened?"

"Morrosco caught the bow in the middle of the back. He knocked us all down. Hitting him flung the spears out prematurely."

"How is he?"

"Out like Lottie's eye," replied Jackson.

Chopping the vine had triggered the simplest of booby traps, a tree limb bent backward with a cup on the end full of what looked like giant toothpicks. The darts were about eight inches long and thicker than a propelling pencil. They would go through a man's body like an arrow. The trigger was in the direct flight path of the darts. When the limb struck Morrosco at the end of the line, the darts were flung out as if it had been at full arc. Morrosco had knocked the others out of the way, and I had been saved only because the arc had allowed me time to go to ground. A man could diagnose these pieces of luck until he went mad. It had not killed us, and that was that.

This booby trap almost cracked us. It was the simplest thing in the world, a typical Cambodian cum Viet Cong device laid in the predicted path of any unit moving in the area. But this one was brand-new and well prepared. It must have been laid for us. No one spoke for a long while.

We could not stop to bring Morrosco around. We grabbed him up and kept moving. He came around when we went into the river and dragged him through the water. The branch had gone up his back before slamming into his head. He was semiconscious and had to be carried for two hours. We crossed under the highway and went into high ground east of there, where we rested.

We were exhausted. Carrying Morrosco and watching for booby traps had been an almost unbearable strain. While we stopped, Tan worked on the radio. He could still not get any sense out of it because he could not tune out the static. He reconstructed the mouthpiece in a bush way. The head man had ripped it out, and the pin plugs were missing, but Tan broke into the radio and twisted wires together, and he got life out of the microphone.

I was only half aware of what Tan was doing, because I was thinking about the ever-increasing intensity of action over recent days. I no longer discounted the wildest theories about our predicament. I grew convinced we had been dangled on a string, and now the puppeteers were closing in on us. There had been a lull when we struck east because we had caught someone unprepared; they—whoever they were—expected us to hang on to the myth of a Mekong crossing. But that had been denied us so many times we had reached a point where we needed a new goal. A different way of thinking.

"Does anybody know Ban Houaysan?"

"The old air base?" Jackson asked. "I worked out of there several times before they closed it."

"It's within four or five miles of the South Vietnamese border," I explained to the others. "It's a perfect place for us to be picked up. If we can get the radio working. Just moving that way, we have a good chance of running into someone. If we can't get picked up, we can cross the border, push on into South Vietnam."

Tan was not getting any joy out of the radio by scanning the band without fine tuning. A couple of times we thought we picked up American units conversing, but the static was so heavy, we could not be sure.

"Stick it on the Mode H emergency band," I told him, "and broadcast blind."

Tan began fiddling with the dials.

"Yeah, do that," said Jackson. "There must be somebody left in Indochina who don't know where we are. We got the Pathet Lao on our ass. And the VC and the NVA. We got the Cambos coming north. And maybe our people. The last time the phone rang, it wasn't exactly good news. Why don't we think about this a minute?"

"If we're not going to use the radio, we might as well leave it here," said Tan.

"Let's be sure we use it to help us then," said Morrosco.

"Let's go to high ground, where we're protected, and get better transmission," I said. "We put out a code three, special forces emergency call. We don't say who we are. Only that we need help, we're east of Ban Houaysan and on our way there. We'll take a look at the next hamlet, try to figure out what it is, and transmit that we are east of there."

"Are you really afraid to say who we are?"

"Yeah."

"You think we have been eyeballed for elimination?"

"Is there anybody here who doesn't?"

"Do you think they dare use direct action against us?"

"Depends on who's behind it. If the decision to send us in the first place came from below high command, it will be done indirectly. This whole bloody nonsense could have been started by a colonel. Some maniac wondering how well we'd do. If that's the case, he must be pretty bloody surprised by now. He never expected to see us back knocking at his door. Well, he can't very well call in the B-52s on us without a lot of explaining. So he'd have to hire Cambos or something like that. Maybe this lunacy did start at the top. Either way, our embarrassment factor supersedes our importance. They don't want us home."

"Yeah, well they can forget about that," Morrosco said. "Because we're going back. There's no stopping us."

Our morale was very good in one sense; we had become, not survival-happy, but success-happy. If anyone were ever to survive a mission like this, we were the people. We felt as if we could go on getting away with things as long as we were a unit. Ended as a unit. We saw ourselves as the supreme test of man's ability to survive. And we were up to it.

Our loyalties to external forces had been shredded beyond repair. As soldiers . . . as Americans . . . Koreans . . . Australians . . . we were finished. We were flagless people now, which was an almost unimaginable reversal for someone like Tan, who had been the proudest Korean in Southeast Asia. Or Jackson, a soldier's soldier. Or Prather, whose loyalty to Britain had been beyond question. He swore he would expose the thing if we got back. If they knew us as well as they should have, they knew Prather would come to that conclusion sometime. Which was the same as Prather signing his death warrant. To a certain extent, we were all being judged by Prather's frame of mind. By someone who knew we were alive. I was certain we were not meant to return.

We moved out toward a populated area where we knew RFI units had operated. If we did not find any, we had agreed to keep moving until we reached South Vietnam. We had decided to expose ourselves to any allied troops we met and face the consequences.

A strange, subdued atmosphere came over the unit. None of us expected to make it, though we would never give up trying. But the other thing did not worry us any longer. Hell, you can only go on fighting for your life for so long.

We followed a river, then left it for high ground above the village of Ban Maloua to break the ice and try to make radio contact. There must be allied units somewhere about that would pick up our distress call. We ducked a well-armed VC patrol and kept climbing. We were within striking distance of highways 9 and 91, so our hopes of finding someone were not unrealistic. Tan set up the radio and switched it on.

"Code three," he said, "code three. Do you read? Over."

A voice responded.

CHAPTER 22

It was garbled. It was unintelligible. But somebody was responding to our calls. We all let out a shout. Tan continued transmitting, and every time he stopped, we were getting reception.

"Mention Highway Nine," I prompted him. "Tell them we'll move along it toward Ban Maloua."

Tan transmitted for ten minutes. The replies kept coming back indecipherable. Little by little deflation set in. I grew irritated, then enraged with frustration.

"Fuck it," I said. "Say the lot. Tell them we've been to China. And if they don't want to hear that, they can come and pick us up."

"Code three. China mission. Fingers Five. Five Fingers. Repeat. Code three China mission. Fingers Five. Five Fingers . . ."

Somebody must have been living through a nightmare somewhere, but I did not give a fuck. At least people knew we were still alive and intended to stay that way. If they wanted to shut us up, let them come and get us.

We broadcast for another quarter of an hour, then headed out for Highway 9. We felt better. The radio was working, and we had been answered. It was so fuzzy with static, it could have been our imagination. Or we could have been listening to two other units converse. But I did not believe that.

Our route brought us to Ban Maloua before we reached the highway. It was dark by now, and the tiny hamlet was quiet. We ran across no dogs. Nor chickens, which was even worse. We were all walking now. Jackson required even less help than I did. We were tired and hungry. I considered stealing food. In the end, we decided to take the place for a short while; that was always safer. Jackson and Prather went to the far side. Tan stayed with me. We crawled in under the houses, and the other two went to wake the villagers. I watched them mount the veranda of one of the huts on the far side of the clearing. They began shouting. There was the usual commotion: people rushing out to see what was happening, then dashing, frightened, back inside. Tan and I were making ready to surface when I realized there had been no reaction from the building above us. I had heard people awakening, but no one had rushed out, no woman had stifled a scream, no child had whimpered. I put my arm on Tan's shoulder and listened. We heard boots scuffling. Metallic sounds. Slow and deliberate movement. I signaled to Tan that I was going under the next building. I heard the same there.

Wiley and Morrosco jumped off the veranda down to the ground. They were waiting for a call to action, and none of us had surfaced. They were momentarily confused, then realized what it meant. Wiley ran under the veranda, and Morrosco dashed beneath the next building. Tan rolled over and joined me. The buildings opposite were now full of hysterical peasants, the buildings above us occupied by people quietly shuffling about.

I rolled out from under the building one way, Tan the other. I threw a grenade through the veranda window. It exploded with a tremendous roar and engulfed the dry thatch in flames. A band of VC came bursting out of the second building, and Tan shot two dead, then heaved grenades in behind them. That building too went up in flames. Burning bodies threw themselves through the walls, and Tan and I shot them down as they came. Morrosco and Wiley leapt up and ran together to back us up. There was a flash behind them. My face was hit by the roar of a concussion grenade. Morrosco and Wiley were snatched up by an invisible hand and thrown in our direction, their limbs flying like marionettes as they hurled through the air. They hit the ground, rolled, and stopped. Neither gave a sign of life.

Tan and I killed everyone on the south side of the village, and Prather and Jackson dashed in from the north to find where the grenade had come from. Prather leapt up the steps and piled into the building where we had heard the most noise from the peasants. I heard screams and fighting inside. The peasants were killing Prather. I dashed across the clearing, firing from my hip through the sides of the buildings. Tan and I arrived together and burst inside. To find Prather untouched.

"They were killing VC," he shouted. "They were prisoners."

Three bodies lay on the floor, drenched in blood. Their heads were battered and their limbs twisted grotesquely. I glanced about and saw two more bodies.

"Someone was firing through the wall," Prather said. "Killed two of these people."

"The place is secure," Jackson shouted from outside.

"See about Wiley and Morrosco," I told him.

Tan was conversing with two old men. Everyone else was sobbing and wailing.

"They want to go into the next building," he said.

"Let them."

I followed them outside. Tan went inside with the old men. I was just about to walk over to Jackson when Tan came running out. He grabbed the veranda and vomited bile from an empty stomach. I walked up the steps.

Through the door, I saw several teen-age boys. The two old men were standing over one, pulling at the wooden stakes that had been driven through all their hands and feet. The flesh had been slashed open up and down their bodies, and they had been disemboweled. The old men were not crying. I turned away.

"They're alive!" Jackson shouted.

I ran to his side. I half expected the peasants to set into me for the two I had killed, but they were very docile. They had seen enough carnage to fill their lives.

Morrosco and Wiley were both unconscious, but Wiley was about to come around, so he was the priority. Jackson rolled him over, then drew back in horror.

"His face has been blown apart."

"Tan," I called out, "tend to Morrosco. Jackson, help me drag Wiley away from the flames."

Half the hamlet was ablaze, and the heat beat on us unbearably. Wiley's clothes had been blown off his back, and his head was bathed in blood. We dragged him some distance away, then I turned to treat his wounds. I almost screamed.

Wiley's left eye was hanging out of the socket, suspended on his cheek by the optic nerve. I drew in deeply with my lungs to steady my nerves. I had no idea what to do. The scene around me was absolute chaos . . . the building aflame . . . peasants running aimlessly about . . . Prather searching frantically for more Viet Cong. I glanced over to Tan, who had ripped Morrosco's uniform open to get at the wounds. Morrosco had caught shrapnel in his back and all up and down his leg. It filled him: his buttocks, his abdomen, his groin. His penis was torn. Blood was spilling out everywhere.

The peasants were gathering their belongings on the run and dropping off for us what we could use; food, water, clean cloth. They had to disappear into the bush before another Viet Cong unit murdered them all. They tore about, they snatched up chickens and tied their feet, they grabbed everything they could carry, and faded into the jungle. To mingle with another village, I guess. Only they knew where they could go. A few stayed behind and helped with Morrosco. It was useless trying to remove the shrapnel. Prather snatched some clean clothing off a woman who started to argue, then ran on. He bound strips over what was left of Morrosco's uniform.

I had Wiley on my hands, and the only man who would know what to do was Morrosco. Wiley began to come around. We had no morphine.

"Tan, you and Jackson hold him down."

"What are you going to do?"

"I don't know."

I had decided to put his eye back, but I did not know how to get hold of it. It did not hang out far, just over the lip of the lower eyelid; it hardly cleared the front of the eye. But the eye socket was bleeding profusely. Blood vessels in the eye itself had burst and were discharging blood.

I tried to take the eyeball in my fingers, but it slipped loose and wobbled on the end of the optic nerve. I knew not to touch the optic nerve or the retina, but beyond that I was helpless. Then Wiley was conscious. And this guy had guts.

"I'm blind," he said. "I'm blind. No. I can see! I can see something."

He must have been seeing a little out of his other eye, though it was covered in blood as well and swelling shut from the bruising.

"Everything is red," he said.

"Can you hear me?" I asked.

"Yes, but I can't see anything. Only red. I see a glow. It hurts."

He tried to raise one arm to shield his face from the flames. I propped him up against me and pulled the shreds of his shirt up around his face. Jackson grabbed a burning stick for light.

"Listen to me. A concussion grenade hit you in the back of the head. It knocked one of your eyes out."

"I'm going to be blind."

"Listen. The eye is still there. I'm going to put it back in. You've got to help."

I did not know whether to take it in my hand or in a rag or what. Wiley began to tremble. He started to shake all over uncontrollably. If I did not do something soon, he would go into shock and die. I lowered him across my knee and cradled his head in my arms. I waited. And waited. And I thought, Jesus, I can go on like this forever, thinking about how I am going to do it. I cupped his eye in the palm of my hand.

"My head!" he screamed. "The back of my head! I can't stand it!"

"You're making it harder for me!" I shouted over his screams. "Open your eyes as wide as you can."

He tried. His eyebrows went up. One eye opened. And the other eye socket never opened; it was covered in bits of loose skin that just hung there.

I lowered his head and tilted the eye into the socket. The eye went in from the bottom and fell under the loose flesh. I pressed gently with the palm of my hand. The eye popped out. I put it in again and held my hand over it for ten seconds. I lifted my hand. The pupil looked straight at me, then the eyeball rotated inward until I saw only white. There was nothing more I could do. I had blinded him.

"It's in now," I said. "But you can't see anything now."

"I can't see out of either eye now."

"Try to open your eyes," I said, not really knowing why. "Try as hard as you can."

He strained until he screamed again. The eyelids fluttered, then opened slightly. As I watched, the eyeball began to center. The socket was weeping profusely, washing and lubricating the eye. The iris and pupil surfaced, moved a bit more, then the movement stopped off center. At least he might have some sight.

We bandaged his hair back and left the eye to bleed and weep.

I turned to Morrosco, who was now conscious. Most of the bleeding had been stemmed, but the groin wounds were being poisoned by uncontrollable dysentery. To my astonishment, Morrosco could stand. Even walk. We left.

The unit was dying. We carried Wiley, sometimes three of us, sometimes four. He tried to walk, but it was hopeless with him stumbling into everything. Dysentery was weakening Tan and me by the hour. Tan had the first signs of malaria, already well advanced in Prather. The symptoms had shown a day or two earlier in the latter; he was shaking and trembling without ceasing now, suddenly seized by chills or fits of raging fever. Jackson was walking, but his leg was badly infected. My wounds were infected. My leg was as stiff as if it were made of wood. We were all in the latter stages of malnutrition; our eyes, sunk deep into their sockets, were surrounded by pink swollen flesh that contrasted with the blackness of our faces. Our bodies had exhausted the ability to fight decay, to heal us from within; the slightest abrasion meant instant infection. The blow from the rifle across Morrosco's face had raised a great bruise that was covered with pepper spots where poison was pushing against the skin. Tan had lost almost complete use of his arm; it was paralyzed from the elbow joint to the shoulder. The flesh was dying around the wound on Prather's arm. Jackson had once been lean and wiry; now he walked bent and stooped, like a man who had aged forty years. I did not expect Morrosco to recover, nor Wiley. How much longer could the rest of us go on?

Morrosco began to cry. From pain, from exhaustion, from the sheer ordeal of it all. He cried like a little boy, tears running down his face as if he had been hit by his sister. I said nothing, but I hated him for it. My hatred was the only emotion within my grasp now. I was hardened to every circumstance; I had met it head-on, and I defeated it, until finally there was nothing left to fight with but insensitivity. To myself. To other people. My hatred subsided. I felt compassion for the poor dying boy.

It was too great an ordeal to talk. Conversation was reduced to checking one another's condition. I'll carry that. Help me with this.

Daylight came, and I saw clearly the state we were in. Our uniforms mirrored our physical condition. I had no shirt, just pieces of cloth that clung to me in several places. I threw those aside. Morrosco's shirt hung in tatters like that of a circus clown. Fatigue legs were missing entirely or flapping loosely as we walked. The canvas of our boots was torn in a dozen places. We had not had our boots off for weeks, because our feet would have run away from us, would have swollen immediately, and we would not have got them back on. If any man's feet had packed up, he was finished.

We could not gain Highway 9 immediately because it was elevated high above the river and passed over it in a narrow ravine. To join it, we had to leave the river. I sent the others ahead and dropped behind to fill our canteens.

I started to dip my canteen into a still backwater when by the early morning light I caught my reflection in the surface. I set the canteen aside and stared at the image before me. What had I become?

My precision was breaking down. Back at the village, I had mouthed off at the gun and needlessly killed two people, something I would never have done if I had been me. My mind was slipping. I needed time for mental analysis, to pull myself together, to be on my own. I was shattered. For the first time, I noticed that my hands were trembling. I could not stop them shaking. All of a sudden, I wanted something . . . a fuller life than I had known.

I sat for a while, looking into the pool. I saw faces of people I had known before I had got into this thing. Snatches of scenes from my childhood drifted by, times as a boy when I had stopped to take account of myself. I began to think of the soft parts of life, moments of pure pleasure . . . the beauty of looking at snow . . . the beauty of catching fish in the river . . . the beauty of being with someone. Beautiful things I had once enjoyed and almost taken for granted, and now I might never see again, came rushing back. I saw a dog at play, and a horse being chased by a foal around a green field. I met someone, and being with her instilled in me a great appreciation of the beauty that was everywhere around me.

It also made me recognize the other extremes of life. The idiots and the fanatics who had gotten me to the side of this river. I found myself asking if we were among those idiots and fanatics. And this jolted me back to the present. Perfectionism. I had been hunting for the word. It was this we were losing. We were not used to making mistakes . . . were not used to seeing someone muck up bringing a man down with his knife . . . or getting careless with his weapon. I recalled the perfection with which I had attacked the mission three months earlier. Three months! We had been in this for three months. I had accepted my orders with total confidence; I could do the job. I saw us sitting on that hillside in China, when my killer instinct had been tuned and balanced in a most perfect way. And then I saw the way we had blown a village apart. We had destroyed and killed with such . . . relish. It was too much.

I caught up with the others. We moved out on a trail that would carry us to Highway 9. Because of our condition, we were not pointing but moving close together.

"Freeze," Jackson said. "Booby trap."

We stopped in our tracks. Jackson had his rifle on his shoulder, his finger on the trigger. I could not see the booby trap. But I could see the fear on people's faces. We were in grotesque positions; standing on one leg, leaning forward, bending to one side. Everyone was afraid to move, to blink. I was waiting for the thing to happen, because maybe it had already been set off.

Maybe we were already dead and just waiting for it to happen.

The stop by the river had calmed me, gotten some things out of my system. I had regained some presence of mind. But the tension in the others was going to kill us. Everyone wanted to do something quickly. That really got to me. These were guys who had acted coolly for three months in moments of extreme duress. And I saw the panic in their faces. Maybe it had been there before, and I had ignored it. Morrosco whimpered. He must have felt things ripping into his body. But nothing happened. He stopped. We grew completely silent.

"Everybody stay put and stay cool," I said, not feeling cool myself. "What is it?"

"Strings left and right," Jackson said.

"Height?"

"My rifle barrel."

"I can't see anything."

"It's under the loop."

I was third in line, with Morrosco in front of me. He was trembling so badly I thought he might fall down.

"Morrosco," I said sharply, "unlock your knees. Breathe deeply. You're going to be all right. For God's sake, don't move. I'm coming forward, Jackson," I said and started inching my way toward him.

"Don't move! Don't move!" Jackson shouted.

"I'm clear," I said and kept coming.

"You're not clear!" he screamed.

Then I saw the string stretched across his barrel. I followed it with my eye. It went out to a nearby limb and crossed back over the path. Behind me. I had walked underneath it. We all had; Jackson and Morrosco and I were so bent and crippled we had passed under a cord set to catch us at the throat. Jackson's rifle barrel had caught it on the second crossing; the weapon was tipped back under the tension, because the trigger needed a body weight to trip it.

"Don't move your feet," I ordered. "Crouch down. Watch for head-high wires. And trip wires."

I saw the string loop off around a tree, then I could not see a damn thing. We all stood there, trying to figure this device out. Then very slowly I made my way out to the tree around which the twine was looped. The sweat was crawling off me. Never taking my eyes off the line, I worked my way around the tree. My boot came up against something. I looked down. My toe was resting against a branch that had been bent off the same tree and driven into the ground. The line would be attached somewhere to the end of it.

"I've found it!" I yelled out.

I followed the branch to where it entered the ground. Beyond, a line of earth had been turned where the string was obviously buried and anchored with something heavy I had not yet spotted. I still did not understand how the device worked. The line of earth led to a distant tree, where the string had some job to do, but I bloody well was not going to walk that far to find out what it was about.

I scraped a bit of dirt away from the end of the branch, and the earth started to move next to my hand. The branch had been anchored, not the string, and it was breaking out. Slowly the line of soil began to shake.

"Take your rifle off the string!" I shouted.

Jackson did it without hesitation, with complete trust in me. The limb stopped moving.

"Make your way over here, Jackson. Watch out for trip wires."

He crawled to me on his stomach while I waited for the body vibration to set something off.

"I've seen this son-of-gun before," he said. "That line will lead to where a lot more lines are gathered. They'll be tied to pins in mines scattered all over the joint, probably on the end of a branch. That string across the path is holding a stick in place somewhere."

I searched along it again, and on the far side of

the tree I found a wooden pin, restrained by the line, gripping another branch. This branch went over our heads, and it was connected to the line in the ground. One of the two lines would lift a cluster of mines over our head and set them off at the same time. But for some reason, both lines had stopped moving.

We edged under the wire and inched our way to the road, watching for trip wires at every step. We were bathed in sweat and shaking when we got clear.

"I'm going to set that thing off," Jackson said.

"Don't," I said. "You don't know what other devices you might set off."

"I don't care. I'm going to do it anyway."

We moved to the far side of the track. He lobbed a grenade behind him, then hit the ground. The earth erupted. Four or five clusters of these things came flying out and blew the jungle apart, showering us with stones, dirt, and branches. No one could have survived it.

The dust settled. We got up and were brushing ourselves off when we heard voices and the sound of men running. A dozen guys came piling down the road toward the booby trap. They must have set it, and they thought we were all dead. We lay beside the road, and when they came alongside us, I launched two grenades into their midst. Half of them were killed on impact. One guy went over backward, then scrambled back to his feet. He began a frenzied search for his weapon. As his eyes darted down the road, they met mine, then stopped and looked me square in the face. He let out a great roar of fear and hatred, then reached for his rifle at his feet.

I was so fatigued, all I could think was, here we go again. I found myself switching my weapon on single shot. And I stood up in the road and exposed myself.

It was completely wild. It was against every instinct and all my training. The guy fumbled with his weapon, trying desperately to draw a bead to me. And

I was filled with anger for this man, a great loathing that started down in my boots and coursed through me. I did not hate the soldier on the road; he was just a face. It was a searing wrath for what I found myself in.

The scene became a fantasy acted out in slow motion. The man's features became so clearly defined that I could see the stubble on his chin. His body started churning over, and his eyes grew so wide they almost popped out of their sockets. I watched the man clamoring for his life, trying to beat the bullet he knew was on its way.

I was mesmerized. I felt myself sinking into the gun at my shoulder. My chin found comfort on the stock like a sleepy head on a pillow. Nothing else mattered now. The rest of the world retreated beyond my sight. There was just me, the weapon, and this guy.

I pulled off . . . one . . . two . . . three. I drew him from his head to his waist. Ping, ping, ping. I cut him in half. While he was still thinking about the first bullet, the third was tearing into his stomach. The guy's reflexes were still happening, but he was already dead.

In a way, it was quite funny. I was watching a human being who had as much chance as anybody. But he never really had any chance at all, so why bother to move in the first place. Because he was just a normal guy trying to survive an environment he did not want to be in anyway.

I felt completely a winner. I had beaten the opposition, won the game. I snapped out of it, and I was back on the road.

Everyone was firing. Prather jumped to his feet and ran in among them, blasting away from the hip. He was over the top now; he did not care what happened. We finished them off in two minutes without being touched. They wore parts of American uniforms and carried a mixture of arms, mostly new, mostly American. Tan identified them as Cambodian. We fell back into the trees and waited for the next lot; we were in no condition to run. No one came.

Finally Prather went down the road. A minute after he had disappeared out of sight around a bend, we heard a high-pitched scream. There were more around the corner, I thought, and Prather had shot one. But no weapon had been fired.

"Help me," Prather called out.

At first we could not see him. Then he appeared in the middle of the road, dragging along on his stomach.

"Help me! Someone come and get me!"

"Don't anybody move!" I said.

"Please! For Christ's sake, come and get me!"

For all I knew, there were a dozen guns trained on him.

"It's a booby trap. I'm hit by a booby trap. There's no one here. But booby traps."

Jackson climbed to his feet and started for Prather. One of the Cambodians on the road surfaced and fired at Jackson. He missed. Morrosco shot the man. And he kept firing. Round after round thudded through the lifeless body. I knocked the barrel down to the ground. Tan ran past Jackson and Prather and went around the corner. I heard two grenades go off. He ran back to us.

"There's nobody else. I set off more booby traps, so watch out."

One by one, we joined the prostrate Prather on the road. He had been speared through the side by a stake the size of a night stick. It had entered the flesh above his hip, and the point was exiting beside his kidney. We dragged him to the side of the road and debated leaving the stake in him for fear of dragging out his stomach or kidneys, and because he was not bleeding. But no one could carry this spear in his side.

"Pull it out! Out!" he cried hysterically.

He began to tremble so much we could hardly hold on to him. I looked at Tan. He hit Prather a vicious punch in the temple. Prather fell back unconscious. Morrosco staggered forward and fell down beside Prather.

"Bring Wiley forward," I said to Jackson.

"Why don't you bastards let us die," Morrosco said. "Leave us alone. Let us both die. What's the point anymore?"

"Get Morrosco out of here," I told Tan.

He led Morrosco away just as Jackson brought Wiley forward. Wiley was very calm. He felt that death was a matter of waiting, and he was prepared to wait.

"Morrosco is in terrible shape," I told him. "Look after him. Keep him quiet."

"He needs me. I'll take care of him. Until it all ends. Where is he?"

Jackson led Wiley to Morrosco's side. Wiley spoke softly to Morrosco, calming him.

"All right, here we go," I said to Tan. "As I lift the point of the stake, you cut the flesh behind it."

As soon as Tan started cutting, the bleeding began. The pain brought Prather around, so Jackson sat across his chest while we worked. By the time the stake was out, Prather's entire side was exposed. The stake had rested on the hip bone but hit no vital organs. We improvised a bandage and tied him tightly.

We gathered weapons and stripped the bodies of their uniforms and put them on. By now we were dressed half in uniform, half in peasant garb. We put a complete uniform on Prather. Night was approaching. We moved down a trail in what we hoped was an easterly direction. We gave up on Highway 9; from what we had seen, we could expect ambush at every bend in the road. Prather could walk, though he went into delayed shock an hour later. Wiley could see enough from one eye that he did not have to be led. It was a good thing we did not have the physical burden of carrying these two, because the booby traps had shattered us mentally. Because we could never outwit luck. I saw Wiley pouring water from his canteen over his face. It went through my mind to stop him, but I did not bother. Even water seemed unimportant now.

We started to break into the hamlet of Ban Palai. We needed that place more than we had needed any stop on the trip, and we passed it by; we were too weak to face any resistance. We continued east until we could go no farther. We fell out by a river for the rest of that night and part of the following day. The sound of crying and moaning never ceased.

I carried wounds for a hundred men, and I was the fittest of us all. As I listened to the cries of men I had lived with for three months, my resolve to survive redoubled. I would see this thing through. I would carry these men until somebody, somewhere in an American uniform would have to welcome us. Or look me in the eye and kill me. Nobody else was going to kill me. I had Stacey's face before me. The briefers . . .

We pushed out at noon the next day. The men were impossible to move with words, so I got up and started to leave, and they decided to come with me. Morrosco begged to be left to die, but Wiley made him come. No one could have slowed us down, because none of us could move faster than the others. Wiley had never panicked from his loss of sight, and now he was almost serene. He had a strange application, where he felt he was going nowhere, so there was nothing to see. He devoted himself to Morrosco. I think going blind had had an effect on him similar to mine at the river when I stopped for water. His values had changed. There was nothing more important to him than the men around him. And his inner thoughts, I supposed. I did not know.

We were moving along hill contours, still hoping to go to Ban Houaysan. We stopped once, and I tried the radio. It was transmitting as before, but we were not getting feedback, even as static. We were too low. I decided to leave the others and climb to high terrain to the east for transmission. I would catch them up or meet them at the airfield.

"You're not leaving," Tan said.

"We stay together," Jackson said.

"We'll never separate again," Wiley said.

We walked together into high ground, onto an eastward-facing slope. I transmitted for half an hour, and this time we were heard. The response was worse than ever; our batteries were failing. I was calling out for someone to come and save our lives, and all the answer we got was white sound. I could stand it no longer.

"Listen to me!" I screamed into the mouthpiece. "Five Fingers! We've been to China. To kill Giap. Rivers. Prather. Wiley. Morrosco. Jackson. Tan." I hesitated. "Toliver. We want out! Get me the White House. I want the White House to get us out of here. Nixon. Westmoreland. They sent us in here. They get us out, or I'm going to kill them. Do you hear me? Kill them! Stacey. Tell Stacey he's a dead man. Five Fingers! . . ."

Jackson took the microphone away from me and put one hand on my shoulder.

We returned to Highway 9. I was ready to push off when Tan brought me up short.

"Why are we going to take the highway to the airport? It's safer and shorter across the countryside."

"Don't ask me why anything anymore."

We set out on a direct bearing toward Ban Houaysan. We passed under the road once, then lost sight of it. Helicopters passed behind us, moving very fast. Half an hour later, we saw a massive bunch of choppers to the south, along the highlands. Then Skyraiders carrying out an attack to the northwest. It looked as if there was a major battle raging along the border.

I decided again to go to high ground on my own and transmit. I walked away with the radio, and no one tried to stop me. But the hill was murder to climb because of my leg. Half an hour later, Tan was beside me. He took the radio and sent me back to the others. He kept his weapon and ammunition and gave me the rest of his gear. I watched him go, then turned down the hill. His belt dragged on the ground, his canteen banged into my leg. It was hot. The gear was heavy. I dropped it and walked on. Tan came back a quarter of an hour later, moving very fast.

"I couldn't get to the top. There's NVA ahead of us. Directly in our path, between us and the airfield. We've got to get out of here."

"Where do we go then?"

"Let's go to Vietnam."

"How far?"

"Ten miles. Five maybe. You could see it if you went high enough. Just across the river."

"What do we do when we get there?"

"Whatever."

We forgot about the airfield. We decided to break into one last hamlet, rejuvenate ourselves, make one final effort with the radio, then push for the border. We would cross the river and move to high ground, hopefully to be picked up. We went into the first hamlet we reached after nightfall. The peasants were terrified; they babbled about a VC unit that had been through, asking if a NVA unit had made an arms drop for them. Obviously both units would be coming back. We cranked up our radio once more, but the batteries were flat. The head man kept begging us to leave. We ransacked the place for food and bandages, with the villagers frantically trying to clean up behind us. We wrapped Morrosco in clean clothes and moved straight out. We expected to hit the border that night or early the next morning; it was very near, but we were moving bloody slowly. We sought high ground so that when the sun came up, we could look down on the border.

A VC unit overtook us on the trail. We went to ground. As they filed past, Morrosco began to shake and whimper. His body shrank as if he were curled up against the bullets that were about to slam into him. I leapt on him and clamped his mouth with my hand. I tried to intimidate him by putting my face down on his, but Morrosco was preparing himself to die. His eyes were rolling as if he did not know I was there. This made me very angry, because I was determined to get as many of us out as possible. I knew we were coming up to the last effort I would ever get out of these guys. They all promised only to keep moving until we were in South Vietnam. Then the hell with it.

We did not have much left to fight with. Jackson and I were leaning on Prather for support. Morrosco's bowels never ceased flowing, and he was growing weaker with each step. Tan's malaria was worse; he and Prather never stopped shaking.

We reached the border at daybreak. When the sun rose, we had Vietnam before us. As we rested on an outcrop overlooking the Nam Mo Valley, I asked myself why we should go on. Why not try the radio again, transmit from here? And wait to be picked up. It would be easier than moving this lot. Prather spoke before I could suggest it.

"We're going to make it," he said. "We're going to walk to that clearing over there. And sit there until they come and pick us up."

He pointed to a bare patch on a hill facing us about four miles away on the far side of the Nam Mo. His remark bowled me over. After all this struggle, it was so badly timed . . . or was it? I looked to the others. Morrosco had not heard, or did not have the strength to reply. Wiley was going to walk as long as the rest of us did; progress, safety, home, none of it seemed to register with him. Tan's only reaction had been to stiffen perceptibly. I saw him gazing toward the far hill. Jackson exchanged glances with me.

"Maybe it's because I'm a Londoner . . ." Prather sang in a throaty, broken voice.

Prather raved on about the high road and the low road, and he was growing happier by the minute. The malarial shaking had gotten worse, and at first I thought he was delirious. But he was not talking through a fever. He was believing it and was trying to make us do the same, trying the old "chin up, men" repertoire. I could not stand it. I dared not relax for one moment, or I was finished. I walked away, out to where I could look to the east. I had a different purpose from the others—not different from Tan perhaps—I was determined to see the faces that had sent us in. And I had the feeling that we were not going to be allowed to make it home.

"Come on, Pete," I heard Prather say. "Today's the last day. We walk up that hill, and it's all over. Barry and I will help you. We'll stay with you. There's only a little more now."

Jackson joined me.

"We should be running into Yanks soon," I said.

"That's a pretty view," he answered.

I looked out and saw it for the first time. Vietnam stretched before us green and lush. The Nam Mo twisted below us like fallen tinsel. It was a spectacular view. I started to talk about my home in New Zealand.

"You know," Jackson said. "I'm never going home."

"What do you mean?"

"I'm going to walk out of here, and I'm never going back to America."

This was a wild statement for a guy who was . . . well, he was not now the Green Beret I had left with. I think I had misjudged the depth of Jackson's insight, or it had grown as the trip progressed.

"Those sons-of-bitches . . . those sons-of-bitches . . . and I'll never know . . ." he said.

Was he talking about not learning? Or about dying? I was in no frame of mind to dig and pry and discuss. We were just having one of those conversations where two people are thinking aloud to one another.

Jackson returned to the others, and I sat there on my own. I was roused out of my reverie by a swoop of jets taking up the attack where they had left off the night before. They came rushing out of nowhere and hit the ground very hard due north of us. I made up my mind to get to the far hill and bleed the radio dry and shout and go no farther.

We moved out. We had almost no gear left. I had an Armalite, but had lost the shotgun somewhere. I still had my sidearm, but I had thrown Tan's away the day before. Prather was carrying an Armalite, but he had no clips. The others were all very low on ammunition. We stumbled down to the Nam Mo in half an hour. The river was deep and very swift. We walked up and down for an hour without finding a good crossing point. We linked arms. Tan led us into the current. Halfway across our footing broke, and we were swept downstream for a hundred yards, still clinging to one another. The line swung around, and I made the shore first from the tail end. The others clambered ashore. Prather and Jackson had lost their weapons, and Morrosco his sidearm. We were virtually unarmed now.

Water had filled the bandages about Morrosco's waist; they must have felt like a lead weight, because he began tearing at them. The bandages were filled with excreta. He started bleeding profusely.

"Leave the goddamn bandages the way they are," Jackson shouted.

Morrosco pulled at another.

"I mean it," Jackson said, rising to one knee.

Morrosco stopped and fell back exhausted. I turned to Wiley. The water had washed away the dirt and encrusted blood, and I was filled with horror when I saw his condition. His entire face and one side of his neck were swollen like a goiter. One eye was blood red and rolled in to his nose. The other peeped through a slit in a great swollen lump of flesh. His nose was twisted and swollen twice its size.

We lay by the riverbank, then panicked briefly when someone mentioned the radio. The dialing face had been smashed, but the radio still worked. We struck out for the last bare patch, three miles away.

When we got high, we saw people by the river behind us. From the distance, they looked like VC.

They must have followed us all night. They were searching for a crossing point. We lost sight of them as we crested a ridge.

Prather grew stronger with every step. He moved from one to the other of us, pulling us toward that distant clearing. We were making slow progress, so I left him to herd the others, and Tan and I climbed higher to use the radio.

We got immediate response to our transmission, though it was unintelligible. Someone had heard us earlier and was listening for us. I called out for help, giving rough co-ordinates as Tan fed them to me. I described the land we were standing on. Four miles east of the river. I yelled out that I could see helicopters to the south and off to the east.

"The batteries are going," Tan said.

"For bearing! For bearing!" I shouted. "Get a directional finder on us. For bearing . . ."

The radio died. Tan and I played with it until the others caught up, then we abandoned it and continued to climb a hill like a thousand other hills we had climbed. We moved out on open shrubland, and the going grew easier.

We heard the crump of heavy artillery and the scream and whir of battle aircraft. We were within a quarter of a mile now of the clearing. I fell back to help Morrosco, and Prather pulled out slightly ahead of the rest of us. We could all see the clearing now; beyond that we would not go. Morrosco sagged, and I looked up for Prather to help. He was striding out with something close to a smile on his face. We had made it, he was telling himself. I could not stand even that little bit of carelessness, so I went forward to tell him to be more cautious, to slow down a bit. Prather was completely unarmed, his arms swinging freely at his side. He was rambling on and looking nowhere. And I saw his foot open up the ground . . . and an explosion rushed skyward . . . and Prather disappeared before my eyes.

CHAPTER 23

And where he had been, another mine came flying up . . . and another nearby . . . the sun was pouring through the trees and seemed to freeze the metal cylinders in time. . . .

I heard my voice scream No! but the sound never left my head . . . as if all of a sudden I knew I was going to die . . . it was like shouting under water . . . the impact hit me . . . I began to fly . . . for a second I was numb, then coils of barbed wire tore the flesh from my limbs . . . I wondered if my genitals had been blown away . . . I blacked out. . . .

I awoke . . . I was being hurled along the ground, bouncing and hitting things . . . the sound of the explosion seemed to go on for hours. I hit the ground, feeling nothing from the waist down . . . I was a bust being hurled by a volcano . . . I blacked out. . . .

I awoke, but it was dark, and I could hear no sound . . . how strange to be dead . . . but I was still bumping into things, still rolling . . . and then I stopped moving.

I felt completely relaxed . . . it was all over . . . I wanted to smile at my death . . . then I felt blood on my cheek, streaming from my eyes . . . I was alive, and I began to see through a red film.

For a minute nothing moved . . . I was deaf . . . then I felt that I was being blown up again . . . the earth erupted all around me . . . but my body only rocked, and a great wind was rushing over me.

I recognized the downwash from the helicopters, though I could hear nothing. I was conscious, and I waited through a long, naked silence until a figure stood alongside me, and hands that I could not feel touched me.

I blacked out again and awoke when I crashed to the floor of the helicopter. I could hear noises now. Gunfire. We were in a great hurry to leave. Another body crashed alongside me. I saw a boy's face . . . eighteen perhaps . . . very close to mine. It was the face of a baby. A second man stood alongside, holding a plasma bottle.

"Adrenalin!" the boy shouted.

A great spear was driven into my heart, and my chest was filled with fire. I rose upright and screamed, then collapsed.

When I came around, I could see the man beside me. His stomach was open, and his guts were hanging over me. He was dead. I wanted to turn his head, to look in his face, to see who he was, but my body would not move.

I was on and off a stretcher, in and out of hospitals. Hue. I remembered wakening once there. I underwent a field operation. I came around in a different hospital. The nurses were not in field uniform. The main base hospital in Saigon, I think.

Someone came to see me . . . a face I did not know . . . then Stacey . . . the people who had been involved in the briefings . . . the colonel . . . the civilians . . . only one face moved . . . the one I did not know . . . they stayed there for a long time . . . then the drugs would take me elsewhere. . . .

How long had it been? I was flown out to another hospital in Japan or Hong Kong or Singapore . . . a flight in a Cavac Jet . . . always people around me . . . a subtropical hospital with ceiling fans . . . I reached for my dog tags, but they were gone . . . a couple of months? . . . Welcome to Alice Springs. . . .

I was in Darwin at the main military hospital, on a huge base. I began to collect my thoughts. I had gone through about a thousand bed changes and half a dozen hospitals, and I was still in intensive care. Why had they moved so many times a man so badly hurt? To protect me? To hide me? To get me as far away as possible? Or simply to save my life?

I had been literally blown apart from the waist down, and my chest and back and arms were filled with shrapnel. Much of the bone was missing from the heel of my left foot, and the muscle had been sliced half away. For four months the doctors grafted bone to bone and flesh to flesh. It was like driving hot needles into me. Then the drugs would carry me away, but that was terrible, because my sleep was filled with nightmares.

"Where are the others?" I asked.

"What others?"

"The rest. Tan and Wiley and Jackson, and Toliver and Morrosco and Prather and the others. The Five Fingers. Are they all dead?"

"You need rest."

"How can you bring a man half-dead into your hospital and you don't know anything about him, and you can't answer anything?"

They would put me out again. The pain subsided. The hospital, the doctors and nurses, all the sterile unreality of the present drifted away, and I was back with the team . . . Jackson dashed across the road into a hailstorm of fire, yet none touched him . . . we washed blood from our bodies by dawning sun, and Tan made brothers of us all . . . a man's hands on my throat . . . Toliver saved me, then dragged me to the others . . . where was Toliver? . . . oh yes, he was buried deep, where the wild animals would never touch him . . . "That's it! Abort!" Morrosco had shouted . . . Wiley's hands trembling, his eyes aflame with fear and anguish . . . a bridge ablaze, Jackson's body torn apart; my fault? . . . a river, fresh water for my canteens, a look into another world . . . Jackson would never go home . . . but Prather was so sure, so cocky . . . he simply disappeared.

My condition improved. I could hear and see and sit up for a while. I had a room alone. I learned to walk in the garden. An orderly befriended me.

"Would you find out about these guys for me?" I asked. I gave him their names. He returned, shrugging his shoulders. He had contacted personnel in Saigon. Nothing came back.

"Tell them to ask Colonel Stacey," I pleaded. "He'll know."

This time he had a reply.

"Stacey's no longer in Vietnam."

"Where is he?"

"He's retired."

"Where's he retired?"

"How the hell should I know?"

"Do me a favor. There's a thing called the Five Fingers Exercise. China mission. Find out what you can. I've got to know what happened."

He avoided me for ten days. One afternoon I caught him in a corridor.

"Did you learn anything?"

"Listen, mate. If you want to know about any exercise, you go find out for yourself. I got my ass in a crack asking questions."

"What did they say to you?"

"Look, I don't want to know anything more about what you or anybody else has been up to. Just leave me alone."

It was six months now. Six months my mind had been twisted by pain and drugs. Six thousand miles since I had lain beneath a helicopter, my body broken.

I had become a recluse, turned inward to find the answers denied me by others. I spent days trying to make sense of it until my head was burning with brain fever.

I finally accepted that the mission must have been genuine. Then someone in the Pentagon or the White House decided that détente was the better part of valor. As the man said, there had never been a mission like ours in China. There must have been good reasons. So we had to go. The Five Fingers were very special people, but the powers that be were going to push and keep pushing us until we faded out. It was like wringing a rag until there was nothing more to squeeze.

The only thing that had kept us alive so long was that we had seen ourselves being run out, and we had turned in upon ourselves, until we, alone, were responsible for our survival. We were in the shit on our own.

In the end . . . it was a strange thing I thought about for many hours. Maybe we turned inward so deeply that we could not save ourselves when friendly hands had reached out to take us in. I could not pinpoint a single incident when we had not acted correctly, and yet . . . Surely there must have been shorter alternatives to the two-month journey out of China. We had been mad to look for help in South Vietnam; the area we entered was as contested as any in Southeast Asia, it was crawling with enemy.

By the end, we had had enough. I do not believe we could have walked away from that bare patch of ground on a hillside if the helicopters had not come. We could have taken no more.

Now I found myself clutching at small mercies. The fact that I had been blown out of Indochina meant that I did not have to go through the transition back to a normal world. That explosion closed a chapter, just like slamming a book. If I had walked out of that jungle and climbed into a helicopter whole and intact, the pain would have been greater than a thousand surgeons' knives, the scars deeper than those lacerating my body.

Little by little, I began to forget. The only alternative was to lose my mind. Days passed without a thought of the mission. More slowly were my nights freed of the terrible dreams. I decided to go away. Walk away from my past. Build a new life. Revenge? Even that lost its sharp edge as the months slipped by. I thought about going to the other side of the world. America. Maybe South Africa.

I was asleep in my room one hot January day. A young nurse shook me awake.

"There's someone to see you."

A very young, very cocky New Zealand adjutant strode in. Under his arm was a soft leather brief case.

"Good afternoon, Gayle," he said with an enormous forced smile.

"Hello, Captain," I said.

"Uh . . . Lieutenant," he corrected me.

I waited.

"I'm glad to see you looking so fit. I've been in several times to check on you, but you were either in therapy or asleep. The doctors tell me you are about fit to go."

I made no reply.

"Uh . . . first, I want to extend the deepest apologies from the New Zealand Government for having notified your parents that you had . . . died. Please extend my . . . uh . . . apologies for any suffering we may have caused. You are, of course, to be immediately discharged. Now you are qualified to receive a substantial disability pension. Or a cash settlement. I'm sure you'll want to think about that. When you know what your plans are. Have you thought about your future?"

"Stay out of my life."

"Well . . . Gayle . . ."

"Get me the cash."

"I'll be seeing you before you leave. . . ."

I spent another month in the hospital. One day as I was walking in the garden, the adjutant turned up again. He gave me four thousand pounds in Singapore dollars.

"Where are my discharge papers?"

"Oh, those. They've been forwarded to your house."

"Do you want a receipt for the cash?"

"No . . . no . . ."

He gave me a one-way plane ticket to Hong Kong.

"I've put a suitcase in your room. Clothes as per your request. Call me when you're discharged from the hospital, and I'll have a car take you to the airport."

I flew to Jakarta. And from there to Hong Kong.

ABOUT THE AUTHORS

GAYLE RIVERS (a pseudonym) was the youngest man on the team but second in command. His target was General Giap.

JAMES HUDSON was born in Dallas, Texas. After serving in the army, he studied at the Sorbonne and then took a job with *The New York Times* International Edition. He has been Paris Correspondent for two major Dallas newspapers, as well as a free-lance journalist. He now lives with his wife and two sons on the island of Mallorca.

BANTAM WAR BOOKS

These action-packed books recount the most important events of World War II. They take you into battle and present portraits of brave men and true stories of gallantry in action. All books have special maps, diagrams, and illustrations.

☐	12657	**AS EAGLES SCREAMED** Burgett	$2.2
☐	12658	**THE BIG SHOW** Clostermann	$2.2
☐	13014	**BRAZEN CHARIOTS** Crisp	$2.2
☐	12666	**THE COASTWATCHERS** Feldt	$2.2
☐	*12664	**COCKLESHELL HEROES** Lucas-Phillips	$2.2
☐	12141	**COMPANY COMMANDER** MacDonald	$1.9
☐	12578	**THE DIVINE WIND** Pineau & Inoguchi	$2.2
☐	*12669	**ENEMY COAST AHEAD** Gibson	$2.2
☐	*12667	**ESCORT COMMANDER** Robertson	$2.2
☐	*11709	**THE FIRST AND THE LAST** Galland	$1.9
☐	*11642	**FLY FOR YOUR LIFE** Forrester	$1.9
☐	12665	**HELMET FOR MY PILLOW** Leckie	$2.2
☐	12663	**HORRIDO!** Toliver & Constable	$2.2
☐	12670	**THE HUNDRED DAYS OF LT. MACHORTON** Machorton	$2.2
☐	*12668	**I FLEW FOR THE FÜHRER** Knoke	$2.2
☐	12290	**IRON COFFINS** Werner	$2.2
☐	12671	**QUEEN OF THE FLAT-TOPS** Johnston	$2.2
☐	*11822	**REACH FOR THE SKY** Brickhill	$1.
☐	12662	**THE ROAD PAST MANDALAY** Masters	$2.2
☐	12523	**SAMURAI** Sakai with Caidin & Saito	$2.2
☐	12659	**U-BOAT KILLER** Macintyre	$2.2
☐	12660	**V-2** Dornberger	$2.
☐	*12661	**THE WHITE RABBIT** Marshall	$2.
☐	*12150	**WE DIE ALONE** Howarth	$1.

*Cannot be sold to Canadian Residents.

Buy them at your local bookstore or use this handy coupon:

Bantam Books, Inc., Dept. WW2, 414 East Golf Road, Des Plaines, Ill 60016

Please send me the books I have checked above. I am enclosing $_____
(please add 75¢ to cover postage and handling) Send check or money order
—no cash or C.O.D.'s please.

Mr/Mrs/Miss _____

Address _____

City _____ State/Zip _____

WW2—5/79

Please allow four weeks for delivery. This offer expires 11/79.

THE SECOND WORLD WAR

The full drama of World War II is captured in this new series of books about a world on fire. In addition to paintings, there are maps and line drawings throughout the text at points where they are most informative.

☐ 11642 **FLY FOR YOUR LIFE** $1.95
   by Larry Forester
   Amazing story of R.R. Stanford Tuck, one of Britain's foremost air aces.

☐ 12927 **THE FIRST AND THE LAST** $2.25
   by Adolf Galland
   Unique view of German air war by commander of all fighter forces in the Luftwaffe.

☐ 12523 **SAMURAI by Sakai with Caidin** $2.25
   and Saito
   Sakai's own story by the Japanese combat pilot responsible for shooting down 64 allied planes.

☐ 13014 **BRAZEN CHARIOTS by Robert Crisp** $2.25
   Vivid story of war, of fighting in tanks in the wide spaces of the Western Desert told by Major Robert Crisp.

These large format (8½ X 11), full-color art books capture the spirit of men and machines in action.

☐ 01063 **THE AVIATION ART OF KEITH FERRIS** $7.95
   Canada $8.95
☐ 01049 **THE AVIATION ART OF FRANK WOOTON** $6.95
☐ 01004 **THE MARINE PAINTINGS OF CARL EVERS** $5.95
☐ 01029 **THE MARINE PAINTINGS OF CHRIS MAYGAR** $6.95

Buy them at your local bookstore or use this handy coupon for ordering:

BOOKS BEHIND THE LINES

The side of war you will never read about in history books